U.S. POLICY AND
THE GLOBAL ENVIRONMENT

MEMOS TO THE PRESIDENT

A Report of the
Environmental Policy Forum
July 8 - 11, 2000
Aspen, Colorado

A Project of the Aspen Institute's
Program on Energy, the Environment, and the
Economy

Donald Kennedy and John A. Riggs
Editors

For additional copies of this book, please contact:

The Aspen Institute
Publications Office
109 Houghton Lab Lane
PO Box 222
Queenstown, MD 21658
Telephone: (410) 820-5326
Fax: (410) 827-9174
E-mail: publications@aspeninst.org
Web: www.aspeninstitute.org

For all other inquiries, please contact:

The Aspen Institute
Program on Energy, the Environment, and the Economy
One Dupont Circle, NW-Suite 700
Washington, DC 20036-1193
Telephone: (202) 736-5823
Fax: (202) 467-0790
E-mail: jriggs@aspeninst.org

The Aspen Institute
One Dupont Circle, NW - Suite 700
Washington, DC 20036-1193

Published in the United States of America in 2000
By The Aspen Institute

Printed in the United States of America

ISBN: 0-89843-303-7
00-037

Because all politics is ultimately ethical at its base—or at least pretends to be—the decision making processes that will save the natural environment must be grounded in moral reasoning fed into political life through education.

— EDWARD O. WILSON

Table of Contents

Foreword vii

Forum Participants ix

A Global Environmental Agenda for the U.S. 1
  Donald Kennedy and Roger W. Sant

Climate Change and its Consequences 9
  F. Sherwood Rowland

The Energy-Climate Challenge 21
  John P. Holdren

Controlling Emissions of Greenhouse Gases 45
  David G. Victor

Feeding the World in the New Millennium 61
  Per Pinstrup-Andersen

Global Water: Threats and Challenges Facing the United States 77
  Peter H. Gleick

Environment and Health 91
  Kirk R. Smith

Biodiversity, Ecosystem Change, and International Development . 103
  Walter V. Reid

Maintaining Diversity in Our Oceans 115
  J. C. Ogden

Red Tides and Dead Zones: Eutrophication in the
Marine Environment 127
  Andrew R. Solow

Population and Consumption 135
   Robert W. Kates

Environmental Scarcities and Civil Violence 147
   Thomas Homer-Dixon

Global Environmental Governance 161
   Eileen Claussen

The New Administration and Setting Environmental Priorities ...175
   Thomas C. Jorling

America's National Interests in Promoting a
Transition Toward Sustainability 183
   William C. Clark

Endnotes and Further Reading 199

Foreword

As part of its 50th anniversary celebration in 2000, the Aspen Institute convened an Environmental Policy Forum to explore the most important global environmental issues of the next 50 years and to discuss what the United States should do about them now.

A distinguished group of science, business and environment leaders met in Aspen from July 8 to 11. They were asked to assume that they were an advisory group assembled in Camp David early in 2001 to advise the new president on global environmental policy. Fourteen memos to the president prepared by experts on a broad range of subjects were the basis of the discussion. The authors were asked to tell the president "what you should know" and "what you should do." This method required very knowledgeable scientists and others to write for non-experts. The resulting memos printed here are excellent summaries of complex scientific and policy issues, and they will be valuable to interested citizens as well as policy makers.

The Forum was honored to have as its co-chairs Donald Kennedy and Roger Sant. Their extensive experience across a broad range of environmental issues, their ability to frame the issues in a wide-ranging dialogue, and their deft personal touch allowed them to focus the discussion, explore interconnections, and find broad areas of agreement. Their thematic summary of the group's broad conclusions, also written as a memo to the president, is the introductory essay in this volume. It is an effort to reflect the views of the group as a whole, but all participants were not asked to agree with its final wording.

The memos in this volume were critical to the success of the Forum, but an equally important element was the lively dialogue and the expert contributions from all of the participants who are listed in the next section. The Institute is grateful to them for their thoughtful comments, whether to support, supplement, or challenge the recommendations of the authors.

The Aspen Institute seeks to improve the conditions for human well-being by fostering enlightened, responsible leadership and by convening leaders and policy makers to address the structural challenges of the new century. Using the rigorous discipline of informed dialogue and inquiry, the Institute's programs enhance the participants' ability to think clearly about complex issues, mindful of the moral perspective and the value of differing viewpoints. This Forum exemplified that mission.

We also gratefully acknowledge the John D. and Catherine T. MacArthur Foundation, the Summit Foundation, and the Winslow Foundation for their grants in support of the Forum, and Georgia-Pacific Corporation and Texaco Inc. for financial assistance to publish this book. Without their generosity and confidence in our work, the Forum could not have taken place.

John A. Riggs

Forum Participants

Donald Kennedy, Co-Chair, is Bing Professor of Environmental Science, President emeritus of Stanford University, and editor-in-chief of *Science*, the journal of the American Association for the Advancement of Science.

Roger W. Sant, Co-Chair, is Chairman of the Board of the AES Corporation, a leading global power company that he co-founded in 1981. He also chairs the boards of The Summit Foundation and the World Wildlife Fund U.S.

R. Hays Bell is Director, Health, Safety & Environment, and Vice President of Eastman Kodak Company. Prior to joining Kodak in 1982, he served as a member of the Senior Executive Service in the U.S. government and was director of the Technical Support Directorate at the Occupational Safety and Health Administration.

Georgia A. Callahan is Vice President, Environment and Health for Texaco. She worked for many years at the U.S. Environmental Protection Agency, serving as Branch Chief in the Office of the Comptroller and as Assistant to the Director for climate change and air programs. She joined Texaco in 1990.

William C. Clark is the Harvey Brooks Professor of International Science, Public Policy and Human Development at Harvard University's John F. Kennedy School of Government. Trained as an ecologist, he has served as co-chair of the National Research Council's study of science for sustainable development.

Eileen Claussen is President of the Pew Center on Global Climate Change, and President and Chairman of the Board of Strategies for the Global Environment. She formerly served as Assistant Secretary of State for Oceans and International Environmental and Scientific Affairs, and as a Special

Assistant to the President and Senior Director for Global Environmental Affairs at the National Security Council.

Kathryn S. Fuller has been president and CEO of World Wildlife Fund since 1989. Before joining the WWF, she practiced law with the U.S. Department of Justice. She serves on a number of nonprofit boards, including those of Brown University and the Ford Foundation, and is a member of the Council on Foreign Relations.

Peter H. Gleick is co-founder and President of the Pacific Institute for Studies in Development, Environment, and Security in Oakland, California. In 1988 he received a MacArthur Foundation Research and Writing Fellowship for work on the global change for water and international security. He serves on numerous editorial boards and Boards of Directors.

John P. Holdren is the Teresa and John Heinz Professor of Environmental Policy and Director of the Program on Science, Technology, and Public Policy in the Kennedy School of Government, and Professor of Environmental Science and Public Policy in the Department of Earth and Planetary Sciences at Harvard University. He is a member of the President's Committee of Advisors on Science and Technology and chaired its panel on energy R&D strategy for the climate-change challenge.

Thomas Homer-Dixon is the Director of Peace and Conflict Studies Program, and Associate Professor in the Department of Political Science, at the University of Toronto. Much of his memo herein is condensed and abstrated from his *Environment, Scarcity, and Violence* (Princeton University Press, 1999).

Thomas C. Jorling is Vice President, Environmental Affairs, for International Paper. He worked as Commissioner of the New York State Department of Environmental Conservation, as a member of the faculty at Williams College, and as Assistant Administrator for water and hazardous material with the U.S. Environmental Protection Agency.

Robert W. Kates is a geographer, independent scholar, and University Professor (Emeritus) at Brown University. He is Chair of the National Academies' Coordinating Committee on a Transition to Sustainability, an Executive Editor of *Environment* magazine, and Associate of the Belfer Center for Science and

International Affairs, Kennedy School of Government, Harvard University. He is a recipient of the 1991 National Medal of Science and the MacArthur Prize Fellowship (1981-85).

Fred Krupp is Executive Director of Environmental Defense. A member of the President's Advisory Committee on Trade Policy and Negotiations, Krupp also serves on the boards of the H. John Heinz III Center for Science, Economics and the Environment, and the National Environmental Education and Training Foundation.

Kenneth L. Lay has been Chairman and CEO of Enron, one of the world's leading electricity, natural gas and communications companies, since 1986. He previously served in executive positions at Continental Resources Company, Continental Group, Transco Energy Company and Houston Natural Gas and as Deputy Undersecretary of the U.S. Department of Interior.

Dennis R. Minano is General Motors' Vice President, Environment and Energy, and Chief Environmental Officer. He has worked with GM since 1971, where he began as an attorney on the corporation's legal staff. He has served on President Clinton's Federal Fleet Conversion Task Force and the President's Council on Sustainable Development.

John C. Ogden has been Director of the Florida Institute of Oceanography (FIO) and Professor of Biology at the University of South Florida since 1988. After two years at the Smithsonian Tropical Research Institute in Panama, he built the West Indies Laboratory (WIL) in the Virgin Islands, where he served as Director for seven years.

David Olsen is former President and CEO of Patagonia, Inc. He now serves as President of the CEO Coalition to Advance Sustainable Technology, and as Senior Wirth Fellow at the University of Colorado. He is a director of International Utility Structures, Inc., a manufacturer active in more than 100 countries. Earlier, he developed renewable power projects in more than 20 countries.

Per Pinstrup-Anderson, a native of Denmark, joined the International Food Policy Research Institute as its director general in 1992. Prior to this, he was professor of food economics at Cornell University. He is a member of the National

Research Council's Committee on Biotechnology, the Working Committee on Biotechnology under the State Department's Advisory Council on International Economic Policy, and the World Health Policy Forum and its General Council.

Paul R. Portney is President of Resources for the Future (RFF), an independent, non-partisan research and educational organization specializing in natural resources and the environment. He has worked at RFF since 1972. In 1979-80, he was Chief Economist at the Council on Environmental Quality in the Executive Office of the President.

Walter V. Reid works independently on environment and development policy issues internationally and in the United States. He is Science Director of the Millennium Ecosystem Assessment. For six years, he was Vice President for Program at the World Resources Institute, where he is currently a Visiting Fellow.

John A. Riggs is Executive Director of the Program on Energy, the Environment, and the Economy at the Aspen Institute. Previously, he was Principal Deputy Assistant Secretary and then Acting Assistant Secretary for Policy at the Department of Energy, and staff director of the House Subcommittee on Energy and Power. He also has taught energy policy at the University of Pennsylvania.

Leslie Roberts is Deputy News Editor at the weekly journal *Science*. From 1994 until 1999, she worked at the World Resources Institute, the United Nations Development Programme, the United Nations Environment Programme, and the World Bank. She has also been a senior writer at *U.S. News & World Report*, and editor-in-chief of *Issues in Science and Technology*.

F. Sherwood Rowland is the Donald Bren Research Professor of Chemistry and Earth System Science at the University of California, Irvine. He and his former colleague Mario Molina were the first scientists to warn that chlorofluorocarbons (CFCs) were depleting the earth's ozone layer, for which they were awarded the Nobel Prize in Chemistry in 1995.

Victoria P. Sant is President of The Summit Foundation and The Summit Fund of Washington. Board memberships include: Population Action International, National Co-Chair; The Reproductive Research Institute; The Foundation for the National Capital Region; The Phillips Collection, President; The National

Campaign to Prevent Teen Pregnancy; the DC Campaign to Prevent Teen Pregnancy; and WETA.

Kirk R. Smith has been Professor of Environmental Health Sciences at the University of California, Berkeley and Associate Director for International Programs, Center for Occupational and Environmental Health of UC Berkeley, Davis, and San Francisco since 1995. He is chair of the UCB Division of Environmental Health Sciences and Director of the UCB campus-wide Graduate Program in Health, Environment, and Development.

Lee M. Thomas is Executive Vice President, Paper and Chemicals, at Georgia-Pacific Corporation. He previously worked with the U.S. Environmental Protection Agency as Administrator and Assistant Administrator, and at the Federal Emergency Management Agency as Executive Deputy Director and as an associate director. He also worked in state and local governments in South Carolina.

David G. Victor is the Robert W. Johnson, Jr., Fellow for Science and Technology at the Council on Foreign Relations, where he leads a project on energy technology and global warming. His memorandum is based on his book, *The Collapse of the Kyoto Protocol and the Struggle to Slow Global Warming* (Princeton University Press, 2001).

Timothy E. Wirth is President of the United Nations Foundation. From 1993 to 1997, he was Undersecretary of State for Global Affairs. He represented Colorado in the U.S. Senate from 1987 to 1993, and in the U.S. House of Representatives from 1975 to 1987. He was a White House Fellow under President Lyndon Johnson, and served as Deputy Assistant Secretary for Education in the Nixon Administration.

MEMORANDUM TO THE PRESIDENT

From: **Aspen Institute Environmental Policy Forum**
               Donald Kennedy and Roger W. Sant, Co-Chairs

Subject: **A Global Environmental Agenda for the U.S.**

The group of science, environment, and business leaders who produced and discussed these memoranda share a strong conviction that you and your administration face an array of historic and urgent challenges—the kind that, with bold leadership, can be turned into exceptional opportunities.

Many of the recommendations for specific areas involve policies and tools that will not slow the nation's economy and may even provide economic opportunities and help resolve real humanitarian concerns. This article presents a sketch of the broad outlines of the environmental problems confronting humanity and suggests some paths toward their resolution.

The first two challenges, emerging into the public consciousness only in recent decades, are rooted in the unprecedented pace of global change. The global economy is linking nations and people in new and different ways. But people are only beginning to realize the extent to which human actions are radically reshaping the global environment. Without awareness of the consequences of these actions, people have taken control of the planet.

The first change affects the atmosphere: By adding carbon dioxide and other greenhouse gases, people are altering the global climate at a pace that could threaten human livelihood within this century. The second set of changes is taking place on the land itself. Almost half of the world's land surface has been put to human service; people control half of its primary production and have commandeered the natural cycles of nitrogen and other vital elements. Not only has this footprint been large, but humans have handled the land and oceans roughly, depleting their capital stocks of natural resources and threatening the greatest loss of species in 65 million years.

These vectors of change will converge on a more persistent, chronic challenge—the misery that is the regular lot of much of the human family. Eight hundred million of the world's people are hungry, and hundreds of millions of children face uncertain futures because diarrhea, acute respiratory infections, and malaria threaten their health and well-being. These circumstances offer the grim prospect of becoming worse because they afflict some of the most rapidly growing parts of the developing world. The United States is a nation with a conscience, yet its performance in aiding development and supporting welfare improvement in these countries is inconsistent with its national beliefs.

It would be easy to conclude that the twin challenges of climate change and resource degradation, on one hand, and the continuing problems of global inequity and human deprivation, on the other, are too difficult to handle simultaneously. However, the opposite is true. Complex public policy choices inevitably involve tradeoffs, but done wisely and cost effectively, actions to address the climate and depletion problems can help ameliorate the adverse economic and social conditions around the world that produce human suffering. Responding to the near-term challenges will help the United States deal with the chronic one: Benefits will come especially to the poor, hungry, and sick if the United States can succeed in its efforts to stabilize climate and restore environmental quality.

> **Complex public policy choices inevitably involve tradeoffs, but done wisely and cost effectively, actions to address the climate and depletion problems can help ameliorate the adverse economic and social conditions around the world that produce human suffering.**

Indeed, part of the argument for action is that people in the developing world will take the brunt of the assault from global environmental change. To protect them will be in the best interests of the United States. The relief the United States can provide could dispel the need for repetitive, costly interventions of the kind undertaken in Somalia and Haiti and could mitigate many of the increasing threats to global public health that could affect U.S. citizens. Possible improvements also carry the prospect of new markets and new opportunities for democracy around the world. Equally important is this reality for people in the United States: Continued deterioration of the health and welfare of people elsewhere, in this rapidly globalizing society, presents the caring citizenry of the United States with the unacceptable prospect of enduring moral agony.

What challenges face the United States? Climate change, loss of biodiversity and the human services that depend on natural ecosystems, and the depletion of such resource stocks as clean air, fresh water, and ocean fisheries. These relentless engines of change have three things in common. They are nonlinear, dynamic events that promise surprises. They are complex, with many interactions among them. And they are caused by human action. These commonalties indicate that they will be difficult to solve—and the potential roads to solution will wander between and among the categories. For example, climate change will affect every other issue: agricultural capacity, especially in the tropics; infectious disease, by altering the range and efficacy of important vectors of viruses; coastal marine ecosystems, by changing sea level. Deforestation influences climate. Hunger contributes to deforestation and overfishing. Population growth influences everything else. Consumption patterns and behavior determine how great that influence will be. And resource availability affects so many other conditions of life that it may become a source of civic instability and, sometimes, violent conflict.

Nor is the process of change constant: it is accelerating. People in developed and developing countries alike confront a future in which world population growth (headed for 9 billion in mid-century) and economic development will combine to place exploding demands on land, water, and atmosphere. There is now a scientific consensus that the average temperature will continue to rise throughout this century and that it will have significant impacts on quality of life unless steps are taken now to retard greenhouse gas emissions—especially those from carbon dioxide—and to plan the means by which humans might soften our impact on Earth.

No one should believe that the problems are too many, too big, or too complex to solve. The United States has already largely overcome similar obstacles in meeting its domestic environmental challenges. In every U.S. city, air quality is now better than it was two decades ago. Water quality everywhere has improved.

The United States has gained substantial control over such environmental hazards as lead, second-hand smoke, and toxic wastes. The country has secured protection for many of its most valuable natural resources through the designation of public lands and through the commitments of U.S. citizens to private conservation efforts. In almost every one of these respects the United States is better off than at any time in the 20th century.

The United States's heavy economic dependence on energy supplied by carbon-dioxide yielding fossil fuels presents real concerns: The road to emissions reduction will have costs. Yet people in the United States have displayed, in abundance, their willingness to respond to circumstances of resource scarcity. In the oil shocks of the 1970s or faced with regional water shortage, U.S. citizens have engaged in conservation measures so successful that they exceeded the most optimistic predictions of most economists and other experts. The United States's capacity for technological innovation—the "Yankee ingenuity"—is undiminished. When the need is there, the United States has shown that it can accomplish difficult tasks.

Government actions alone cannot meet such comprehensive challenges. Industry must play a leading role, and many of the recommendations to the new presidential administration will require partnerships with industry, citizen groups, and other

Government actions alone cannot meet such comprehensive challenges.

domestic and international organizations. The problems are global, but they have strong domestic components. The extraordinary success of the U.S. economy has given the nation a special capacity and obligation to lead. That same success has also given it a major role in causing environmental problems, so the United States's capacity to lead will require taking steps domestically to reduce that contribution. The following recommendations, taken from discussions that ranged over the entire terrain covered in the various memoranda to the new presidential administration, deserve special emphasis.

In the climate change area, it is important to exert leadership to commit the United States to reduce the rate at which its activities emit carbon dioxide and other greenhouse gases. The final goal must be long-term stabilization of the atmospheric concentration of these gases. Even if it is premature to set a numerical target for that goal, immediate action is required to reduce the rate at which the United States is adding to the problem. In the future, additional emissions limits and efforts at sequestration will be needed, in the United States and elsewhere, if the concentration of greenhouse gases is to remain at acceptable levels. The United States cannot hope to persuade others unless it, acknowledged world leader as well as champion emitter, begins today. Corporations in the United States and elsewhere are taking voluntary actions. These actions should be encouraged and rewarded. Technological innovation is at the core of the success of the 20th century and the promise of the 21st century. Research and development programs to encourage alternatives to carbon-based fuels should be expanded promptly, and eliminating regulatory, tax, and trade obstacles to innovation and the export of advanced technologies must be a high priority. In advance of a commitment to an international regime for emissions limitation, there is much the United States can do to show leadership—and starting early means getting it done at lower cost.

The loss of critical resources that support the living planet presents an equally urgent challenge. Natural ecosystems—those complex, diverse assemblies of living things—not only have great intrinsic value, but are also sources for an extraordinary range of human benefits. They supply a vast array of goods and services that people need as well as other satisfactions that are difficult to measure economically. Indirectly they support much of what humans do in self-interest: harvesting, irrigating, supplying clean water, and stabilizing the climate.

The United States should move toward a strategy that emphasizes the conservation of these systems on land and in the sea. In the short term, the U.S. president can set an example by establishing aggressive domestic goals for reducing the number of plant and animal species at risk of extinction. At longer range, it is important to develop and implement ways to evaluate the vulnerability of existing regions and to set priorities for their conservation. Attention to land-use development patterns, especially those that fragment forests, wetlands, grasslands, and managed forest and agricultural lands, can help reduce biodiversity loss and the disintegration of intact ecosystems. Establishment of significant new protected zones in the ocean and in terrestrial environments is an important mechanism for sustaining the health of more extended ecosystems. A longer range domestic objective should aim at maintaining the health of representative examples of all globally outstanding U.S. ecoregions. Biological diversity is an attribute of great human value, and extinction is an irreversible endpoint.

Resource depletion—the exhaustion of capital stocks of natural endowments that all people need—is a central element of the human condition in the world's poorest countries. Water deprivation is a fact of life in many places. Loss of soil fertility has stalled agricultural growth in parts of the developing world. Infectious disease, brought on by poor water quality and ecological change, is the major cause of deaths worldwide. Deforestation affects water quality at great distances and impacts soil quality.

There are known solutions for many of these problems. Vaccine development and the export of modern sanitation technology represent major opportunities for improving public health. These efforts will become more critical as climate change alters the distribution of vectors for infectious disease and as new agents emerge—threatening not only distant populations but, because people are as globalized as economies, U.S. citizens as well. Support for international agricultural research and for the maintenance of public-sector banks of genetic resources is essential to meet the needs of a growing population.

These steps will require partnerships with international organizations. The United States's limited financial support of these organizations and the skeptical view some U.S. citizens have taken of their ability to perform has damaged the nation's capacity to form successful partnerships. It is important that the new administration select a small number of the most promising organizations and that it lead an effort to improve their performance and to rally their support by the industrial democracies. They offer research programs that are desperately needed in the developing world and also the regimes required to resolve the allocation of common-pool resources.

With respect to population and consumption, the United States can function as a source of help and as a model. It is necessary to continue work on the central problems of population growth abroad by eliminating poverty, providing economic opportunity, extending family planning services, and supporting the education and improved status of women. These and other international efforts will succeed or fail depending on how U.S. involvement is perceived by other countries. Presently the country's allocation to overseas development assistance falls far short of what other industrial democracies deliver. Your leadership in continuing to improve the U.S. contribution to aid for environmental objectives and to meet basic human needs will be critical during the next four years.

Much can be done to reduce the human footprint on the planet. The United States can offer tax breaks and other incentives for industry to adopt life-cycle analysis, employ take-back strategies, improve carbon efficiency, and practice sustainable design and production techniques. Decision makers can consider policy changes that will tax pollution and

> **No single factor will more vitally affect the United States's ability to meet these global challenges than presidential leadership.**

consumption rather than productive work, savings, and investment. When the government regulates, it can improve its own efforts to set clear environmental priorities, ensuring that private and public funds are wisely aimed at the most important and cost-effective targets.

The U.S. economic system still suffers from misplaced incentives and dysfunctional subsidies—many of them discouraging to wise environmental management in the United States and other nations. It is possible, though at some political cost, to eliminate these. The new presidential administration needs to lead a national examination of this problem followed by actions to get the prices right. Markets can help to achieve this goal, and market-based solutions are often preferable to "command and control" regulatory systems. But markets work well to protect environmental quality only when the information is available and accurate and the economic signals reflect the full external costs of activity. Steps like these, taken in the nation with the world's largest, most successful, most market-oriented, and most consumptive economy, can provide a model for what is possible elsewhere.

Many of our recommendations, delivered in the memoranda that follows, deal with specific aspects of the problem. They are the meat of the advice because in the complex and vital domain of environmental quality, simple, global solutions are hard to come by. We urge you to transmit these to your administration with an unmistakable call to action.

Some of the major themes that warrant your personal attention are highlighted here in the hope that they might provide some thematic guidance for your administration's actions. No single factor will more vitally affect the

United States's ability to meet these global challenges than presidential leadership. So it is essential to lead—in educating the public about the critical challenges it faces and in charting a course of action that will help preserve and enhance the life of all peoples and the planet that sustains them.

MEMORANDUM TO THE PRESIDENT

From: F. Sherwood Rowland

Subject: Climate Change and its Consequences

PROBLEM

The Earth's climate is changing, in large part because of the activities of humankind. The simplest measure of this change is the average temperature of the Earth's surface, which has risen approximately 0.7 degree Celsius over the past century, with most of the increase occurring in the past two decades. In other words, the Earth is undergoing global warming. The simplest predictor of this climate change is the steady growth of the amount of carbon dioxide (CO_2) in the atmosphere. The concentration of CO_2, the most important greenhouse gas, has increased by more than 16 percent in the past 40 years and by more than 30 percent since the beginning of the industrial revolution 200 years ago. This additional CO_2 comes from the burning of coal, oil, and natural gases, which together account for about 85 percent of the industrial energy used by humans.

Although there are several consequences of climate change other than this increase in global average temperature, the most significant fact as we face the future is that scientists have, at best, an imperfect understanding of the global climate system. The possibility exists for noticeable deterioration of the climate in the United States even on a decadal time scale. Furthermore, unless the drivers of climate change are successfully addressed and controlled, no future stabilization point can be identified against the otherwise inexorable warming of the globe. As CO_2 continues to accumulate,

> . . .unless the drivers of climate change are successfully addressed and controlled, no future stabilization point can be identified against the otherwise inexorable warming of the globe.

doubling and then tripling in concentration, the expected warming will continue to increase. The further this proceeds, the greater the possibility that new chemical or physical processes will be triggered that release still more greenhouse gases. Many of the time scales for these processes, both human and geophysical, are decades to centuries in length, and major efforts must be begun before any irreversible processes begin.

BACKGROUND

Changes in Atmospheric Composition

Abundant evidence exists that the composition of the Earth's atmosphere has changed substantially during the 20th century—especially in the last few decades:

Carbon dioxide. The atmospheric concentration of CO_2, which was 280 parts per million by volume (ppm) in 1800, had increased to 315 ppm in 1958 and is now 368 ppm.

Methane. Atmospheric methane increased from 0.70 ppm in 1800 to 1.52 ppm in 1978 and is now 1.78 ppm. Important emissions sources for methane influenced by humankind include the cultivation of rice, with release to the atmosphere through the plants themselves while the rice fields are inundated, and releases from ruminant mammals, such as cows.

Nitrous oxide. The concentration of atmospheric nitrous oxide has grown from 0.270 ppm in 1800 to 0.300 ppm in 1980 and 0.315 ppm currently. Much of this increase appears to be related to the greatly expanded usage of nitrogenous fertilizers in agriculture.

Chlorofluorocarbons (CFCs). Atmospheric concentrations of the human-made CFCs have increased from zero in 1900 to 540 parts per trillion by volume (ppt) now for CFC-12. For CFC-11 the concentration increased from zero to 270 ppt, for CFC-13 to 85 ppt, and for carbon tetrachloride to 100 ppt. All of the CFCs have been synthesized as essentially inert gases for various technological uses, each of which eventually involves release to the atmosphere of the unchanged molecules.

Tropospheric ozone. The concentration of ozone near the Earth's surface has increased during the past century by a factor of 5–8 in the Northern Hemisphere summer and by a factor of 2–4 in the Northern Hemisphere winter and during both seasons in the Southern Hemisphere. The added surface ozone is an important deleterious component of urban smog, arising from the mechanization of urban transportation. The formation of this ozone involves sunlight together with the release from automobiles of nitrogen oxides, carbon monoxide, and simple hydrocarbons, such as ethylene, acetylene, and many others.

Stratospheric ozone. The stratosphere contains about 90 percent of all ozone, and average concentrations there have been reduced since 1975 by 5–10 percent in the north temperate latitudes (depending upon the season) and much more drastically in the polar regions. For example, in early spring, ozone levels over Antarctica—colloquially described as the Antarctic ozone hole—now regularly reach only 35 percent of the values found for the same seasonal period in the 1960s. These losses have been conclusively established, by direct atmospheric measurements, to be caused by the release of atomic chlorine and bromine from CFCs and related molecules.

The Natural Greenhouse Effect

For the past million years, the Earth has had an average surface temperature varying between about 6 and 14 degrees C (and similar values for eons before that). For the past 10,000 years until the mid-19th century, the global average surface temperature had been relatively steady around 14 degrees C. The Earth constantly receives energy from the sun and must give off an equivalent amount of energy to space so as not to undergo a rapid increase in temperature. The radiation emitted from the sun occurs largely in the visible wavelengths (red to violet, between 700 and 400 nanometers (nm)), in the near-infrared (greater than 700 nm), and 5 percent in the ultraviolet (less than 400 nm). Because there is a 20-fold difference in the surface temperatures of the sun and the Earth, the radiation from the latter is emitted at 20-fold longer wavelengths, in the far-infrared (around 10,000 nm). The amount of energy given off increases rapidly with temperature, about 160,000 times more intense per unit of surface area for the sun than for the Earth.

A straightforward physical calculation can be made of the expected average surface temperature of the Earth from three known quantities, if all of the far-infrared radiation emitted from Earth's surface escapes to space:

- the surface temperature of the sun (5,800 degrees C);

- the distance of the Earth from the sun (93 million miles); and

- the albedo of Earth (30 percent), which is the fraction of sunlight—including the solar infrared and ultraviolet—reflected from the Earth directly back to space without ever being absorbed.

The result of this calculation is an average surface temperature for the Earth of -18 degrees C—clearly much lower than the real temperature. This difference of about 32 degrees C is the natural greenhouse effect, a phenomenon that has been present on Earth for millions of years.

The Enhanced Greenhouse Effect

The flaw in the calculation described above is the assumption that all of the infrared radiation emitted by the Earth escapes directly to space. However, some of it does not because atmospheric molecules containing three or more atoms can absorb radiation with wavelengths in the 5–20 micron range. For example, carbon dioxide, methane, nitrous oxide, CFC-12, CFC-11, water and ozone, among others, trap infrared radiation. Because the main components of the atmosphere (nitrogen, 78.0 percent; oxygen, 21.0 percent; and argon, 0.9 percent) do not absorb infrared radiation, the concentrations of gases present only in trace amounts control the escape of infrared radiation to space. However, these molecular absorptions are quite specific for each compound, so that some wavelengths are absorbed quite strongly by carbon dioxide, methane, or other gases while others are not absorbed appreciably by any of these trace species; such infrared radiation does escape directly to space. Observations from Earth-observing space satellites confirm that wavelengths absorbed by carbon dioxide and methane, among other gases, are greatly reduced in intensity. Because the natural greenhouse effect is well-known, the concern expressed over the last several decades about the accumulation of greenhouse gases in the atmosphere has not been about the existence of a greenhouse effect but rather about the effects of the added concentrations of CO_2 and the other trace gases in bringing about a still larger discrepancy—an enhanced greenhouse effect, with the difference between observed and calculated global average surface temperatures rising from 32 degrees C to 33 or 35 degrees C. It is worth noting that when the corresponding planetary parameters for Mars are used, the observed and calculated average surface temperatures are in agreement. The Martian atmosphere, of course, is much thinner (0.7 percent as many molecules) than that of Earth, and essentially all wavelengths in the far-infrared escape directly to space. On the other hand, Venus is many hundreds of degrees warmer than it appears from the simple calculation because its atmosphere is 93 times as thick as Earth's, with 95 percent of the molecules being CO_2. In addition, Venus's surface is continually covered by clouds of sulfuric acid droplets, which also intercept infrared radiation.

Recent Global Increase in Temperature

The instrumentation for accurate quantitative recording of temperatures only dates back about two centuries, and thermometers with geographical coverage widespread enough to permit an accurate estimate of global average surface temperatures was only attained around 1870. Since that time, the average global temperature has risen about 0.7 degree C, with much of that increase coming after 1975. The decade of the 1990s is the warmest decade since thermometry became widespread. Over the past 20 years, in addition to using thermometers, temperatures have been inferred from satellite measurements 500 miles from the Earth's surface. The average temperatures recorded from a broad swath across the lower stratosphere indicate an average decrease of about 2 degrees C in the past two decades—in general agreement with the summed expectations from observed increases in atmospheric CO_2 and from decreases in ozone concentrations in the lower stratosphere. Because the satellite instrument also records responses from a broad swath of the troposphere and these swaths are slightly different when the instrument is looking at the Earth in the nadir and from an angle, attempts have been made to infer near-surface temperatures by subtracting one swath from the other. Although widely publicized over the past decade as showing no temperature increase since 1979, several flaws have been identified in the handling of these satellite data, and the utility to date of this technique for measurement of actual surface temperatures is minimal.

Temperatures have also been inferred retrospectively for layers in glacial ice cores and deep sea sediment cores. The composition of water in an ice core can be used to evaluate the temperature at which the water vapor condensed into liquid water or ice before final precipitation. Air constitutes approximately 10 percent by volume of such ice cores, trapped at the time the weight of snow and ice above has closed off further diffusion through channels in the ice. In Antarctic coastal regions with heavy snowfall, measurements over the past thousand years show nearly constant concentrations of carbon dioxide, methane, and nitrous oxide up to the 19th century and then accelerating increases in concentration that mesh with the direct air measurements made in the past 20–40 years. The isotopic variations in the ice itself distinguish summer from winter and allow a direct count of the passage of the years. By considering a variety of such reconstructed temperature scales, the 1990s also appears to be the warmest decade in the last millennium.

Although over the past million years the Earth's climate has oscillated rather wildly, with a series of ice ages in which all of Canada, the Great Lakes, and Scandinavia were buried under about one mile of glacial ice, during the most recent 10,000 years, the Earth's average temperature has been quite stable. However, within this general stability, substantial regional variations have taken place. For example, about 7,000 years ago most of the current Sahara desert region received annual rainfall of more than 8 inches per year, but it now receives than less than 0.5 inch per year. In the much colder, high altitude regions of Greenland and Antarctica—also deserts in terms of yearly precipitation—the ice cores trace back through the series of ice ages and interglacials that have periodically gripped the Earth. The two-mile-deep Vostok ice core (about 800 miles from the South Pole) has provided such information covering the past 420,000 years. During these extended time intervals, carbon dioxide and methane have exhibited lower concentrations during the ice age periods, mimicking the temperature changes themselves. For both of these gases, the atmospheric concentrations in the year 2000 are the highest recorded for the preceding 420 millennia.

During the time between initial snowfall as a porous, fluffy mass and the accumulation of sufficient weight of snow and ice to produce a compact ice core, the gases trapped within the snow can diffuse both upward and downward. The downward diffusion of atmospheric nitrogen within an ice core (in this case, from Greenland) carries a complex isotopic signal that involves both gravitational separation and the temperature at the surface. The consequence is a measure of the rate of change in surface temperature. During the time period from 16,000 to 10,000 years ago, as the Earth emerged from the most recent ice age, the cores indicate two intervals when the average surface temperature increased very sharply by about 2 degrees C within a single decade. The usual scenario associated with prospective global warming

> . . .the appropriate description of the climate control mechanism may be that of an "off/on switch" rather than a smoothly varying "dial."

and climate change is of gradual, steady warming. However, these ice core results indicate that under some conditions of changing climate, the transition may be rapid—the appropriate description of the climate control mechanism may be that of an "off/on switch" rather than a smoothly varying "dial."

Modeling the Atmosphere

General circulation models (GCMs) are attempts to place within an understandable framework a computational system that reproduces as many as possible of the measured data pertaining to the motions and composition of the atmosphere and the oceans. Basically, the Earth receives more solar radiation per unit area in the tropics than in the temperate and polar zones, creating a gradient of temperature decreasing away from the equator. The flow of heat from hot to cold regions is transported poleward in roughly equal measure by the motions of the atmosphere and by the ocean currents. One simple required test of such a model is its ability to reproduce, through changing angles of incoming solar radiation and variations in the length of daylight, the temperature and other differences between summer and winter. A more difficult test is the simulation of the succession of ice ages over the past million years when the whole globe was alternatively cooler by as much as 5–8 degrees C interspersed with periods characterized by temperatures much like the present. The best current explanation for these drastic changes in global temperature is the variation of solar intensity received during the summer in the high northern latitudes because of periodic cyclic variations under the influence of the multiple gravitational attractions among the sun and the other planets in the solar system. This understanding, put forth 60 years ago by the Yugoslavian scientist Milankovitch, involves three parameters in the sun-Earth relationship:

• the angle of inclination of the Earth toward its orbital plane (now 23.5

degrees);

- the month of the year when the Earth is closest to the sun (now January); and

- the extent of deviation of the Earth's elliptical orbit from circular, (now 3 percent).

The timing of the ice ages agrees with this explanation when measured against fluctuations in the amount of solar energy arriving in the summer at a latitude of 65 degrees North. However, the differences in the amounts of energy arriving are not in themselves able to produce the large temperature changes needed for agreement with the observations. Because the needed amplifying factors triggered by these initial solar energy inputs have not been satisfactorily identified, the evidence for the explanation through the Milankovitch cycles remains only circumstantial.

The Effects of Increasing Trace Gas Concentrations: Feedbacks

In a typical GCM calculation, the model is run with 280 ppm of CO_2 present and then again with 560 ppm of CO_2, a doubling of its content. The infrared wavelengths that CO_2 can absorb are absorbed very near Earth's surface with 280 ppm present and are then re-emitted in all directions in amounts determined by the ambient temperature at that altitude. Then they are reabsorbed at a higher altitude by CO_2 and re-emitted again and again, until finally somewhere in the lower stratosphere at a temperature of perhaps -60 degrees C, some lesser amount of radiation makes it out to space at this wavelength. When the model simulation is repeated with 560 ppm of CO_2, the final escape is even more hindered, and the temperature of the surface must increase to maintain the balance between incoming solar energy and outgoing terrestrial infrared energy. This balance is not quite perfect, and the almost imperceptible excess of incoming solar over outgoing terrestrial energy accumulates over the decades into a higher surface temperature, (i.e., the enhanced greenhouse effect).

After the average global surface temperature has increased, three feedback effects come into play. First, the increased temperature causes an increase in the rate of evaporation of water about 6 percent for each degree C. Because water is itself a greenhouse gas, its higher concentration also traps more outgoing terrestrial infrared radiation, requiring a higher temperature to produce more infrared emissions in compensation. Second, in the polar regions at the margins between water and ice, a warming trend will replace the highly reflective ice (albedo ~ 0.8–0.9) with strongly absorbing water (albedo ~ 0.1). Consequently, less incoming solar radiation will be reflected back into space, and the additional energy absorption will add to the temperature rise. The margin between bare ground and snow cover behaves similarly, again furnishing a positive feedback to augment the original temperature rise. These effects are included in the GCMs, with the consequence that predictions of global temperature change for the polar regions are larger than for the global average. Such preferential warming of the polar regions tends to reduce the latitudinal temperature gradient and diminishes the need for poleward heat transport through the atmosphere and the oceans. A lessening of the Gulf Stream's strength could induce temperature decreases in western Europe in the midst of average global warming.

The Effects of Clouds

The most problematic part of GCM calculations concerns the effects of clouds. As with the greenhouse gases, they, too, absorb outgoing terrestrial infrared radiation. But, in addition, the tops of clouds reflect incoming visible radiation back into space and also emit infrared radiation upward. Because the average temperature decreases with increasing altitude in the troposphere, the top of a high cloud is much colder—and emits less infrared radiation—than the top of a low cloud. With a low cloud, the top reflects incoming solar to space and, because its temperature is not much colder than the ground beneath, emits almost as much infrared radiation as it intercepts. As a result, the formation of a low cloud with increasing temperature represents a negative feedback, working against the temperature increase. However, with the formation of a high cloud, the lower temperature on top reduces the outgoing flux of terrestrial infrared radiation (relative to surface emissions) more than it reflects incoming solar radiation to space. The result is a positive feedback. The real situation is even more complicated because it is not obvious whether an increase in atmospheric temperature will increase or decrease cloudiness or whether it will change the altitudes of the clouds. The individual cloud feedbacks can theoretically be either negative or positive and may well have a different sign over different geographic regions, depending upon the particular circumstances.

The Year 2100

Future calculations with GCMs carry with them not only the manifold imperfections in their simulation of the real world, but also the unknown behavior of the human population during each period. Within these limits, the expected increase in global average temperature by the year 2100 lies between about 1 degrees and 3.5 degrees C. In more detailed predictions for specific regions, the models frequently diverge from one another. For example, using the most recent results from the Canadian GCM, the prediction for the southeastern United States is for an average temperature increase of more than 6 degrees C by 2100 and an even greater increase in the (Dis)Comfort Index from the combination of heat and humidity. Other model calculations do not show such large changes but still indicate substantial warming in the southeast. The underlying difficulty in policy considerations is that none of the available information indicates that the Canadian model (or any of the other models) is wrong—the regional information is simply not precise enough to distinguish among conflicting, plausible models.

In the future, water will play an even more important role than it does now, with increasing global population and the consequent heavy demands for increased agricultural production. A warming climate will have many consequences for water use on the planet. For example, as the atmosphere warms, heat is transferred to the ocean, and it in turn warms—and expands. The warming of the ocean's surface is slowly transmitted downward so the total expansion response of the oceans requires many decades—even centuries—for completion. Additional sea-level rise can also result if the total amount of land-supported ice is diminished and redistributed into the oceans. The estimated sea-level rise by 2100 varies from about 1 to 3 feet. In another example, the increase in surface temperature will cause the rate of water evaporation to increase, with a corollary increase in rainfall. At the same time, a quickening loss of soil moisture could bring about alternating conditions of hotter and drier periods with more intense rainstorms. When hurricanes are traced back to their oceanic birthplaces, the water there is found to be 27 degrees C or warmer—the developing storm requires additional energy to grow to hurricane strength, water vapor condensing into droplets releases the needed energy, and warmer water produces water vapor more rapidly. Plausible arguments can be made for both more big storms and for greater intensity of these storms. In California, most of the precipitation now comes down as rain and snow in the autumn and winter seasons. The winter snow pack then serves as the major water source during the dry spring and summer. With higher winter temperatures, precipitation is more likely to come down as rain than as snow, and the state could have lessened snowpacks and therefore less available water in the summer and heavier runoff and flooding during the winter rains.

RECOMMENDATIONS

As the various examples cited above indicate, a changing climate offers numerous possibilities for extensive, possibly severe, impacts upon society. However, the present and likely situation in the immediate future is that the capability of prediction from the best atmospheric models will not provide accurate smaller-scale forecasts. We need to have much more computational power available, with climate modeling as one of the major applications. Simultaneously, we need to have an appropriate, consistent set of detailed measurements made on a regional scale so that the differential outputs from various choices of input parameters fed into the climate models can be tested for significance in comparison with real world data. Under these circumstances, we should be preparing for adaptation to more rapid changes than have been routinely encountered in the past, while still endeavoring to improve our predictive abilities.

None of the human or geophysical responses to climate change can take place quickly. Even alterations of the transportation fleet takes place over decades, as old cars and trucks are replaced by more fuel-efficient vehicles, or, as is happening now in the United States, by sport utility vehicles with significantly enlarged fuel needs. Most industrial power plants going into operation in the year 2000 will be nearing the end of their useful life in the decade 2040–2050. Conversely, more than half of the current power plants globally will still be in operation 20 to 25 years from now. Harbor facilities that will still be in use in 2075 should be built to accommodate the coming sea-level rise. The removal of the greenhouse gases from the atmosphere by natural processes occurs on a time scale of a half-century or more. Because of the long-term nature of such alterations, the need to begin the process is urgent.

None of the currently available remedial responses, such as the Kyoto Protocol, provide a solution to the problems brought about by climate change.

Rather, they are directed toward slowing the pace of change, amelioration, and adaptation rather than cure. Consequently, the climate change problem will be much more serious by the year 2050 and even more so by 2100. Currently, the best models of the climate system agree reasonably well on hemispheric-scale features, but they have progressive difficulties as the regions for which predictions are desired become smaller

> None of the currently available remedial responses, such as the Kyoto Protocol, provide a solution to the problems brought about by climate change. Rather, they are directed toward slowing the pace of change....

and more specific. Nevertheless, these forward-looking projections indicate the kinds of effects that may arise in the near future. We need to be exploring all of the potential avenues of response to climate change, and we need to do it now because the development of long-term solutions will require decades to develop and decades to put into action.

MEMORANDUM TO THE PRESIDENT

From: John P. Holdren

Subject: The Energy-Climate Challenge

PROBLEM

More than a quarter of a century ago, two immensely important under-standings about the contemporary human condition pushed themselves, almost simultaneously, into public and political consciousness. One of these under-standings—reflected in the occasion of the first Earth Day in 1970, the publica-tion of the report of the MIT-hosted international Study of Critical Environmental Problems that same year, and the convening of the first UN Conference on the Environment in Stockholm in 1972—was that the environ-mental conditions and processes increasingly under siege from the expansion of human activities were too important to human well-being to continue to be neg-lected, as they often had been, in the pell-mell pursuit of increased material pros-perity. People began to realize that ways would need to be found—and could be found—to meet economic aspirations while adequately protecting the environ-mental underpinnings of well-being. The other understanding, which was thrust on the world by the Arab Organization of Petroleum Exporting Countries-induced oil-price shocks of the 1970s and the global economic recession that fol-lowed, was that a reliable and affordable supply of energy is absolutely critical to maintaining and expanding economic prosperity where such prosperity already exists and to creating it where it does not.

Today, these two understandings have long since become part of conven-tional knowledge. Essentially everybody recognizes the importance of energy for economic prosperity and the importance, for human well-being, of protecting the environment. But far less widely appreciated is the close connection between these two imperatives—and the immense challenge arising from it—in the form of the central role played by civilization's principal energy sources in generating the most dangerous and difficult environmental problems facing the planet. Energy supply is the source of most of human exposure to air pollution, most of acid precipitation, much of the toxic contamination of ground water, most of the burden of long-lived radioactive wastes, and most of the anthropogenic alteration of global climate. Moreover, the constraints imposed by these problems on the composition and expandability of energy supply are becoming the most important determinants of energy strategy and, increasingly, of energy's monetary costs. In short, energy is the most difficult part of the environment problem, and environment is the most difficult part of the energy problem. The core of the challenge of expanding and sustaining economic prosperity is the challenge of limiting, at affordable cost, the environmental impacts of an expanding energy supply.

> **In short, energy is the most difficult part of the environment problem, and environment is the most difficult part of the energy problem.**

The most demanding part of this energy/environment/prosperity challenge is the challenge posed by anthropogenic climate change. In terms of the current scale of damage to health, property, ecosystems, and quality of life, climate change is not yet comparable to air pollution, water pollution, or land transformation. But, over the next several decades, it will come to be understood as the most dangerous and the most intractable of the environmental impacts of human activity.

Climate change is the most dangerous part of the energy/environment challenge because climate constitutes the envelope within which all other environmental conditions and processes operate and because, once it has been set in motion, the degree of irreversibility of human-induced climate change is very high. Substantial disruption of the climatic "envelope" places at risk the full array of "service" functions of the environment: the formation, fertilization, and retention of soils; the detoxification of pollutants; the provision of fresh water; the distribution of warmth and nutrients by ocean currents; the natural controls on human and plant pathogens and pests; the bounding, within mostly tolerable limits, of extreme temperatures, precipitation, and storminess; and much more.[1]

As discussed below, the evidence that human-induced climate change is on a trajectory to create major damage to these services within the current century is becoming overwhelming. The complacent notion that society is clever enough and rich enough to fully replace these contributions of the natural environment to human well-being with engineered substitutes is folly—although insofar as a substantial degree of disruption of global climate is already inevitable, we shall have to try.

Climate change is the most intractable of all environmental impacts to address because its primary cause—increasing carbon dioxide (CO_2) emissions—is deeply embedded in the character of civilization's current energy-supply system in ways that would be both time consuming and potentially very costly to change. More than 75 percent of the world's energy supply (and more than 85 percent of that of the United States) currently comes from burning oil, coal, and natural gas.[2] The rich countries of the industrialized world achieved their enviable prosperity based on a huge expansion of the use of these versatile and relatively inexpensive fuels, and the "business-as-usual" energy future would have the developing countries doing the same. Today's fossil-fuel-dominated world energy system (worth some $10 trillion at replacement cost and characterized by equipment-turnover times of 20 to 50 years) could not be rapidly replaced with non-CO_2-emitting alternatives even if these were no more expensive than conventional fossil-fuel technologies have been (and today, the non-CO_2 options are considerably more expensive); nor is the voluminous CO_2 combustion product (some 3 tons of CO_2 per ton of coal or oil) easy to capture with add-on pollution-control equipment for existing engines, furnaces, and power plants.

That the impacts of global climate disruption may not become the dominant sources of environmental harm to humans for yet a few more decades cannot be a great consolation, given that the time needed to change the energy system enough to avoid this outcome is also on the order of a few decades. It is going to be a very tight race. The challenge can be met, but only by employing a strategy that embodies all six of the following components:

- expanded research on climate-change science, geotechnical engineering adaptation to climate change, and increased investments to exploit the resulting understandings;

- increased national and international support for measures that address the motivations and the means for reducing family size;

- incentives for reducing the greenhouse-gas emissions of firms and consumers;

- accelerated research, development, and demonstration of advanced energy-supply and end-use technologies;

- increased international cooperation to ensure the application of these advances in all countries; and

- development of a global framework of commitments to long-term restraints on greenhouse-gas emissions.

Each of these components will be discussed later.

The private sector will clearly need to play an immense role in much of this agenda. In addition, because the problem involves externalities, common property resources, public benefits, and binding agreements among states, government policies must also play a major role. The government of the United States—a country with one-quarter of the world's fossil-fuel use and CO_2 emissions, the world's strongest economy, and the world's most capable scientific and technological establishments—ought to be leading, not following, in this effort that is so crucial to the prospects for a sustainable prosperity for all.

The remainder of this memorandum elaborates on three important aspects of this argument: what the current state of climate-change science allows one to say about the implications of energy business-as-usual (BAU); the extent of the deflection from BAU likely to be required to bring the degree of energy-linked disruption of global climate in this century within manageable bounds; and the content and prospects of the six-point strategy summarized earlier for achieving this deflection.

BACKGROUND

Business-as-Usual and Its Climate Change Implications

It is illuminating to disaggregate carbon emissions to the atmosphere into four multiplicative factors: the size of the human population, the per-capital level of economic activity (measured in purchasing-power-parity-corrected dollars of gross domestic product (GDP) per person), the energy intensity of economic activity (measured in gigajoules per thousand dollars of GDP), and the carbon-emission intensity of energy supply (measured in kilograms of carbon contained in CO_2 emitted to the atmosphere per gigajoule of energy supply). The "business-as-usual" assumption is not that these factors remain constant but rather that their trajectories of change follow recent trends that are adjusted for expected patterns of development. In a typical BAU global energy future:[3]

- World population increases from 6.1 billion in 2000 to 8.5 billion in 2030 and 9.8 billion in 2050, stabilizing by 2100 at about 11 billion. Almost all of this growth occurs in developing countries.

- Per-capita economic growth is higher in developing countries than in industrialized ones but declines gradually over the century in both. Aggregate economic growth (reflecting the combined effect of growth in population and in per-capita GDP) averages 2.9 percent per year from 2000 to 2020 and 2.3 percent per year over the whole century in real terms. As a result, world economic product (corrected for purchasing power parity) grows from about $38 trillion in 2000 to $87 trillion in 2030, $140 trillion in 2050, and $360 trillion in 2100 (all in 1995 U.S. dollars).

- Energy intensity of economic activity falls at the long-term historical rate of 1 percent per year in industrialized and developing countries alike for the entire century. With the indicated economic growth, this produces a doubling of world energy use between 2000 and 2040, a tripling by 2070, and a quadrupling by 2100 (by which time the figure is about 1,800 exajoules (EJ) per year, compared with about 450 EJ per year in 2000).

- Carbon intensity of energy supply falls at a rate of 0.2 percent per year in all countries for the entire century. With the indicated energy growth, this causes carbon emissions from fossil-fuel combustion to triple during the century, going from a bit more than 6 billion tons of carbon per year in 2000 to some 20 billion tons per year in 2100.

Historically, the atmospheric concentration of CO_2 rose from a pre-industrial level of about 280 parts per million by volume (ppm) in 1750 to about 370 ppm in 2000—an increase of 32 percent—driven in the first part of this 250-year period mainly by deforestation and in the latter part mainly by fossil-fuel combustion. Under the indicated BAU scenario for emissions from fossil fuels (and assuming no further contribution from net deforestation), the atmospheric concentration would be expected to reach 500 ppm by 2050 and more than 700 ppm by 2100. Moreover, if this BAU scenario persisted until 2100, there would be almost no possibility that the continuing run-up of the atmospheric CO_2 concentration thereafter could be stopped below 1,100 ppm (a quadrupling of the pre-industrial value).

In addition to the CO_2 increase, atmospheric concentrations of a number of other greenhouse gases—mainly methane, nitrous oxide, tropospheric ozone, and halocarbons—have also increased since pre-industrial times. The warming effect of all of these increases together, as of the mid-1990s, was estimated as roughly equal to that of the CO_2 increase; but this warming contribution of the non-CO_2 greenhouse gases was estimated to be approximately offset by the net cooling effect of increased atmospheric concentrations of particulate matter also caused by human activities.[4] Under the indicated BAU scenario, the concentrations of the non-CO_2 greenhouse gases increase more slowly during the 21st century than the CO_2 concentration does, while concentrations of atmospheric particulates slowly decline. By 2100, the net warming effect of all the greenhouse gases together—less the cooling from particulates—is just slightly larger (about 10 percent) than the warming that would be caused by the increased CO_2 alone. Therefore, one can simplify the discussion of future possibilities, without much loss of accuracy, by associating these possibilities with CO_2 concentrations alone—leaving out the offsetting complexities of non-CO_2 greenhouse gases and particulate matter.[5]

Today the debate about whether the effects of rising CO_2 concentrations on global climate are already apparent is essentially over—resolved in the affirmative.[6] In 1995, when the atmospheric CO_2 concentration was 360 ppm, the Intergovernmental Panel on Climate Change (IPCC) wrote in its *Second Assessment of the Science of Climate Change* that "the balance of evidence suggests a discernible human influence on global climate." This report noted that global mean surface air temperature had increased by 0.3 to 0.6 degrees C since the late 19th century, that this had been accompanied by an increase in global sea level by 10–25 centimeters, and that the patterns of change (in relation to day-night temperature differences, vertical temperature distribution, latitudinal differences, patterns of precipitation, and more) match with quite striking fidelity the patterns predicted, by basic climate science and elaborate computer models alike, to result from the observed increases in greenhouse-gas concentrations, adjusted for the effects of atmospheric particulate matter and the known variability of the sun's output. These patterns are often described as the "fingerprint" of greenhouse gas-induced climate change, and no one has postulated a culprit other than greenhouse gases that would have the same fingerprint.[7] Since the completion of the IPCC second assessment, the evidence has only grown stronger.

By the end of 1999, for example, it was clear that 15 of the 16 warmest years worldwide, in the 140 years since the global network of thermometer records became adequate to define a global average surface temperature, have occurred since 1980. The seven warmest years in the 140-year instrumental record all occurred in the 1990s, notwithstanding the cooling effects of the Philippine's Mount Pinatubo volcanic eruption at the beginning of that decade. Based on evidence from ice cores and other paleoclimatological data, it is likely that 1998 was the warmest year in the last thousand, and the last 50 years appear to have been the warmest half-century in six thousand years. A National Academy of Sciences report that appeared in January 2000, reviewing modest discrepancies between the surface thermometer records and satellite measurements made over the preceding 20 years, concluded that "the warming trend in global-mean surface temperature observations during the past 20 years is undoubtedly real."[8] And a comprehensive survey of ocean-temperature measurements, published in *Science* in March 2000, showed widespread warming of the oceans during the past 40 years.[9] With rather high confidence, then, one can now say that global warming is being experienced and that greenhouse gas increases from human activities are its primary cause.[10]

What is to be expected from continuation of business-as-usual? Because of the large thermal inertia of the oceans, the attainment of the equilibrium temperature increase associated with a given CO_2 concentration lags by some decades the attainment of that concentration. Thus, although the BAU emissions future described above yields a doubling of the pre-industrial CO_2 concentration by 2070, the best estimate temperature increase over the pre-industrial value is only about 1.8 degrees C by 2070, reaching 2.5 degrees C in 2100.[11] On the other hand, these estimates are global land and ocean averages; in general, the increases on land will be higher, and those on land at high latitudes higher still. Sophisticated climate models capable of tracing the time evolution of these changes typically show mid-continent U.S. temperatures in the range of 2.5 to 4 degrees C higher than today's for the middle of the century under the business-as-usual scenario.

The IPCC's 1995 assessment concluded, for the indicated BAU scenario, that sea level would rise by 2100 to a best estimate of 50 centimeters above today's value (and would continue to rise for centuries thereafter) and that other characteristics of the warmed climate would be likely to include increases in floods and droughts in some regions,[12] increased variability of precipitation in the tropics, and a decrease in the strength of the North Atlantic circulation that warms the southeastern United States and western Europe in winter. (A warmer climate overall can make it colder in some places at some times.) The assessment found that the expected climate change "is likely to have wide-ranging and mostly adverse effects on human health" (with the increased damage from heat stress, aggravation of the effects of air pollution, and expanded range of tropical diseases more than offsetting the reduced health impacts from cold winters); that northern forests "are likely to undergo irregular and large-scale losses of living trees;" and that agricultural productivity would "increase in some areas and decrease in others, especially the tropics and subtropics" (where malnutrition is already most prevalent).[13]

The 1995 assessment also emphasized, as all competent reviews of climate-change science do, that many uncertainties about the character, timing, and geographic distribution of the impacts of climate change remain, and that the nonlinear nature of the climate system (in which small causes can have big effects) implies the possibility of surprises that current models cannot capture at all. Such possibilities include increases in the frequency and intensity of destructive storms (which a few models do suggest), larger and more-rapid-than-expected sea-level rise (from, for

> . . ."uncertainty" does not necessarily mean, as the public and policy makers sometimes suppose, that when we learn more, it will all turn not to be as bad as was feared. It can easily turn out to be worse than the best estimates.

example, slumping of the West Antarctic Ice Sheet), and a "runaway" warming effect from the release of large quantities of the potent greenhouse gas, methane, immense amounts of which are currently locked in icy-like solids called clathrates beneath permafrost and on the ocean floor. These examples illustrate that "uncertainty" does not necessarily mean, as the public and policy makers sometimes suppose, that when we learn more, it will all turn not to be as bad as was feared. It can easily turn out to be worse than the best estimates.

Although there is room for debate about whether the impacts of doubling the pre-industrial CO_2 concentration would be unmanageable, any basis for optimism shrinks when the postulated CO_2 level moves to a tripling or a quadrupling.[14] Under the IPCC's assumptions, a quadrupling of pre-industrial CO_2 would yield an equilibrium mean global surface temperature increase of 3 to 9 degrees C with a best estimate of 5 degrees C. Studies by Princeton's Geophysical Fluid Dynamics Laboratory—one of the few groups to analyze this case—found equilibrium average temperature increases of 7–10degrees C (13–18 degrees F) for the mid-continental United States after a quadrupling, drops of June–August soil moisture by 40 to 60 percent over most of the country, and a July heat index for the southeastern United States reaching 43 degrees C (109 degrees F) compared with the prewarming value of 30 degrees C (86 degrees F).[15] The Princeton calculation also showed the North Atlantic thermohaline circulation (which drives the Gulf Stream) shutting down almost completely under a quadrupling of pre-industrial CO_2, accompanied by a rise in sea level at about twice the rate expected for a CO_2 doubling.[16]

Although there are of course uncertainties associated with the projections of this particular study—as for all others—it would be foolish to suppose that the impacts of the degree of climate disruption that any model will show for a quadrupling of atmospheric CO_2 would entail anything other than immense human costs.

How Big a Departure from Business-as-Usual is Required?

Stabilizing CO_2 emissions at or near current levels would not lead to stabilizing the atmospheric CO_2 concentration. Constant emissions at the mid-1990s rate would lead, instead, to a more or less steady increase of about 1.5 ppm per year in the concentration, leading to a value of about 520 ppm by 2100 if the constant emissions rate were maintained throughout this century. Stabilizing the

atmospheric concentration at any level of possible interest—even at a quadrupling of the pre-industrial level—would require that global emissions drop eventually to a small fraction of the current 6 billion tons of contained carbon (GtC)
per year. However, it is consistent with ultimate stabilization of the atmospheric
concentration that emissions rise for a time—as they are destined to do given the
momentum in the current fossil-fuel-dominated energy system—as long as they
peak eventually and then fall to levels well below today's.

For example, to stabilize the atmospheric concentration at 550 ppm—about
twice the pre-industrial value—the BAU trajectory could be followed until about
2020, and the concentration would need to peak at not more than 11 GtC/yr
around 2030 and begin falling by 2035, reaching 5 GtC per year by 2100 and 2.5
GtC per year by 2200. A somewhat different emissions trajectory that would still
be compatible with stabilizing the atmospheric CO_2 concentration at 550 ppm
would depart from business-as-usual sooner (essentially immediately), peak
lower (at 8–9 GtC per year) and later (around 2050), and then fall more gradually, becoming coincident with the more sharply peaked 550 ppm trajectory
between 2150 and 2200.

In addition to the details of their shapes, emissions trajectories that lead to
stabilization of the atmospheric CO_2 concentration at various levels can be characterized by the cumulative emissions they entail between 2000 and 2100.
Trajectories compatible with stabilization at 550 ppm would have cumulative
emissions in the range of 800 to 900 GtC in this century. Trajectories corresponding to stabilization at 750 ppm would have 21st century cumulative emissions in
the range of 1,100 to 1,200 GtC. For comparison, cumulative 21st century emissions on the BAU trajectory would be about 1,400 GtC.

Under the UN Framework Convention on Climate Change (UNFCCC),
which was enacted at the Earth Summit in Rio de Janeiro in 1992 and subsequently ratified by the United States and more than 170 other nations, the parties
agreed to pursue "stabilization of greenhouse gas concentrations in the atmosphere at a level that would prevent dangerous anthropogenic interference with
the climate system." There has been no formal or even informal agreement, up
until now, on the stabilized concentration that would be considered low enough
to meet this criterion. But it is difficult to believe, given the evidence that global
climate change is already doing damage, that any level equivalent to more than a

doubling of the pre-industrial CO_2 concentration could possibly be considered compliant with the convention. Were it not for concerns about the practicality of meeting a lower target—or, stated another way, concerns that the cost of compliance might exceed the benefits—it seems likely that a level at or below today's concentration would be chosen. If the target were a compromise of 450 ppm (a bit closer to today's 370 ppm than to a doubling at 560 ppm), then cumulative carbon emissions over the 21st century would have to be kept below 600 GtC—a figure 2.5 times smaller than that for business-as-usual.

The magnitude of the challenge represented by a target this low can be illustrated by considering what would be required to meet it by emissions reductions alone—that is, without reductions below BAU population growth or per-capita economic growth. With the population and per-capita GDP trajectories at their BAU values, a doubling of the century-average rate of decline of energy intensity (energy divided by GDP), from 1.0 to 2.0 percent per year, and a doubling of the rate of decline of carbon intensity (carbon emissions divided by energy), from 0.2 to 0.4 percent per year, would reduce the 21st century emissions to about 700 GtC, establishing a trajectory that could stabilize the atmospheric concentration at about 500 ppm. If, in this variant, the century-average rate of reduction of carbon intensity were boosted to 0.6 percent per year—three times as fast as business-as-usual—the result would be a trajectory consistent with stabilization at 450 ppm.[17]

Attaining such a trajectory would not be easy, but neither would it be impossible. Higher reduction rates in these intensities than are needed have been achieved in some places and times in the past (although never for as long or as universally as would be required to meet the challenge described here). For example, between 1973 and 1986, in response to the 1973–74 and 1979 world oil-price shocks, energy intensity in the United States fell at an average of 2.5 percent per year. In France in about the same period (1973–91), when that country was rapidly nuclearizing its electricity-generation sector, the carbon intensity of energy supply in the French economy fell at an average rate of 2.7 percent per year. Among global scenarios for energy in the 21st century constructed by IPCC, the joint Global Energy Futures study of the World Energy Council and the International Institute for Applied Systems Analysis, and other reputable efforts, there are high-technological-innovation variants with long-term world-average rates of improvement averaging 1.5 to 2.5 percent per year in energy intensity and 0.6 to 1.2 percent per year in carbon intensity.

RECOMMENDATIONS

Ingredients of Strategy

A sensible strategy to overcoming the energy climate challenge would seek to stabilize the atmospheric CO_2 concentration below 500 ppm while taking additional steps to try to reduce the harm to human well-being that disruptions of climate, even at this level of greenhouse-gas increase, would tend to cause. In principle, there are just four possible approaches to the overall problem from which the ingredients of such a strategy can be assembled, and they can be enumerated as follows:

- reduce greenhouse gas emissions to less than what they would otherwise be;

- remove from the atmosphere greenhouse gases that have previously been added to it;

- intervene to reduce the effects of greenhouse gas increases on climatic variables; and

- adapt to reduce the human impact of the degree of climate change that cannot be avoided.

Working up from the bottom of this list, it is plain that a considerable amount of adaptation will be needed, inasmuch as climate change and adverse impacts from it are already apparent. Adjustments in agriculture, forestry, fisheries, water storage, flood control, public-health measures, transportation management[18] and protection of coastal settlements, among other activities, will be required. Some of this is already under way. But a strategy that relies too heavily on adaptation or not enough on avoidance is likely to be costly, not to mention much less effective in resource- and infrastructure-poor developing countries than in industrialized ones.

Interventions to reduce the effects of greenhouse gas increases on climatic variables constitute what is often termed "geotechnical engineering." An example would be the insertion of reflecting materials into orbit to reduce the sunlight reaching the Earth and thereby offset greenhouse warming. Although such ideas are intriguing, they suffer too much from insufficient understanding of the intricacies of the planet's climatic machinery for us to be confident of achieving the desired effects (or, to be confident of doing more good than harm). Humans are powerful enough to disrupt the climate and smart enough to notice we are doing it, but we are not yet competent enough to fine-tune the complex machinery of climate to our tastes. The possibilities—and the climate system itself—need much more study.

The best means currently known for removing CO_2 from the atmosphere is growing trees. The trick is to increase the inventory of carbon embedded in plant material, of which the most enduring form is wood: Just as net deforestation reduces that inventory and adds CO_2 to the atmosphere (as has happened on a global-average basis during much of the past few centuries), so does net afforestation increase the inventory and remove CO_2 from the atmosphere. Expanding the forested area of the planet is feasible (although not as easy to achieve and to sustain as is sometimes supposed), as is increasing the carbon storage on existing forested land. But given the amount of continuing deforestation in the tropics, it would be a considerable accomplishment just to stay even on a global-average basis during the next century. The best imaginable performance at rapidly ending current deforestation and improving other land-management practices that generate greenhouse-gas emissions,[19] combined with aggressive reforestation and afforestation efforts (including widespread, costly restoration of degraded land), might achieve 20 or 25 percent of what is required for a transition, in this century, from the BAU trajectory to a trajectory consistent with stabilizing atmospheric CO_2 at 500 ppm. Far more study and effort than are happening today will be required to achieve even this much.[20]

The Six-Point Action Program

The foregoing considerations about the adaptation, geotechnical engineering, and greenhouse gas-removal options motivate the first element in this six-point program, namely:

(1) expanded research on the science of climate change, climate-change impacts, enhancement of the uptake of carbon sinks in terrestrial ecosystems and in the oceans, geotechnical engineering to offset the effects of greenhouse gas increases in the atmosphere, and means of adaptation to the degree of climate change that proves unavoidable; and increased investments to exploit the opportunities that this research uncovers.[21]

The same considerations make it plain that no matter how much ultimately proves to be achievable under these headings, prudence also requires pushing forward aggressively on the option of reducing greenhouse gas emissions to below what they would otherwise be. This necessary preoccupation leads back to the determinants of the most important anthropogenic greenhouse gas emissions— those of CO_2—in the form of population, GDP per person, energy use per unit of GDP, and carbon emissions per unit of energy. Although the trajectories of these four factors alone are sufficient to specify the trajectory of total carbon emissions, each of the four is influenced in turn by an array of interacting technical, economic, social, and political factors, wherein reside the leverage points for policy.

The range of plausible world population sizes in 2100 extends at least from 7 billion to 14 billion. The difference between these two figures in terms of ease or difficulty of achieving a low-carbon-emission energy future (as well as for a great many other aspects of the human condition) is immense. We should be striving for a result near the low end of these possibilities.

The principal manipulable determinants of human fertility, and hence of population growth, are the prospective parents' knowledge of reproductive biology, their motivation affecting desired number and spacing of offspring, and the effectiveness and availability of technologies of fertility limitation. Knowledge of reproductive biology is a matter of education—of women even more importantly than of men—which is in turn a matter of development. Motivation about number and spacing of offspring has been shown to depend most directly on the status and education and employment opportunities of women, the survival prospects of offspring, and the availability of a social security system—again, all matters closely related to the process of development itself—as well as government incentives for small families and other factors influencing perceptions about the individual and social costs of large ones. Fertility-limiting technologies (the means of contraception and abortion) are already quite good; the key factor is access to them on satisfactory terms.

Although a few of these fertility-reducing factors have been or could be politically sensitive, nearly all of them are things that most of the world's people want for their own immediate well-being. That achieving them would also bring a large societal gain in the form of reduced population growth and the benefits of that for addressing the energy/climate challenge (and a great many other resource, environmental, and social problems of the 21st century) means that there can be even less excuse than otherwise for failing to push ahead with the second element in the six-point program:

> *(2) increased national and international support for the education, development, social-welfare, and family-planning measures known to be most effective in reducing population growth.*

The GDP-per-person factor in carbon emissions can be dispensed more quickly, at least in respect to policy leverage for reducing those emissions. Much can be said, of course, about how GDP is influenced by the productivity of labor (which in turn is influenced by health, education, training, organization, technology, and natural resources), but policy is rightly focused on how to increase all this, not on decreasing it as a way to reduce environmental harm. In the long run, GDP per person also depends on the allocation of time between economic and noneconomic activities, influenced in turn by conceptions about the relative importance of economic and noneconomic contributions to well-being. However, as much as some might like to see a reorientation of human wants away from economic consumption, advocating this explicitly is not likely to become a part of a major political party's platform for some time to come. It may happen, nonetheless, that bringing more of the external costs of economic growth into the balance sheets of producers and consumers—as overall economic efficiency requires—will raise the price of growth enough that people will not buy so much of it. But the appropriate policy instruments relate to internalizing the external costs—not to suppressing economic growth per se.

This leads to the two more technical determinants of emissions, namely the energy intensity of GDP and the carbon intensity of energy supply. The energy intensity of GDP relates both to "technical efficiency" (the energy requirement to produce a given good or service) and to the composition of economic output (the mix, in the economy, of more and less energy-intensive types of goods and services). The carbon intensity of energy supply depends on the characteristics of fossil-fueled energy technologies (specifically, how much carbon they emit per unit of end-use energy they supply to the economy) and the mix of fossil-fueled and nonfossil-fueled energy technologies in the energy system as a whole. The two elements of the six-point program that relate directly to the evolution of these factors in the United States are

(3) incentives and other help for firms and consumers to make low- and no-CO_2 choices from the menu of energy-supply and energy-end-use-efficiency options available at any given time; and

(4) accelerated research, development, and demonstration of advanced energy-supply and end-use technologies, to steadily expand and improve the menu from which choices are made.

The range of policy measures that can be considered under the third component is wide, including analysis and education of firms and individual consumers about the available options, correction of perverse incentives embedded in existing policies, lowering of bureaucratic barriers to adoption of otherwise desirable options, performance standards (relating, for example, to energy efficiency and to emissions), portfolio standards (relating to the proportion of low- and no-carbon options in the energy-supply mix), preferential financing, tax breaks, and other subsidies for demonstration and widespread deployment of targeted options, overall emissions caps implemented through tradable permits, and carbon taxes.[22]

> **. . .the most potent and economically efficient means to encourage low-carbon and no-carbon choices from the menu of available options and to encourage research and development of better choices of these kinds, would be a tax on carbon emissions.**

Although there is room for innovation and expanded activity on many of these fronts, most economists will argue that the most potent and economically efficient means to encourage low-carbon and no-carbon choices from the menu of available options and to encourage research and development of better choices of these kinds, would be a tax on carbon emissions. They are right. Taxing a widely practiced activity that society has reason to want to discourage has a long and successful history. Taxing "bads" (such as pollution) is preferable to taxing "goods" (such as income and capital investment) for a variety of reasons, and the revenue stream from taxing the "bads" can be used to reduce the taxes on "goods,"[23] to reduce the burdens on hard-hit subpopulations (such as coal workers), and to finance research, development, and demonstration of better low-emission technologies. The money does not disappear into a black hole.

Serious advocacy of a carbon tax has been anathema in U.S. political discourse, but it is far from obvious that the persuasive power of the presidency would not be enough to sell such a tax to the public. One does not have to leap to the levels of $100 or $200 per ton of emitted carbon that feature in scare stories about how damaging this approach would be to the fossil-fuel industries; getting our toes wet with a tax of $20 per ton, as a beginning, would generate a healthy set of incentives for energy firms and individual energy users to start making more climate-friendly choices, and it would raise about $30 billion per year initially in the United States—of which, perhaps, one-tenth could be used to alleviate resulting burdens on the groups hardest hit, one-tenth could be used for additional targeted incentives for the adoption of low-carbon energy options from the existing mix, one-tenth could be used for more than doubling federal support for research, development, and demonstration of improved low-carbon options, and the remaining seven-tenths ($21 billion) would still be left for reducing other taxes.[24]

As economists frequently point out, an effect on the energy marketplace substantially identical to that of a carbon tax can be obtained through the use of an emissions cap implemented through tradable emissions permits. It is often supposed that this approach would be less problematic politically than a carbon tax, and this may be right. But a cap-and-trade system is harder to design, harder to calibrate, and harder to implement than a tax. For the United States, initially, a carbon tax would be more effective. However, ultimately, an international cap-and-trade scheme may be the best negotiable approach for constraining carbon emissions worldwide in an equitable way.

Politically easier than carbon taxes or emissions caps are the increases in
research, development, and demonstration of advanced energy-supply and ener-
gy-end-use technologies recommended as the fourth part of this six-part program. But even this proved problematic in the last administration. The 1997
report of the President's Committee of Advisors on Science and Technology
(PCAST) on *Federal Energy Research and Development for the Challenges of the
Twenty-First Century* concluded that the federal energy-technology research and
development programs then in place were "not commensurate in scope and scale
with the energy challenges and opportunities that the twenty-first century will
present," taking into account "the contributions to energy [research and develop-
ment] that can reasonably be expected to be made by the private sector under
market conditions similar to today's."[25] The panel recommended modifications
to U.S. Department of Energy's (DOE) applied energy-technology (fossil,
nuclear, renewable, efficiency) research and development programs that would
increase funding in these categories from their fiscal year (FY) 1997 and FY1998
level of $1.3 billion per year to $1.8 billion in FY1999 and $2.4 billion in
FY2003.[26]

The administration embodied a considerable fraction of this advice in its
FY1999 budget request (which contained a total increment about two-thirds of
what PCAST recommended for that year) and Congress appropriated a considerable fraction of that (about 60
percent of the increment
requested by the administration). The net result was an
increment about 40 percent as
large as PCAST recommended
for FY1999. In subsequent
budgets, the gap between the
PCAST recommendations and
what the administration was

> ...proposed increases in federal energy
> research and development would not
> only have positioned the country to
> respond more cost effectively to the
> need to reduce greenhouse-gas emis-
> sions. . . it would also lower the mone-
> tary costs of energy and energy services
> below what they would otherwise be. . . .

willing to recommend widened steadily, and Congress continued to appropriate
only a fraction of what the administration recommended. This should not have
been so hard. As PCAST pointed out, its proposed increases in federal energy
research and development would not only have positioned the country to
respond more cost effectively to the need to reduce greenhouse-gas emissions
when and if a national decision were made to do this; it would also lower the

monetary costs of energy and energy services below what they would otherwise be, increasing the productivity and competitiveness of U.S. manufacturing, reducing U.S. overdependence on oil imports, and reducing emissions of air pollutants directly hazardous to human health and ecosystems, among other benefits. In addition, it would only have restored federal spending on applied-energy-technology research and development, by FY2003, to its level in the FY1991 and FY1992 Bush administration budgets (the annual total for which could be raised by an increase of 2.5 cents per gallon in the federal gasoline tax).

Another PCAST study, this one completed in June 1999,[27] fleshed out the arguments for and ingredients of the fifth element of the six-point program recommended here:

(5) increased international cooperation to facilitate the application of the results of first, third, and fourth components in developed and developing countries.

The report from that PCAST study, entitled *Powerful Partnerships: The Federal Role in International Cooperation on Energy Innovation*, noted that enhanced U.S. participation in such cooperation would improve the access of U.S. firms to the immense foreign market for energy technologies,[28] lower the cost of energy-technology innovation for U.S. domestic application, and help other countries participate effectively in the solution of global energy problems that the United States cannot solve by itself. The energy technologies that other countries deploy will largely determine not only the pace of global climate disruption by fossil-fuel-derived greenhouse gases[29] but also the extent of world dependence on imported oil and the potential for conflict over access to it, the performance of nuclear-energy systems on whose proliferation resistance and safety the whole world depends, and the prospects for trade-enhancing and security-building sustainable economic development in regions where, otherwise, economic deprivation will be a continuing source of conflict.

This 1999 PCAST study estimated that federal spending on international cooperation in energy research, development, demonstration, and deployment (ERD[3]) amounted in FY1997 to about $250 million per year, and it recommended that this figure be increased to about $500 million in the FY2001 budget and to $750 million by FY2005. The increments were for specific initiatives to strengthen the foundations of energy-technology innovation and international cooperation relating to it (including capacity building, energy-sector reform, and mechanisms for demonstration, cost-buy-down, and financing of advanced technologies); for increased cooperation on ERD[3] of technologies governing the efficiency of energy use in buildings, energy-intensive industries, and small vehicles and buses, as well as of cogeneration of heat and power; and for increased cooperation on ERD[3] of fossil-fuels-decarbonization and carbon-sequestration technologies, biomass-energy and other renewable-energy technologies, and nuclear fission and fusion. The administration's FY2001 budget request included an increment of $100 million for these initiatives (as opposed to the $250 million increment proposed by PCAST). At this writing, the fate of this increment in an election-year Congress controlled by the other party is unclear.

Addressing the energy/climate challenge should not be a partisan issue. The values at stake—economic prosperity, environmental quality, and international security—are held dear by both parties. The UN Framework Convention on Climate Change was signed by a Republican president. That convention, which, unlike the Kyoto Protocol, has long since been ratified by the U.S. Senate and is therefore the law of the land, already commits the United States to most of the climate-related actions that climate-change skeptics in the 106th Congress have mistakenly associated with the Kyoto Protocol and noisily opposed. For example, Article 4 of UNFCCC commits the parties to "formulate, implement, publish, and regularly update national and, where appropriate, regional programmes containing measures to mitigate climate change by addressing anthropogenic emissions by sources and removals by sinks of all greenhouse gases not controlled by the Montreal Protocol, and measures to facilitate adequate adaptation to climate change," and to "promote and cooperate in the development, application and diffusion, including transfer, of technologies, practices, and processes that control, reduce, or prevent anthropogenic emissions of greenhouse gases. . . ."[30] This covers a lot of ground—and provides a lot of cover for doing what is required.

The 1992 UNFCCC and the unratified 1997 Kyoto Protocol represent early, halting, imperfect steps in the effort to achieve the sixth element of this six-part program of action on the energy/climate challenge, namely:

(6) development of a global framework of commitments to long-term restraints on greenhouse-gas emissions designed for sufficiency, equity, and feasibility.

UNFCCC correctly recognized the asymmetries built into the energy/climate challenge—notably that it has been industrialized countries who mostly consumed, in the course of their economic development, the capacity of the atmosphere to hold anthropogenic CO_2 without entraining intolerable changes in climate; that industrial countries are far better positioned financially and technologically to undertake early corrective action; and that no approach to planetary emissions limits that closed off the path to development for three-quarters of the Earth's population would be acceptable. Article 3 explicitly affirms, accordingly, that "the developed country Parties should take the lead in combating climate change and the adverse effects thereof." This is only sensible.

The Kyoto Protocol negotiation attempted, with insufficient time and insufficient preparation in relation to the complexity of the agenda, both to address a variety of gaps and ambiguities in the UNFCCC's treatment of the coverage and approach of a global framework for limiting anthropogenic climate change and to agree on an initial set of binding numerical targets and timetables for emissions reductions by the industrialized countries. The biggest shortcoming of the negotiation was the degree of preoccupation in the meeting—and in the preparations in individual industrialized-country governments—with these numerical targets and timetables, to the near exclusion of addressing the mechanisms (above all, incentives) that might start to move emissions trajectories in the right direction.

The result was a set of targets and timetables for industrialized countries—expressed in terms of percentage reductions from 1990 levels to be achieved in the 2008–2012 time period—that has been assailed for requiring more than is needed in the short run and for requiring

> . . .arguments and agreements about targets and timetables are essentially irrelevant in the absence of mechanisms that might cause them to be achieved.

much less than is needed in the long run. It has also been assailed for failing to bind developing countries. The criticisms about too much and too little have some validity, but the bigger failure is that arguments and agreements about targets and timetables are essentially irrelevant in the absence of mechanisms that might cause them to be achieved.

The idea that developing countries could have been or should have been included in reductions targets of this character (percentage cuts from 1990 levels) was a nonstarter from the outset—inconsistent with the principles of UNFCCC and not taken seriously by most people outside the U.S. Senate. When it is time to bring developing countries into a framework of commitments to reductions (and this will only happen after the industrialized nations have demonstrated a willingness not just to establish targets but to impose mechanisms to make the targets attainable), the formula will need to be based either on carbon intensities (agreement to reduce the ratio of carbon emissions to GDP at a specified rate) or on tradable emissions permits allocated on a per-capita basis.

A satisfactory global framework for emissions restraints might well employ the two approaches just mentioned in successive stages: commitments based initially on specified annual percentage reductions in the carbon intensity of economic activity, transitioning in the longer term to evolving global emissions caps implemented through tradable permits. If "sufficiency" in a framework of emissions restraints were defined in terms of getting the world onto a trajectory that would stabilize the atmospheric CO_2 concentration at between 450 and 500 ppm, then the initial commitments for reducing the carbon-to-GDP ratio might start in the range of 1.5 percent per year (not far above the long-term historical average) and ramp up over a decade or so to the range of 2.5 percent per year that would be required, as a century-long worldwide average, to achieve stabilization at the indicated level.

The later phase, employing caps, would be based on the insight that the desired stabilization trajectory cannot have a peak higher than about 10 GtC per year around 2035 and must fall thereafter. If one supposes that world population in 2035 will be 8 billion persons (somewhat below the 8.8 billion projected for 2035 in the BAU scenario), the per-capita allocation in 2035 would need to be about 1.2 tons of carbon per person. This is about three times less than what industrialized nations were averaging at the end of the 1990s, and three times more than what developing countries were averaging then. So, in this strikingly symmetric scheme, the per-capita allowances of industrialized and developing countries would have converged from opposite sides, after 35 years, to the geometric mean of their current per-capita emissions.[31] The emissions cap and the associated per-capita allocations would fall gradually thereafter, tracking the trajectory needed to achieve stabilization at 450–500 ppm.

Such an approach would certainly be equitable. It is more likely to be sufficient than variants aiming for stabilization at 550 ppm or more (although worse-than-expected evolution of climate change over time could still show it to be inadequate). This is a feasible approach, at least from the technical and economic standpoints even if not yet from the political one. But, crucially, it does not need to be politically feasible today, because its most politically problematic ingredient—equal per-capita emissions allocations—would not need to begin being phased in before 2015 or 2020, by which time people's everyday experience of the impacts of climate change is likely to have stretched considerably the scope of what domestic and international politics will allow.

As for the Kyoto Protocol, it is, with all its warts, sufficiently important today as a symbol of the world's commitment to move forward collectively to address the energy/climate challenge that a serious effort must be made to either salvage or supplant it. The most important ambiguities in it—relating, for example, to the treatment of carbon sinks and to the operation of the Clean Development Mechanism—have been in the process of being ironed out in Conferences of the Parties (to UNFCCC) subsequent to the Kyoto meeting. As for the binding targets and timetables, these might be made acceptable by designing a set of agreed penalties for noncompliance that are more constructive than punitive. (Industrialized countries could agree, for example, to increase their investments in ERD[3] and international cooperation on low-carbon-emitting energy technologies in proportion to the margin by which they miss their 2008–2012 targets.) If the Kyoto Protocol proves not to be salvageable in these ways, it will be important to have a new and better agreement that the major emitters in the developed and developing worlds alike are prepared to sign at the same meeting when the final demise of the Kyoto agreement is formally acknowledged.

Conclusion

The energy/climate challenge must be met. And it can be met. There is no shortage of persuasive professional knowledge about why doing so is necessary, nor is there any shortage of promising proposals about how to proceed. There is not even a good argument that doing this job would be too expensive: The cost of the needed steps almost certainly would be small compared with the cost of the environmental and economic damages averted, as well as small compared with investments society makes in military forces (in which the degree of certainty about the magnitude of the threat—and about the cost-effectiveness of the proposed investments against it—is actually considerably smaller than in the energy/climate case). What have mainly been missing are simply the public understanding and the political conviction that this is a problem to which the nation and the world must now give high priority. Repairing that deficit is a matter of political leadership, and no one is in as good a position to provide it as the new president of the United States.

MEMORANDUM TO THE PRESIDENT

From: David G. Victor

Subject: **Controlling Emissions of Greenhouse Gases**

PROBLEM

America is in a bind. Public pressure to act on greenhouse warming is growing. Evidence that it makes economic sense to limit emissions of greenhouse gases is mounting.

Yet unilateral action makes no sense. Carbon dioxide, methane and the other gases that cause global warming have long lifetimes in the atmosphere; they waft worldwide, making greenhouse warming a truly global phenomenon. The United States is responsible for one-quarter of these emissions—our actions are significant, but acting alone would not have a dramatic effect on the total problem. Moreover, the United States must coordinate its actions with other nations because efforts to control emissions could be costly and will affect our economic competitiveness.

Yet today there is no viable framework for international action. The debate remains focused on the 1997 Kyoto Protocol, but it is nearly impossible for the United States to comply with that Protocol. This memo explains the origins of the Protocol and our predicament. It explains why we must not ratify the Protocol and outlines the major elements of a better alternative; it also explores the political strategy that will be needed to adopt this alternative since the United States was the leading architect of the Kyoto pact and will be tarred when it collapses.

Throughout, the memo focuses on an international framework for controlling ("mitigating") emissions of greenhouse gases. No country can fully plan its own policies to mitigate emissions until the central elements of an international framework are agreed. It focuses on mitigation because that is the most costly and contentious issue in the debate over how to respond to the dangers of global climate change. However, there are several other dimensions to an effective international global warming strategy in addition to mitigation. International action is needed to coordinate and fund research on the science of greenhouse warming—in that area, the U.S. is already a leader with its multibillion dollar annual investment in climate data and research programs. International action is also needed to help societies adapt to the effects of climate change, such as rising sea levels, possibly more intense storms, and (in some places) scarcity of fresh water. In general, adaptation has not been given enough attention considering that some climate changes are inevitable even if we undertake a vigorous mitigation effort. Finally, some international coordination is also needed for further research into "geoengineering"—for example, space mirrors that could reflect the sun and cool the planet. Geoengineering raises many severe concerns (what if the space mirrors cool the planet too much, or if they suddenly fail?), but a rational strategy would develop such exotic tools in case scientists discover an inevitable lurking climatic catastrophe. At present, U.S. and world investment in geoengineering research is inadequate.

BACKGROUND: The Road to Kyoto

In the late 1980s the major industrialized nations faced growing internal pressure to slow global warming. Environmental groups and a small group of concerned scientists were the prime movers. The hot summer of 1988 focused and multiplied the political pressure that these entrepreneurs had mobilized—first in the United States and then abroad.

The initial response in 1988 was to create a scientific body to review the evidence—the Intergovernmental Panel on Climate Change (IPCC). IPCC reported in 1990, noting that the effects of greenhouse warming were highly uncertain but could be adverse. IPCC has since become a permanent body, reporting every few years and also issuing special reports on various technical topics. Although the IPCC has become large and unwieldy, the United States government has wisely supported it because there is no realistic better alternative. The IPCC has probably helped to forge international consensus on the science of greenhouse warming; it has also engaged scientists from developing countries in an effort to encourage developing countries to take the climate issue seriously. Getting them involved is in our interest because within the next two decades developing countries will account for more than half of the world's emissions of greenhouse gases.

With the first IPCC report in hand, negotiations on an international treaty to control global warming began in 1991. As only one year remained before the "Earth Summit" in Rio—at which nations were slated to adopt the treaty—diplomats deferred most of the substantive issues and instead negotiated a loose framework for future cooperation: the Framework Convention on Climate Change. The United States quickly ratified the Convention, as did nearly every other nation on Earth—the calculus was easy because the Convention required little action beyond what most nations were doing anyway. The Convention's main obligations require all nations to submit periodic reports on greenhouse gas emissions and policies for controlling emissions. In addition, the Convention requires that industrialized nations contribute to an international fund that helps developing countries comply with the treaty's obligations. Most nations, including the United States, had already committed to such funding because they knew how essential it was to engage developing countries.

Since the Framework Convention contained only vague obligations to control emissions, negotiations began in 1995 on a stronger treaty—a "protocol"—that would augment the Convention. Diplomats set a meeting for December 1997 in Kyoto as their deadline. Governments squandered most of the intervening two years with symbolic postures and debate on dozens of poorly fleshed-out proposals. Most proposals focused on mandating "targets and timetables" for controlling emissions of greenhouse gases. The European Union set the scene with a bold proposal for all industrialized nations to cut emissions of greenhouse gases 15% below 1990 levels by the year 2010. Although the EU had no plan for meeting its own target, horse trading around the European target dominated the public debate rather than sober assessment of what nations actually could implement.

In Kyoto, delegates finally agreed that the industrialized nations—known as "Annex I" countries—would, on average, cut emissions about 5% below 1990 levels during the period 2008-2012. The collective 5% goal was parsed into targets for each of 39 Annex I nations. For example, Japan committed to a 6% reduction, and the United States accepted a 7% cut. The European Union committed its 15 members to cut 8% collectively and has since doled out that target to each of its members, requiring Germany and the U.K. to cut deeply while Portugal and Spain actually increase their emissions. The Kyoto targets were averaged over five years, from 2008 to 2012, instead of aimed at a single year, to help soften the effects of the business cycle. Emissions rise and fall with the economy, so predicting emissions for a particular year is especially tricky. However, the 5-year period is somewhat arbitrary—real business cycles vary in length.

The Kyoto Protocol includes three mechanisms that can lower the cost of compliance by giving nations more flexibility in meeting their targets. First, the Kyoto targets apply to a "basket" of all six of the major greenhouse gases. Most global warming (70%) is caused by carbon dioxide, but methane (20%), nitrous oxide (6%) and other gases are also significant. An exchange rate known as the "global warming potential (GWP)" governs the tradeoff between the gases. For example, the current GWP for methane is about 21, which means that cutting a ton of methane would earn the same credit under the Kyoto Protocol as cutting 21 tons of carbon dioxide. In some countries and settings, the cost of controlling 21 tons of carbon is more than the cost of mitigating a ton of methane—in those situations, the extra flexibility of the "basket" approach saves money. In practice, however, making the multigas approach work requires overcoming some extremely difficult technical problems. Among them is the difficulty of measuring the emissions of nearly all the greenhouse gases. Of the major greenhouse gases, only emissions of carbon dioxide caused by burning fossil fuels can be measured with acceptable accuracy (within about 5% to 10%). In addition, scientists calculate GWP values by relying on arbitrary parameters that have no relationship to the real economic choices; some alternative schemes that don't require GWPs have been proposed, but they are complex and still not adequately fleshed out.

Second, the Protocol allows "emission trading"—Annex I nations may trade credits and debits so long as the tally for the group complies with the emission targets. The program is modeled on the successful emission trading program for sulfur dioxide here in the United States. In principle, trading makes economic sense because it is much cheaper to focus emission controls in Hungary, for example, than in the United States. The Hungarian economy is relatively wasteful of energy, whereas the United States economy already uses energy relatively efficiently. Buying some of the Hungarian quota would allow us to save money while the Hungarians get better technology. Since the emissions mix worldwide, it doesn't matter exactly where emission mitigation actually occurs.

Emission trading remains extremely contentious. In Kyoto, some environmental groups as well as many European and developing country delegates viewed trading as an American ruse to avoid serious action to control emissions. With this controversy swirling furiously, delegates in Kyoto agreed in principle to create an emission trading system, but

> **. . .designing a workable emission trading system is no easier than inventing a new monetary system.**

deferred agreement on the rules that would govern the system. Diplomats still have not settled those rules because they are discovering that designing a workable emission trading system is no easier than inventing a new monetary system. Care is needed because much is at stake. If an emission trading system were created, the targets allocated in Kyoto would define the number of emission permits that each country could claim as its own. Reasonable calculations suggest these permits would be assets worth more than $700 billion, perhaps more than $1 trillion. (The asset value is the underlying worth of the asset—like the value of a house, rather than the cost of merely renting a house for a year.)

Third, the Protocol allows industrialized countries to purchase emission credits from developing countries. Developing countries often use energy extremely inefficiently and offer a cornucopia of low-cost ways to limit emissions. Yet developing countries have adamantly refused to set targets for controlling emissions because they fear that policies that would be needed to mitigate emissions would also undermine economic development, and without targets they can't participate in emission trading. The solution is a scheme, known as the Clean Development Mechanism (CDM), which allows developing countries to earn tradable emission credits on a project-by-project basis. For example, a firm in the United States could invest in a project to build an efficient natural gas power plant in India. The American investor would earn credits for the difference between the actual emission level and the emissions that would have occurred without the project. The Indians would get the technology. Both sides win, and the climate is cooled while costs are controlled.

CDM, like emission trading, is highly contentious. The most important objection is technical: it is difficult to estimate the "baseline" of emissions that would have occurred without any particular project, and thus it is difficult to determine the level of credit that should be awarded. There is no simple and transparent method for solving the "baseline" problem and thus no way to ensure that only worthy credits are distributed. Already without the lure of emission credits there is nearly $200 billion per year in private investment in developing countries, of which perhaps ten percent is in the energy sector. Companies such as Enron are already building efficient natural gas-fired power plants in India. With so much money already flowing there is great danger of rewarding projects that would have occurred anyway—issuing excessive credits will undermine the integrity of the credit system, just as printing money undervalues a currency through inflation. One solution is to empower an international regulatory body to review every CDM project individually. The problem, however, is that individual review would introduce large transaction costs and high uncertainty that would severely dampen the incentive for firms to invest. Indeed, the United States has a program under way known as the "United States Initiative on Joint Implementation" that operates with project-by-project review. The result is exactly as expected—the program is useful but cumbersome, and consequently the actual investment is far less than the potential.

RECOMMENDATIONS

Your immediate decision concerns whether to prepare for ratification of the Kyoto Protocol. The United States can't ratify the Protocol unless you and the Senate are confident that the nation can comply with the Protocol's obligations. Three strategies could bring the United States into compliance with the Protocol. However, none advances our interests, and thus none should be pursued; even if all were pursued simultaneously we would not be able to comply with the Kyoto emission targets at an acceptable cost.

First, the United States could attempt to control emissions within its borders and meet the Kyoto limits without having to resort to the controversial international emission trading or CDM. That scenario is impossible. U.S. emissions of carbon dioxide from fossil fuels, as shown in figure 1, are already 15% above 1990 levels and on track to rise perhaps another 10% by 2008. Yet Kyoto requires a 7% cut below 1990 levels. There is no way, even if the United States began in earnest, to cut 32% from our emissions in less than a decade. The lifetime of energy equipment is long (2 decades or more); by the end of 2000, 80% of U.S. electric power generating capacity in 2010 will have been already built. We could comply only by shutting down a large part of the economy or by replacing existing energy equipment before the end of its economically useful lifetime.

The problem of compliance does not become much easier if the United States makes full use of the "basket" of gases to achieve compliance. Only 18% of U.S. emissions are from non-CO_2 gases, most of which is methane. The EPA already has several useful programs in place to help firms implement low-cost controls on methane, and we can achieve more before 2008-2012. However, it is unlikely that the United States can earn more than about 5% of the needed 32% reduction from non-CO_2 gases. Carbon dioxide matters most to solving the environmental problem.

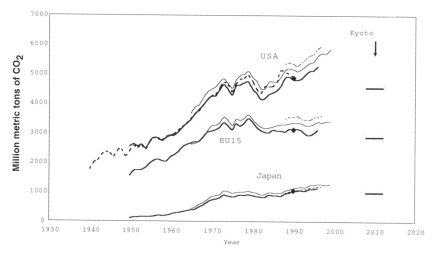

Figure 1: Trends in CO_2 emissions from combustion of fossil fuels. Chart shows historical data from four semi-independent data sources and thus indicates the low uncertainty in the data. The large diamonds show the official data reported by countries for 1990, the base year for determining compliance with the Kyoto targets, which are shown as bars from 2008-2012. U.S. emissions have continued to rise steeply since the early 1990s, but emissions in Europe and Japan are more flat. Data exclude carbon sinks (e.g., forests and soils) as well as non-CO_2 greenhouse gases. Data sources: Oak Ridge National Laboratory (solid heavy lines), IIASA/WEC (dashed heavy lines), BPAmoco (solid light lines), EIA (dashed light lines).

The best chance for the United States to comply with the Kyoto targets is to play accounting tricks with carbon dioxide. The Kyoto Protocol includes not only emissions of CO_2 but also CO_2 sinks. When plants grow they accumulate carbon in their biomass—in the trunks, stems, roots and leaves as well as in surrounding soils. Two carbon sinks are especially important. One is trees. United States forests are growing rapidly as former farmland reverts to forest. More than two-thirds of Connecticut used to be pastures and crops; today, nearly all the state is woodland. All told, as much as 1 billion tons of carbon dioxide are sequestered every year in these growing forests; that offsets our emissions of greenhouse gases, which total about 6.6 billion tons of carbon dioxide equivalents today. (Carbon dioxide "equivalents" are the sum of all emissions of all greenhouse gases, weighted by the GWP exchange rate; of that total, 5.3 billion tons are in the form of carbon dioxide and the rest is other greenhouse gases.) The other sink is agricultural soils. Starting in about 1910—when tractors made it easier for farmers to plow deeper—intensive tilling has reduced the carbon content of America's soils. Since the 1950s, to help slow soil erosion farmers have shifted to "no till" techniques that have also caused the carbon content of soils to rise. There are no good data on exactly how much carbon the soils are absorbing, but luck and clever accounting could deliver a large number.

The problem with using these sinks for a large fraction of our Kyoto commitment is that both trends long pre-date concern about carbon emissions and global warming. Rules that will govern credits for these sinks have not yet been adopted, but the Kyoto Protocol implies that credit should be awarded only for activities that are caused by humans and somehow relate to efforts to slow global warming. Should you instruct your diplomats to secure rules that let us take credit for these sinks and twist our books into compliance? This is unwise for several reasons:

- Most other industrialized countries are in a similar or better position to take advantage of lenient rules. Russia's carbon sink from trees is perhaps twice the size of the U.S. sink, maybe larger; and in Europe, Japan and Australia the forests are also growing.

- We don't know the trends in agricultural soil carbon, but countries with historically poor agriculture practices might be in even better position than the United States to claim credit for agricultural sinks as they improve soil management techniques.

- Fundamentally, no sound method yet exists for determining the credit that should be awarded for soils and forests. Good methods exist for verifying the carbon balance at particular well-monitored plots, but methods are not yet adequate for measuring the carbon balance of whole countries. (Under international legal agreements such as the Kyoto Protocol, ultimate responsibility lies with countries and thus good accounting is needed at the country level.) It is important to develop good methods for including forest and soil carbon, but pushing this agenda now, just for the sake for finding a way to comply with the Kyoto Protocol, would build a foundation of sand for future emission accounting systems.

In short, time has run out for America to comply with the Kyoto targets mainly through actions within our borders. We must look to other countries for credits.

A second strategy is to comply by purchasing credits through the emission trading system. The problem with this scenario is that Russia and Ukraine are by far the cheapest source of emission credits—not because the Russians and Ukrainians have had an epiphany about the risks of global warming but rather because their savvy negotiators got an emission target in Kyoto that far exceeds the likely level of emissions. Russia and Ukraine agreed in Kyoto to freeze emissions at 1990 levels, but the collapse of the Soviet economy in the early 1990s means that their emissions are already far below that target and unlikely to recover fully by 2008. Selling the windfall to nations in emissions deficit—notably the United States—could earn Russia and Ukraine $50 to $150 billion. (About four-fifths of that windfall would flow to Russia.) Since the windfall is free—completely an artifact of the luck and skill of the diplomats in Kyoto rather than the result of any effort to control emissions—these permits would squeeze out bona fide efforts to control emissions. That buys paper compliance but no reduction in global warming. Don't expect Congress to be fooled by this ploy, not least because big financial transfers to Russia are not politically popular.

None of the proposed solutions to the problem of windfall permits—also known as "hot air"—is attractive. For example, the European Union has proposed a general rule that would cap the use of emission trading at 50% of each country's effort towards the Kyoto targets, but that rule would not halt the flow of windfall permits from Russia; rather, it would cause more harm than good by ensuring that each country filled its cap with windfall permits and probably eliminate any bona fide permits from the international emission trading market. Moreover, the proposed cap would set a bad precedent for the future because an emission trading system would be most efficient if trading were unlimited. The real problem is not the trading rules but that the Kyoto allocation of quotas is severely biased in favor of Russia. Reallocating the permits would require renegotiating the targets adopted in Kyoto, which in effect would require renegotiating the entire protocol

Finally, a third strategy envisions using the CDM to earn credits. However, it is unlikely that the United States could earn more than perhaps five percent of its Kyoto commitment through the CDM. Firms can't sensibly parachute into developing countries with tens (or hundreds) of billions of dollars in additional investments in efficient power plants, afforestation projects and other activities that earn large quantities of CDM credits before 2008-2012. Even though the clock is ticking, governments still have not agreed on the rules that would govern the CDM system; nor have they built the institutions that would be needed to oversee and approve CDM projects. In principle, the CDM is extremely important because it is a concrete way to engage developing countries and to diffuse modern technology into developing economies. But there should be no illusion about the difficulty, time and expense of building a viable CDM system; time has run out for the CDM to play a major role before 2008-2012.

All the other industrialized countries also face difficult choices, but most are not nearly in as tough a bind. For them, the first strategy—meeting the Kyoto targets mainly through their own actions—is much easier because special factors and sluggish economic growth have kept emissions low. For example, in Britain the collapse of the coal industry and the shift to gas and nuclear power have reduced emissions of carbon dioxide. Compared with coal, natural gas emits only half the carbon dioxide per unit of energy; nuclear power causes essentially no emissions of carbon dioxide or other greenhouse gases. No wonder that Tony Blair has suddenly become one of Kyoto's greatest advocates and the U.K. government is seriously considering cutting emissions beyond its Kyoto-related obligations. In Germany, the incorporation of the former communist East has also sharply cut emissions, mainly through economic recession and the replacement of inefficient equipment in the East. Together, Britain and Germany have propelled the European Union remarkably close to its Kyoto target. In Japan, persistent economic troubles have kept emissions low. The silver lining to a cloud of economic trouble is that the European Union and Japan are both already close to compliance and can plausibly claim that the Kyoto targets are achievable, although in reality they, too, will find it difficult to comply with the Kyoto targets fully. In contrast, since the mid-1990s U.S. emissions have continued to increase strongly—and the gap between actual U.S. emissions and the Kyoto target has widened—thanks mainly to the unprecedented robust growth of the U.S. economy.

> . . .since the mid-1990s U.S. emissions have continued to increase strongly—and the gap between actual U.S. emissions and the Kyoto target has widened—thanks mainly to the unprecedented robust growth of the U.S. economy.

Since the United States can't comply with Kyoto, we should make no effort to ratify it. However, you should not openly make that decision because doing so will incur the wrath of Kyoto's supporters here and overseas. For many, supporting Kyoto is synonymous with the mission of slowing global warming—rejecting the former will call into question your commitment to the latter, not least because the United States was the main architect of the Kyoto pact. Formally rejecting Kyoto will put the U.S. government on the defensive and undermine any effort to build a sensible alternative. Instead, you should make no formal decision about Kyoto. Over the next few years it will become clear that the Clinton administration has put you in a bind because the United States can't meet its Kyoto commitments—that fact is already clear to close observers of the scene. It is better that the bad news seep slowly and that fingers point to the previous administration than for you to paint a bull's eye on your administration by announcing a formal decision to abandon Kyoto.

Moreover, formally rejecting Kyoto will destroy a framework that continues to be useful. The Kyoto process is leading to the development of generic rules and institutions—for example, carbon accounting systems for forests and agricultural soils—that will be needed in any international cooperative effort to slow global warming. Those precedents will form the starting point for the effort to build a successor to Kyoto. U.S. diplomats are deeply involved in these efforts; they should be instructed to pursue rules that make economic and scientific sense and not to adopt any rules whose main purpose is simply to make the Kyoto emission targets for 2008-2012 easier to honor.

After Kyoto

Given the resources already invested in Kyoto, there will be very strong political pressure—in the United States and abroad—to leave the basic framework intact. As it becomes obvious that the United States and some other nations will not ratify the agreement, Kyoto's backers will merely want to stretch out the timetables and adjust the targets to make it easier to comply. However, the problems with the Kyoto Protocol are not merely the result of unrealistic targets and timetables that could be fixed through diplomatic tweaking. Rather, the problems are fundamental, and fixing them will require a different framework. The United States should take the lead in developing this alternative. Its exact form should emerge through consultation with your top advisors and key allies. A few elements to help start the rethinking process are outlined below. If you agree that an alternative is needed you should be prepared to back it with action and resources—the United States will be blamed for Kyoto's collapse, and an alternative will not gain acceptance unless it generates tangible and prompt results.

> . . .a superior framework must emerge from consultations with about six of the largest emitters of greenhouse gases—the United States, the European Union, Japan, China, India and Brazil.

First, a superior framework must emerge from consultations with about six of the largest emitters of greenhouse gases—the United States, the European Union, Japan, China, India and Brazil. Let us call this group the Climate 6 (C6); they account for most emissions of greenhouse gases today and include the main developing countries that will be the largest emitters of greenhouse gases in the future. A small group is needed because the current United Nations framework is too unwieldy for serious thinking about alternatives to the Kyoto architecture, and some of its members (e.g., oil-rich Saudi Arabia) actively work to undermine progress. The U.N. can remain as a global framework for cooperation, but a small group must lead with a foot outside the U.N.

Second, we should focus on controlling emissions of carbon dioxide caused by burning fossil fuels. This is the most important cause of global warming and, luckily, it is also the easiest flux to measure. Building a viable international framework for mitigating emissions of carbon dioxide will be hard enough without clouding the agenda with other gases that are much less important, harder to measure, and require use of the dubious GWP concept. Rather, we should expand the system to include other fluxes only after we develop a sound framework for fossil fuel CO_2.

Third, we must take a long-term perspective and set long-term goals. Governments have little leverage over the short term because most of the technologies that cause emissions of greenhouse gases, such as electric power plants and automobiles, are long-lived. The problem, however, is that it is difficult to use binding international legal agreements as instruments for negotiating long-term goals. Goals are most effective if they are ambitious and unequivocal, but many governments (including the U.S.) have been wary of negotiating such goals in binding treaties because circumstances change and compliance may not be possible years down the road. Thus, with the C6 we should start with nonbinding objectives and focus our international cooperation on packages of actions that countries will implement to achieve those objectives, such as commitments to remove fossil fuel subsidies, promote energy efficiency, and raise the cost of emitting carbon dioxide. Such a nonbinding framework would send clear long-term signals that emissions will be controlled, and it would promote focused and quantitative debate on the objectives beyond the short 2012 time period of the Kyoto Protocol. Crucially, by focusing on actions and long-term goals, the C6-led system would shift governments' energy away from the unrealistic short-term targets that have characterized global warming diplomacy to date and toward implementation and performance, which have been lacking.

Fourth, we must be sure that the long-term focus includes investment in new carbon-reducing technologies. Those investments should include not only efforts to improve existing technologies, such as making today's gas-fired power plants even more efficient. We should also invest in more radical schemes—such as hydrogen energy carriers and the next generation of nuclear power—that the private sector won't fund adequately on its own but which could eventually make feasible a carbon-free economy. The reports from the Clinton Administration's Presidential Committee of Advisors on Science and Technology (PCAST) established good plans for beginning that effort—we should fund those plans more fully. We will need to work with other major centers of innovation—in particular, Europe and Japan—to ensure that they make comparable new investments in basic research and technology.

Fifth, starting within the C6 we should implement programs to invest in carbon-saving technologies in developing countries. The U.S. government already participates in modest programs to diffuse energy technologies to developing countries, and the potential for earning CDM credits has led the private sector to make small additional investments in projects that reduce emissions of greenhouse gases from developing countries. We should subsidize a much larger effort—perhaps a few hundred million dollars per year at peak. That investment would demonstrate the tangible benefits to developing countries of participating in efforts to control emissions of greenhouse gases, and it would help demonstrate that the United States is taking this problem seriously. Such a practical program would also help analysts refine methods for measuring "baselines" and solve other technical problems that have plagued efforts to implement the CDM. It would increase the chance that future CDM rules will be based on real experience that is consistent with U.S. interests and the interests of U.S.-based vendors of energy equipment for the developing world.

Sixth, as experience grows—perhaps over 5-10 years—it will be necessary for the C6 and other nations to codify basic obligations into binding treaties. A nonbinding framework, advocated above, can set norms and provide direction, but it will not be adequate as the cost of action rises and the incentives to "free ride" mount. A ratified, binding treaty will be needed to assure countries that others are making comparable efforts.

Negotiating a new binding treaty must start with a clear understanding of why the Kyoto Protocol has not worked. In principle, the Kyoto approach—setting emission targets and allowing trading of emission credits—is an elegant market-based mechanism for controlling emissions of greenhouse gases. In practice, however, the approach impedes international cooperation because it requires creating and allocating new property rights (emission permits) that are worth hundreds of billions of dollars. Making that allocation is extremely difficult for two reasons. First, nations will be extremely wary of getting a raw deal because they are mindful that circumstances could change and they could be saddled with unexpectedly high compliance costs. Indeed, the surprising surge in U.S. emissions after Kyoto—and the decline in British and German emissions—reveals just how much can change in only a few years. Second, allocation of such large assets is especially difficult under international law because countries that are dissatisfied with the outcome can defect. If enough nations defect—as the United States must from the Kyoto pact—then it will not be possible to "cold start" an international emission trading program. Even if the program were started, the threat of defection would loom like a cloud over the trading system. Securing property rights so that markets can operate efficiently requires strong rule of law, which is not available in the international system.

One widely discussed alternative to Kyoto-like emission targets and trading is to coordinate emission taxes. The tax approach makes the most economic sense, but it is impossible to monitor and enforce under international law and must therefore be rejected. The best option is to combine the two mechanisms— trading and taxation—into a hybrid system that regulates both the quantity of emissions as well as the price. Countries would set emission targets and allow trading, but if the price of controlling emissions ever exceeded a "trigger" level then governments could raise the quota by selling more tradable permits at the trigger price. By capping the price the hybrid mechanism would help assure that the cost of controlling emissions would not be unexpectedly large, which would make governments more willing to adopt meaningful binding commitments, ease the process of allocating permits, and make an international agreement less prone to defection if circumstances change.

If the initial cuts in emissions are modest—as surely they will be—then the hybrid approach has another especially attractive feature: most of the economic advantages of this hybrid approach could be achieved without international emission permit trading. Thus the United States could justify implementing this approach at home even before a full international framework was in place. That would send a clear signal to firms that they should begin to control emissions, demonstrate that you are taking the global warming problem seriously, and make it more likely that a similar system would be adopted at the international level. Starting with a generous allocation of permits and a low trigger price could achieve all of these benefits while minimizing the cost imposed on U.S. business. To sweeten the economic and political advantages of this approach, the U.S. government could use the proceeds from auctioning and selling permits to offset capital gains and labor taxes—making it possible for you to build a winning coalition that could also benefit the U.S. economy by promoting investment and work. As you start work with the C6 you will be under pressure to make concrete efforts to control emissions—implementing the hybrid approach here in the United States and working with the others to do the same overseas would be a wise first step.

Global warming is the toughest international environmental problem that the community of nations has confronted. Solutions require a long-term perspective because the greatest risks of climate change lie many years ahead and there is little that we can do to leverage emissions over only a decade. That long-term perspective requires new legal instruments and institutions; we can play a constructive role in building those, but none of the sensible paths start with ratifying the Kyoto Protocol.

MEMORANDUM TO THE PRESIDENT

From: **Per Pinstrup-Andersen**

Subject: **Feeding the World in the New Millennium**

PROBLEM

One of every five people in the developing world is hungry. The new U.S. administration must put solutions to this catastrophe high on its agenda—and encourage other nations to do likewise—for six reasons:

- Hunger spawns illness, instability, violent conflict, and refugees—problems that are seldom contained within national borders and often spill into the United States;

- poor and hungry people do not make good trading partners;

- developing countries offer the most promising future market for U.S. goods and services;

- hunger fuels environmental degradation as desperate people try to eke out a living on ever more marginal land and migrate to urban slums in search of livelihoods;

- environmental degradation in developing countries affects the United States; and

- it is the morally right thing to do.

BACKGROUND

Poverty and Hunger

About 1.2 billion people in developing countries—almost five times the U.S. population—live on $1 a day or less.[1] These people often cannot afford to buy all the food they need, although they may spend 50–70 percent of their incomes trying,[2] and many do not have access to land to produce food.

The number of hungry people has fallen since 1970, but 800 million people in developing countries (18 percent of the total) remain chronically undernourished.[3] Severe undernourishment is rare in industrialized countries, but many low-income people have difficulty meeting their food needs. The U.S. Department of Agriculture (USDA) considers 31 million people in the United States—about one in ten—"food insecure," i.e., unable to regularly afford an adequate diet.[4] The rising economic tide of the 1990s has left many boats stuck on the bottom.

> . . .800 million people in developing countries remain chronically undernourished.

The largest number of hungry people is in the Asia-Pacific region, especially South Asia (the Indian subcontinent). The other global hunger hot spot is sub-Saharan Africa, the only region in which the number of hungry people is expected to increase during the next 20 years. If the international community does not make significant policy changes, the developing world's hungry population will only fall to 650 million by 2015, with hunger even more concentrated in Africa and South Asia. This is far short of the 1996 World Food Summit goal, agreed to by the United States, to reduce hunger by half by 2015.

Malnutrition among preschool children is of particular concern. Each year, it contributes to 5 million deaths of children less than 5 years old in the developing world—this is ten times the number of people that die from cancer annually in the United States. Even when they reach their fifth birthdays, malnourished children frequently suffer impaired physical and mental development. The silent scourge of malnutrition robs the human family of countless artists, scientists, community leaders, and productive workers. Currently, there are 150 million malnourished preschoolers in developing countries (27 percent of the total number of children less than five years old there). Malnourished mothers frequently have low-birthweight babies who are vulnerable to malnutrition, in effect passing hunger across generations.[5]

The International Food Policy Research Institute (IFPRI) projects that by 2020, without any changes in national and international policies, the number of developing-country malnourished preschoolers will still be 135 million (25 percent). The number will increase substantially in Africa, and 77 percent of all hungry preschoolers will live there and in South Asia.[6] Acute malnutrition is rare among U.S. children, but USDA estimates that 40 percent of the people in the United States who are food-insecure—12 million—are children. The reduction in global child malnutrition between 1990 and 2020 will not reach 25 percent, even though the World Summit for Children in 1990 pledged to halve preschooler malnutrition by 2000.[7]

Hunger is not just a problem of consuming too little food. Diets may also lack vitamins and minerals. Roughly 75 percent of people in the developing world consume too little iron; one billion suffer from anemia as a result. Iron-deficiency anemia is also a problem in wealthier countries, including the United States. It can lead to mothers dying during childbirth, newborn deaths, poor health and development among surviving children, and limited learning and work capacity. In some developing countries, iron-deficiency anemia reduces national income by as much as 1 percent annually. Inadequate vitamin A intake among developing-country children causes blindness, infections, and tens of thousands of deaths. Pregnant vitamin A-deficient women face increased risk of death in childbirth and mother-to-child HIV transmission.[8]

The Supply Side

For the past 25 years, total global food production has consistently been more than adequate to provide everyone with minimum calorie requirements if food were distributed according to needs. However, in recent years, food production has been stagnant or declining in countries the United Nations has designated "low-income food deficit." Poor weather, economic difficulties, and violent conflict create short- and even long-term food shortages affecting millions of people.

IFPRI estimates a gap between food production and demand in several parts of the world by 2020. Population growth, urbanization, changes in income levels, and associated changes in dietary preferences all affect demand. World population is projected to increase 25 percent to 7.5 billion in 2020. On average, 73 million people—equivalent to the population of the Philippines—will be added each year, virtually all in developing countries. Urban population in developing countries is expected to double. When people move to cities, they shift to foods that require less preparation time and to more meat, milk, fruit, and vegetables.

Average incomes in all developing regions are expected to increase through 2020, but income inequality is likely to persist within and between countries. Poverty is likely to remain entrenched in South Asia and Latin America and to increase considerably in Africa, where the average income per person will be less than $1 a day. Many millions of impoverished people will be unable to afford the food they need even if it is available in the marketplace.

A 58 percent increase in global meat demand is forecasted between 1995 and 2020, with almost all of it coming from the developing world. This livestock revolution is already under way and will double developing countries' feedgrain demand during the next two decades. Farmers will have to produce 40 percent more cereals in 2020, with 80 percent of additional output coming from yield increases rather than farmland expansion. However, in both developed and developing countries, rates of increase in cereal yields are slowing as low cereal prices have reduced fertilizer use, and levels of investment in agricultural research and technology are low. Poorly functioning markets and lack of infrastructure and credit also contribute. Africa is falling behind other regions.

> **Farmers will have to produce 40 percent more cereals in 2020, with 80 percent of additional output coming from yield increases rather than farmland expansion. However . . . rates of increase in cereal yields are slowing.**

IFPRI projects that developing countries' cereal production will not keep pace with demand through 2020. Net cereal imports will increase by 80 percent between 1995 and 2020. With a 34 percent increase projected in net cereal exports, the United States will continue to capture a large market share, providing about 60 percent of the developing world's net cereal imports. However, competition will increase from Eastern Europe, the former Soviet Union, the European Union, and Australia.[9]

Constraints on Ending Hunger

Several factors could significantly influence the food outlook during the next few decades:

Trade Liberalization. Many developing countries have liberalized food and agricultural trade since the 1980s. Developed countries have not taken reciprocal measures, maintaining barriers to high value commodities from developing countries, such as beef, sugar, peanuts, dairy products, and processed goods.

Developing countries must be encouraged to participate effectively in upcoming global agricultural trade negotiations, pursuing better access to industrialized countries' markets. However, without appropriate domestic economic and agricultural policies, developing countries in general and poor people in particular will not fully capture potential benefits from trade liberalization. The distribution of benefits will be determined largely by distribution of productive assets, such as land, water, and credit. In addition, many developing countries lack the infrastructure and the administrative and technical capacity to comply with global trade rules. The African share of world agricultural trade continues to decline rapidly. The effect of current trade agreements is likely to be adverse for most African countries.

Low-income countries must try to strengthen their bargaining position and pursue changes in both domestic policies and international trade arrangements:

- enact domestic policy reforms to remove biases against small-scale farmers and poor people while facilitating access to benefits from more open trade;

- seek elimination of industrial countries' export subsidies, taxes, and controls that exacerbate price fluctuations;

- provide technical assistance and financial support for poor countries' agriculture;

- create strong animal and plant health standards and technical support to help developing countries produce for developed-country markets; and

- convince donors to target adequate levels of food aid to poor groups in ways that do not displace domestic production.10

Decreasing Aid. Aid to agriculture and rural development shrunk by almost half between 1986 and 1997. The share of aid going to agriculture dropped from 25 to 14 percent. Aid to education has similarly declined, and overall development aid fell about 17 percent between 1992 and 1997.[11] Yet research has found that aid to developing-country agriculture not only is effective in promoting sustainable development and poverty alleviation, but it also leads to increased export opportunities for developed countries, including increased agricultural exports as agricultural growth spurs more general economic growth and demand for food products.[12] In addition to reversing the aid decline, donors, including the United States, must rethink their 20-year emphasis on reducing government's economic role, which has contributed to developing countries' public disinvestment in agriculture.[13]

In the post-cold war era, the United States has fallen to last place among donors in terms of aid as a percentage of gross national product (less than 0.1 percent). In absolute terms, U.S. aid has consistently ranked second to Japan's.[14]

In the late 1990s, the United States expanded food aid after substantial reductions mid-decade.[15] Fluctuations stemmed from domestic market conditions rather than developing-country needs, as the United States continues to tie food aid to U.S. farm products.

Conflict, Refugees, and Food Security. Since the end of the Cold War, internal conflicts have proliferated in developing and transition countries, particularly in Africa. Fourteen million refugees have fled these struggles, which have displaced another 20 million to 30 million people within their own countries.[16] Uprooted people are vulnerable to malnutrition and disease and need humanitarian assistance to survive. Postconflict reconstruction takes years. Violent conflict not only causes hunger, but hunger often contributes to conflict, especially when resources are scarce and perceptions of economic injustice are widespread.[17]

Soil fertility management. Policies and investments are needed to eradicate hunger and protect natural resources, thereby breaking the vicious cycle of poverty, low productivity, and environmental degradation.

Low soil fertility and lack of access to affordable fertilizers, along with past and current failures to replenish soil nutrients in many countries, must be rectified through efficient use of organic and inorganic fertilizers and improved soil management. Reduced chemical fertilizer use is warranted where heavy application is harming the environment. Nevertheless, it is critical to expand fertilizer use where soil fertility is low and a large share of the population is hungry, especially in Africa. This will help boost production and reduce the serious land degradation that affects 20 percent of African farmland.[18]

Pest management. Preharvest losses to pests (insects, animals, weeds, and plant diseases) reduce the potential value of farm output by 40 percent; postharvest losses cost another 10 percent. In developing countries, losses greatly exceed agricultural aid received.[19] Developing countries' share of the global pesticide market is expected to increase significantly during the early 21st century. Insecticides now used in developing countries are often older and acutely toxic and often banned in developed countries except for export.

Until recently, developing-country governments and aid donors encouraged use of chemical pesticides. Now, consensus is emerging on the need for integrated pest management, emphasizing alternatives to synthetic chemicals except as a last resort. Alternatives include use of natural predators and biological pesticides as well as breeding pest-resistant crops.[20]

Water. Globally, water supplies are sufficient to meet demand through 2020. But water is poorly distributed across countries, within countries, and between seasons. Competition is increasing among uses. Developing countries are projected to increase water withdrawals 43 percent between 1995 and 2020, doubling domestic and industrial uses at the expense of agriculture.

Policy reforms can save water, improve use efficiency, and boost crop output per unit of water while reducing the risk of armed conflict between countries sharing surface or ground water sources. These reforms should include establishing secure water rights, decentralizing and privatizing water management, and setting conservation incentives.[21] (See Gleick memo.)

Wild and marginal land. Poor people in developing countries tend to depend on annual crops (which generally degrade soils more than perennial crops) and on common property lands (which generally suffer greater degradation than privately managed land). They often cannot afford to invest in land improvements. Degradation and lack of access to high-quality land frequently push poor people to clear forests and pastures for cultivation, often at the expense of wildlife habitat, contributing to further degradation. Policies should raise the value of forests and pastures, offer incentives for sound management, and help create nonfarm employment opportunities.[22]

Broad-Based Agricultural Development is Critical

Despite rapid urbanization, poverty remains overwhelmingly rural in developing countries and is likely to remain so for decades. Hence, agriculture is key to reducing poverty. Even when rural people are not farmers or farm workers, they work in jobs closely related to agriculture, such as employment in enterprises producing processed food, tools, household goods, or services for agriculture.[23] Research has shown that for every new dollar of farm income earned in developing countries, income in the economy as a whole rises by as much as $2.60 as increasing farm demand generates employment, income, and growth economywide.[24] Agricultural growth also helps meet rising food demand and creates incentives for sustainable management of the natural resource base necessary for agriculture.

> **Agricultural growth ... creates incentives for sustainable management of the natural resource base. ...**

Sound public policies are essential to guarantee that agricultural and rural development is broad based, creating opportunities for small-scale farmers and other poor people. Markets have a critical role but by themselves cannot assure equity. Key public investments include

- assuring poor farmers access to yield-increasing crop varieties (including drought- and salt-tolerant and pest-resistant varieties), improved livestock, and other yield-increasing and environment-friendly technology;

- access to tools, fertilizer, pest management, and credit;

- extension services and technical assistance;

- improved rural infrastructure such as roads and effective markets;

- particular attention to the needs of women farmers, who grow much of the locally produced food in developing countries; and

- primary education, health care, clean water, safe sanitation, and good nutrition for all.

The policy atmosphere must promote poverty reduction, must not discriminate against agriculture, and should provide incentives for sound natural resource management, such as secure property rights for small-scale farmers. Policies and programs must engage low-income people as active participants, not passive recipients; development efforts seldom succeed unless affected people have a sense of ownership. Unfortunately, public investment in agriculture is on the decline in developing countries. On average, these countries devote 7.5 percent of government spending to agriculture (and the figure is even lower in many African countries).[25]

Agricultural Research Is Essential

Public investment in agricultural research is crucial to food security. The private sector is unlikely to undertake research needed by small-scale farmers in developing countries—even though societal benefits may be extremely large—because it cannot expect sufficient gains to cover costs. Currently, low-income developing countries grossly underinvest in agricultural research: less than 0.5 percent of the value of agricultural production, compared with 2.0 percent in higher-income countries.[26]

Research should focus on productivity gains on small farms, emphasizing staple food crops and livestock. More research must be directed to appropriate technology for sustainable intensification of agriculture in resource-poor areas, where many poor people live. All appropriate scientific tools and better utilization of indigenous knowledge should be mobilized to help small-scale farmers in developing countries. These tools include not only new technologies that rely on external inputs, but also agroecology, which focuses on locally available farm labor and organic material as well as improved knowledge and farm management. In addition to the strengthening of national agricultural research in developing countries, international agricultural research, particularly the work by the Consultative Group on International Agricultural Research (CGIAR), should be supported.

Developed countries stand to gain from support for agricultural research for developing countries. For example, high-yielding varieties of wheat and rice bred by the Future Harvest centers for use in developing countries are now widely planted in the United States as well as in the developing world.[27]

The Role of Modern Agricultural Biotechnology

Modern biotechnology[28] is not a silver bullet for ending hunger, but, used in conjunction with traditional and conventional agricultural research methods, it may be a powerful tool that should be made available to poor farmers and consumers. It has the potential to help enhance agricultural productivity in developing countries in ways that reduce hunger and poverty and promote sustainable natural resource use.

Current applications of molecular biology-based science to agriculture are oriented toward industrial country farmers and commercial farmers in a few developing countries. The United States alone cultivates more than 70 percent of genetically modified (GM) crops.[29]

Strong opposition to GM food in the European Union has resulted in severe restrictions on modern agricultural biotechnology. Opposition stems from perceived lack of consumer benefits, uncertainty about possible negative health and environmental effects, and widespread sentiment that a few large corporations will be the main beneficiaries. Consumers outnumber farmers by 20 to 1 in the European Union and spend only a tiny fraction of their income on food. U.S.

agriculture employs 2.6 percent of the workforce, and people spend an average of 12.0 percent of their income on food.[30] These numbers contrast sharply with comparable developing-country figures noted earlier.

Modern agricultural biotechnology offers many potential benefits to poor farmers and consumers in developing countries. It may help achieve the productivity gains needed to feed a growing global population, introduce resistance to pests without high-cost purchased inputs, heighten crops' tolerance to adverse weather and soil conditions, offer more nutritious foods, and enhance products' durability during harvesting or shipping. Bioengineered products may reduce reliance on pesticides, lowering crop protection costs and benefiting the environment and public health. By increasing yields and lowering unit production costs, biotechnology could help reduce food prices, greatly benefiting poor consumers. Biotechnology-assisted research developed broader-leafed rice that denies weeds sunlight, increasing farm incomes in West Africa and reducing the time women farmers spend weeding, allowing more time for the child care essential for good nutrition. Development of cereal plants capable of capturing nitrogen from the air could contribute greatly to plant nutrition and soil health while helping small-scale farmers who cannot afford fertilizers. Biotechnology may offer cost-effective solutions to vitamin and mineral deficiencies, such as vitamin A- and iron-rich rice. By increasing productivity, agricultural biotechnology could help conserve wild and marginal land and biodiversity.

> **Modern agricultural biotechnology . . . .may help achieve the productivity gains needed to feed a growing global population. . . .**

Public policy must guide research. In addition to increasing the public resources for agricultural research, including biotechnology research, the public sector can entice the private sector to develop technologies for poor people by offering to buy the exclusive rights and make technologies available to small-scale farmers.[31]

Before GM crops and foods are introduced, a country should have sound food safety and environmental regulations to assess the risks and opportunities involved. Health risks include the transfer of allergy-causing traits through genetic engineering. GM foods need to be tested for such transfers, and those with possible allergy risks should be labeled. Environmental risks requiring assessment include the spread of traits, such as herbicide resistance to unmodified plants (including weeds), the buildup of resistance among pests, and unintended harm to other species.

Recent mergers and acquisitions in the biotechnology industry may lead to reduced competition, monopoly or oligopoly profits, exploitation of small-scale farmers and consumers, and extraction of special favors from governments. Institutions to promote competition and an effective antitrust system must be established in developing countries.

The biggest risk is that modern agricultural biotechnology will bypass poor people in a kind of "scientific apartheid."[32] Opportunities for reducing poverty, food insecurity, child malnutrition, and natural resource degradation will be missed, and the productivity gap between developing- and developed-country agriculture will widen for the benefit of no one.

RECOMMENDATIONS

There is nothing inevitable about this rather pessimistic forecast regarding world hunger. It is possible to meet and even exceed the World Food Summit's goal. If the new administration takes the appropriate actions, world hunger could decrease significantly by 2020. Achieving this will require concerted and committed action by governments, citizen groups, and the international community to empower poor people; mobilize new technological developments—including those in biotechnology—to benefit poor and hungry people in developing countries; invest in the factors essential for agricultural growth, including agricultural research and human resource development; and harness the political will to adopt sound antipoverty, food security, and natural-resource management policies. Failing to take these steps will mean continued low economic growth and rapidly increasing food insecurity and malnutrition in many low-income developing countries, environmental deterioration, forgone trading opportunities, widespread conflict, and an unstable world for all.

The United States should make the eradication of hunger the top priority of its relations with developing countries, as the Presidential Commission on World

Hunger recommended 20 years ago. Leadership of global cooperation to end hunger requires new policies:

Domestic hunger. The United States must address domestic hunger with employment policies to ensure adequate incomes for everyone to meet their needs, along with a nutrition safety net. This safety net should include full funding of the Special Supplemental Nutrition Program for Women, Infants, and Children (WIC). Every dollar invested in WIC saves up to $3.50 on Medicaid and special education. All schools should provide breakfast and lunch, with free meals for low-income children. Food stamp benefit levels should increase by 10 percent, and eligibility restrictions should be loosened.

Increased aid. The United States spends a smaller percentage of national income on development assistance than any other Organisation for Economic Development and Cooperation (OECD) country. As the world's wealthiest country, the United States can afford to increase aid to developing countries. It would cost an additional $12 billion annually to bring the United States up to the industrialized-country average of 0.24 percent of GNP devoted to aid, a figure equivalent to half of U.S. annual sales of sporting goods and one-quarter of U.S. spending on tobacco products. The increase comes to $44 per person per year. Such an expansion would leverage additional funds from other countries and accelerate progress toward ending hunger. Polls consistently show public support for aid aimed at reducing poverty and hunger.

Need-based aid. The United States should target aid resources based on need (i.e., to countries with high levels of poverty and hunger, particularly in South Asia and Africa). Aid should go to countries where government policies support poverty alleviation and sound natural resource management. Investment in building prosperity, peace, and stability in these countries promises the United States the potential for future commercial relationships. It is a win-win proposition.

Improved aid. Qualitative improvements in aid are needed, such as giving priority to human capital development and high-impact interventions. These include aid to broad-based agricultural and rural development and national and international agricultural research (including increased support for CGIAR and international programs at Land Grant universities and colleges), clean water, safe sanitation, universal primary education, access to basic health care, access to credit, land reform, natural resource management, and democracy and popular participation in development. Resources should be redirected from higher income recipients and military aid to these priorities.

Social development. Research has shown that improvements in female education, food availability per person, health care, and women's social status all enhance child nutrition. Educating girls has an especially strong impact. Increased national incomes and democratic governance are also important.[33] Aid programs must include conflict prevention and resolution components. Postconflict assistance must focus on reconstruction and underlying social tensions.

Food aid. Food aid for humanitarian emergencies is essential. It should also be used to help ease transitions and dislocations caused by economic reforms and trade liberalization, maternal and child health activities, school meals and building, and restoring roads and irrigation systems through "food for work." The United States should continue to provide food aid through international organizations and nongovernmental organizations, allowing them to sell commodities to generate funds for high-priority development activities. The United States should significantly increase the use of food aid resources to procure food in recipient countries and other developing countries and for direct purchase of seeds, fertilizers, tools, and livestock for poor farmers.

Biotechnology. The United States should support agricultural biotechnology research oriented toward poor farmers and consumers in developing countries and assist developing countries in building capacity to enact and enforce food safety, biosafety, and competition-enhancing and antitrust regulations.

Agricultural trade policy. In light of the continuing importance of the United States as a supplier of food and agriculture products to the global market, domestic farm policies should promote productivity gains and sustainable natural-resource management to assure continued viability of the food and agriculture sector. Policies should focus on preserving and enhancing family farming operations because small- and medium-sized farms are at least as efficient as larger commercial operations. They tend to provide sound management of soil, water, and wildlife; and decentralized land ownership produces more equitable economic opportunity for rural communities and greater social capital.[34]

With respect to agricultural trade policy, maintaining current inequities in the global trading system does not develop long-term, mutually beneficial relationships between developing and developed countries. Allowing higher-value agricultural products from developing countries into U.S. markets without escalating tariffs and encouraging other industrialized countries to take similar steps could greatly benefit developing countries and enhance global public opinion regarding the trading system. In addition, the United States should end export subsidies (both explicit and hidden) and encourage other industrialized countries to eliminate policies that exacerbate global price fluctuations. The United States should also seek a global intellectual property rights framework that balances rights of seed companies and other plant breeders with farmers' rights to save and reuse seed.

MEMORANDUM TO THE PRESIDENT

From: Peter H. Gleick

Subject: Global Water: Threats and Challenges Facing the U.S.

PROBLEM

Four critical challenges and threats related to freshwater resources are likely to require U.S. unilateral, bilateral, or multilateral action during the new presidential administration. Several others will require the special attention of senior members of the administration. These issues have the potential to affect U.S. diplomatic relations with neighboring countries and allies and are likely to affect economic and political security in the United States. Below is a short assessment of these top problems and specific recommendations for addressing them.

   Threats to national interest and security. There is a growing risk of political insecurity and instability in regions where access to fresh water is a problem. These include the Middle East, southern Africa, the central Asian republics, and south Asia, including India, Pakistan, Bangladesh, and Nepal. Other less predictable hot spots are likely to appear. Diplomatic efforts to reduce the risks of conflict must now include an environmental component; military preparedness should also include environmental threat analysis.

   A continuing global water crisis. Access to basic water services, including clean drinking water and sanitation services, is still unavailable for between 2 and 3 billion people worldwide. International efforts to spotlight this problem are necessary, as are multilateral efforts to solve it. The failure to provide basic services will lead to direct and indirect public health ramifications for the United States. The United States should play a leading role in addressing these problems, in redirecting foreign aid budgets, and in encouraging international aid organizations to refocus efforts toward meeting basic water needs.

Lack of a national water policy. The nation's limited freshwater endowment is used inefficiently and ineffectively, in part because of the lack of basic national water policy. If this waste continues unabated, it will impoverish this and future generations, destroy the limited remaining aquatic ecosystems, and threaten the world's future food supply. Increasing the productive use of water nationwide will benefit farmers, cities, and the natural environment. Federal and state programs and top-level political support are required.

Growing consequences of the greenhouse effect. Global climate change is increasingly likely to affect vital U.S. sectors in the coming years, including many related to freshwater resources. Climate change will affect the reliability of the nation's water supply and quality, hydroelectric generation, and food security. The nation could also begin to see changes in the magnitude, frequency, and costs of extreme events, such as flooding and drought. The recently completed national assessment highlighted many of the most important problems, but follow-up work is still needed on the part of the nation's water community.

BACKGROUND

Water Availability and Use in the United States

The United States, as a nation, is well endowed with water. However, the country's resources are unevenly distributed and inefficiently used. The United States has spent billions of dollars over the last century to develop an engineering infrastructure (including dams, reservoirs, aqueducts, waste treatment facilities, and flood control levees) necessary for the management of water resources. These facilities have had tremendous positive effects on the nation and its economy, but they have also been accompanied by severe negative effects, including degradation of natural ecosystems, a false sense of protection against floods, and complacency toward water-quality problems.

An average of around 4,200 billion gallons of precipitation fall each day on the United States, while 2,800 billion gallons per day evaporate back into the atmosphere. Of the remainder, only 100 billion gallons are consumptively used by the nation's farms, cities, and industry. These numbers suggest—misleadingly—that the nation as a whole has no problem with water scarcity and that far more water could be used.

Several additional factors must be taken into account. First, water availability varies enormously by region and time. Second, the western United States receives far less precipitation and has far more evaporation than the eastern portion of the country. Third, water that humans do not use is not "wasted"—it meets critical ecological needs for flora and fauna. "Instream" uses of water (i.e., water left in a river or stream to meet environmental and other needs), only recently recognized by a few federal and state laws, must be maintained to keep fish and other wildlife populations healthy. Finally, although humans only "consume" around 100 billion gallons per day, far more water is withdrawn for human uses. Most of the time, this additional water is returned to the stream, river, or lake after use. Sometimes it is taken from one watershed and returned to another. Sometimes the water itself is returned but degraded in quality. Thus the overall impact of human water use is far greater than that suggested by the measure of how much water is consumed.

Building water infrastructure, including reservoirs, dams, aqueducts and pipelines, has required an enormous economic investment. In the United States, total capital investment for water infrastructure during the past century has been estimated at $400 billion (unnormalized); most of this money took the form of federal subsidies that will never be repaid. In the western United States, limited availability and growing demand for water led to the construction of hundreds of the world's most massive dams on every major river. By the mid-1990s, the United States (largely though the actions of the U.S. Bureau of Reclamation and the Army Corps of Engineers) had built more than 80,000 dams and reservoirs, nearly 90,000 megawatts of hydroelectric capacity, and more than 15,000 municipal wastewater treatment plants. During the same boom in construction, more than

60 percent of the inland wetlands of the United States was lost, half of all stream miles was significantly polluted, and many major fisheries were destroyed.[1]

As the new century begins, these traditional approaches to water planning, although still firmly entrenched in many water-planning institutions, are beginning to change. Water needs in the United States are no longer increasing, even though the economy and population continue to grow. Concern for the environment has led to restrictions on when and where new projects can be built. And the costs of new water infrastructure now often exceed the costs of improving water-use efficiency and productivity.

Throughout the first three-quarters of this century, water withdrawals increased, as shown in Figure 1. In 1900, estimated U.S. water withdrawals for all

Total water withdrawals in the United States: 1900–1990

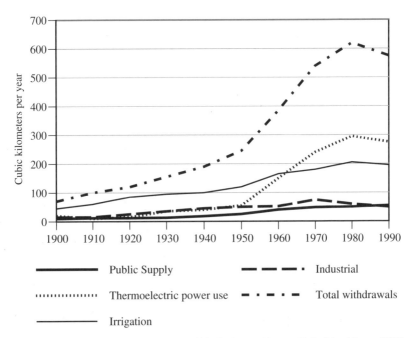

SOURCE: P.H. Gleick, *The World's Water 1998–1999*, (Washington, D.C.: Island Press, 1998).

Figure 1

Total U.S. population and per-capita water withdrawals: 1900–1995

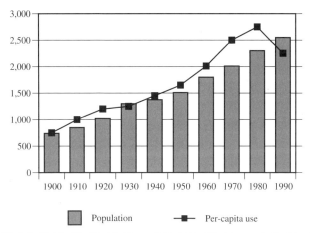

SOURCE: P.H. Gleick, *The World's Water 1998–1999*, (Washington, D.C.: Island Press, 1998).

Figure 2

purposes were 56 cubic kilometers per year (km³/yr). By 1950, total water withdrawals were 250 km³/yr, and by 1970, withdrawals doubled to more than 500 km³/yr. Water use in the United States peaked in 1980 at more than 610 km³/yr—a tenfold increase in water withdrawals during a period in which population increased by a factor of four. Water withdrawals were not only growing in an absolute sense, they were growing in a per-capita sense (see Figure 2). In 1900, freshwater use was less than 700 cubic meters per person per year (m³/p/yr). By the late 1970s and early 1980s, it had increased to nearly 2,300 m³/p/yr. These increases in water demands, more than any other factor, drove the incredible burst of construction of water infrastructure.[2]

Beginning in the early 1980s, these trends of increased water withdrawals ended in the United States and withdrawals began to decline despite continued increases in population and economic wealth—a dramatic departure from the expectations and experience of water planners. Water withdrawals have now dropped nearly 10 percent from their peak in 1980, as shown in Figure 1. The two largest components of U.S. water use—irrigation and water for thermoelectric power plant cooling—have declined by about 10 percent. Industrial water use has

U.S. GNP and water withdrawals

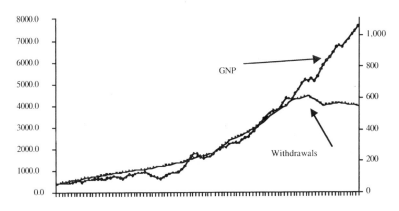

NOTE: U.S. gross national product (in 1996 dollars) and total U.S. water withdrawals (cubic kilometers per year), from 1900 to 1999. Note that the two curves diverged in the late 1970s/early 1980s, indicating that the United States has become more efficient in its use of water per dollar of GNP.
SOURCE: P.H. Gleick, Pacific Institute for Studies in Development, Environment, and Security, Oakland, California.

Figure 3

dropped even more dramatically, falling nearly 40 percent from its height in 1970 as industrial water-use efficiency has improved and as the mix of U.S. industries has changed. Yet industrial output and productivity have continued to soar, clearly demonstrating the possibility of breaking the link between water use and industrial production. Figure 3 shows how the link between water use and gross national product (GNP) changed dramatically starting in the late 1970s. The key message here is that improving the productive use of existing water resources, through reducing waste and inefficiency, is a relatively fast and inexpensive way to meet new water needs.

Water and U.S. Security Interests

In the past decade there has been a major rethinking of the field of international security. With the end of the cold war and the break up of the Soviet Union, the world has witnessed growing concern over regional conflicts, civil, religious, and ethnic wars within regions, and, particularly, the connections between environmental degradation, scarcity of resources, and regional and international politics and disputes. These latter issues have loosely been grouped under the term "environment and security" and interest in them has engendered a wide range of innovative studies.[3] (See Homer-Dixon memo.)

History shows that access to resources has been a proximate cause of war, resources have been both tools and targets of war, and environmental degradation and the disparity in the distribution of resources can cause major political controversy, tension, and violence. In 1989, then Secretary of State James Baker said, "The strategic, economic, political, and environmental aspects of national security and global well-being are, today, indivisible."

In 1994, then UN Ambassador Madeleine K. Albright stated, "We believe that environmental degradation is not simply an irritation, but a real threat to our national security. . . . Left unaddressed, it could become a kind of creeping Armageddon. . . it could, in time, threaten our very survival."

In 1997, Secretary of State Albright said, "Not so long ago, many believed that the pursuit of clean air, clean water, and healthy forests was a worthy goal, but not part of our national security. Today environmental issues are part of the mainstream of American foreign policy."[4]

The argument and focus of debate has now shifted from "whether" to "when, where, and how" environmental and resource problems will affect regional and international security. In the past several years there has been considerable progress in understanding the nature of the connections between water resources and conflict and in evaluating regional cases where such connections may be particularly strong. There has also been progress in identifying policies and principles for reducing the risk that freshwater disputes will lead to conflict.

Progress has been more than academic. For example, in October 1994, Israel and Jordan signed a peace treaty that explicitly addressed water disputes in the Jordan River Basin. U.S. diplomats, academics, and nongovernmental organizations played leading roles in facilitating this treaty. In 1996, India and Bangladesh signed a treaty that moves toward resolving their long-standing dispute concerning river flows in the

Ganges/Brahmaputra system. In 1997, the International Law Commission finalized the Convention on the Non-Navigational Uses of Shared International Watercourses, which was approved by the United Nations General Assembly.

The ultimate goal of U.S. foreign policy related to the risks of conflicts over water must be efforts to reduce those risks. Various approaches exist for reducing water-related tensions, including legal agreements, the application of proper technology, institutions for dispute resolution, and innovative water management. Unfortunately, these mechanisms have never received the international support necessary to resolve many conflicts over water. Efforts by the United Nations, aid agencies, and local communities to ensure access to clean drinking water and adequate sanitation can reduce the competition for limited water supplies and the economic and social impacts of widespread waterborne diseases. Improving the efficiency of water use in agriculture can extend limited resources, increase supplies for other users, strengthen food self-sufficiency, reduce hunger, and decrease expenditures for imported food. In regions with shared water supplies, third-party participation in resolving water disputes can also help end conflicts. The United States can play important roles in each of these areas.

> **The failure to provide basic sanitation services and clean water to billions of people around the world is perhaps the greatest failure of human development in the 20th century.**

Global Water Crisis and Human Health

The failure to provide basic sanitation services and clean water to billions of people around the world is perhaps the greatest failure of human development in the 20th century. As a result of this failure, water-related diseases such as cholera, dysentery, and parasitic diseases are on the upswing in many developing countries. Nearly 250 million cases are reported every year, with between 5 million and 10 million deaths. Yet the world is falling further behind in its efforts to provide these basic services. Between 1990 and 1997, 300 million more people were added to the 2,600 million already without adequate sanitation services. The failure to completely satisfy basic human needs for water and water services is the result of rapid population growth, underinvestment, growing urbanization, and misdirected priorities.[5] The United States is at risk from water-related diseases that may increasingly be imported by travelers and visitors to the country and from diseases that may get a toehold in the continental United States itself. Recent experience with West Nile fever should be studied carefully for lessons on public health education, prevention, and detection.

Eliminating water-related diseases requires more than merely constructing infrastructure or providing clean water. It also requires maintaining and operating that infrastructure, teaching children about adequate hygiene habits, identifying other transmission routes such as unclean handling of food, and controlling disease vectors. In some regions, governmental intervention may be necessary to provide basic water needs; in other places these needs can be met by traditional water providers, municipal systems, or private purveyors within the context of market approaches. Although additional financial resources are necessary, more than money is needed. The U.S. government can play a major role in changing the priorities of aid organizations regarding how money is currently spent. And the United States can play a major role in encouraging the United Nations and other international organizations to refocus efforts in this critical area.

Climate Change

Leading climate scientists believe that humans are now on the verge of changing the Earth's climate. Indeed, a growing number of scientists believe that some human-induced climatic changes are already beginning to occur or are unavoidable even if efforts to reduce gas emissions begin now. These climatic changes—the so-called "greenhouse effect"—will have widespread consequences for every aspect of life on Earth. Among the most important will be impacts on water resources, including effects on both the natural hydrologic system and the complex water-management schemes that have been built to alter and control that system.[6]

Water managers, policy makers, and the public must begin now to think about the implications of climatic change for long-term water planning and management. Changes may be necessary in the design of projects not yet built. Modifications to existing facilities may be required to permit them to continue to meet their design objectives. New projects may need to be built or old projects removed: New institutions may need to be created or old ones revamped to cope with possible changes.

Global climate changes will have major effects on the timing and magnitude of precipitation, evaporation, and runoff. Although specific regional impacts will depend on future changes that are only incompletely understood, some consistent and robust results can be described. In the arid and semiarid western United States, modest changes in precipitation can have large impacts on water supplies. In the Rocky Mountains and the Sierra Nevada, warming will increase the ratio of rain to snow, accelerate spring snowmelt, and shorten the overall snow season, leading to more rapid, earlier, and greater spring runoff. Sea-level rise will affect coastal aquifers and developments.

Climate-induced changes will affect the size, frequency, and consequences of extreme events, which have great economic and social costs for U.S. residents. Flooding, the nation's most costly and destructive natural disaster, could become more common and more extreme. Recent research suggests that greenhouse warming is likely to increase the number of intense precipitation days and flood frequencies in more northerly portions of the nation and that the frequency and severity of droughts could also increase in some regions.

Climate change will also affect water quality, though much less research has been done on this aspect of the problem. Potential negative impacts include reduction in dilution flows, increased storm surges, and higher water temperatures. Low flows in western rivers could increase salinity levels; warmer waters could threaten aquatic life directly and by reducing dissolved oxygen levels. An increase in days with more intense precipitation could increase agricultural and urban pollutants washed into rivers and streams.

There are many opportunities for reducing the risks of climatic variability and change for U.S. water resources. The precautionary approach taken in many international agreements, including the United Nations Framework Convention on Climate Change is applicable:

> *Parties should take precautionary measures to anticipate, prevent or minimize the causes of climate change and mitigate its adverse effects. Where there are threats of serious or irreversible damage, lack of full scientific certainty should not be used as a reason for postponing such measures, taking into account that policies and measures . . . should be cost-effective so as to ensure global benefits at the lowest possible cost.*[7]

Decisions about water planning in the United States, the design and construction of new infrastructure, the type and acreage of crops to be grown, urban water allocations and prices, reservoir operation, and management have traditionally relied upon the assumption that future climatic conditions would be the same as past conditions. This reliance on the past

> **This emphasis on planning and demand management rather than construction of new facilities marks a change in traditional water-management approaches....**

record now may lead people to make incorrect—and potentially dangerous or expensive—decisions.

One of the most important coping strategies must be to begin planning for future changes. The academic community has advocated this position for a decade. In 1990, the Climate and Water Panel of the American Association for the Advancement of Science concluded:

Among the climatic changes that governments and other public bodies are likely to encounter are rising temperatures, increasing evapotranspiration, earlier melting of snowpacks, new seasonal cycles of runoff, altered frequency of extreme events, and rising sea level. . . . *Governments at all levels should re-evaluate legal, technical, and economic procedures for managing water resources in the light of climate changes that are highly likely* [Emphasis in original].[8]

Similarly, the Intergovernmental Panel on Climate Change urged water managers to begin "a systematic re-examination of engineering design criteria, operating rules, contingency plans, and water allocation policies" and stated with "high confidence" that "water demand management and institutional adaptation are the primary components for increasing system flexibility to meet uncertainties of climate change." This emphasis on planning and demand management rather than construction of new facilities marks a change in traditional water-management approaches, which in the past have relied on the construction of large and expensive infrastructure.[9]

In 1997, the American Water Works Association, the largest professional association of water utilities and providers in the United States, published a set of recommendations asking both governmental and private water managers to

- re-examine engineering design assumptions, operating rules, system opti-
  mization, and contingency planning for existing and planned water-management systems under a wider range of climatic conditions than traditionally used;

- explore the vulnerability of both structural and nonstructural water systems
  to plausible future climate changes, not just past climatic variability; and

- re-evaluate legal, technical, and economic approaches for managing water
  resources in the light of possible climate changes.[10]

RECOMMENDATIONS

Advance preparation will position the United States to avoid the worst of the
coming problems and will also permit the nation to play a constructive role in international affairs related to water. Below are specific recommendations for action.

A New Water Policy for the American People

Most water policy decisions can and should be made at the local, regional, or
state level. But some water-management decisions and policies affect interstate
interests, involve federally managed resources, or involve agencies of the federal
government. In the middle of the last century, President Truman established a
water resources policy commission. The commission issued a report on national
water policy directions in 1950.[11] This water policy is out-of-date and the commission should be revived to assess the current state of the nation's water systems
and recommend where and how the federal government should take action to
improve water planning and management and reduce the risks that the nation
will suffer from water-related problems in the future. Such a policy needs to
include expanded data collection and improved data dissemination on national
water resources availability and use.

Water and U.S. Security Interests

The links between water and security suggest two separate areas where U.S.
policy actions may be appropriate. The first is to ensure that U.S. foreign policy and

security organizations are prepared to identify and analyze potential threats to U.S. interests. The second is to enable U.S. diplomatic systems to participate in reducing the risks of conflicts around the world.

More attention by military planners is needed to explicitly monitor and track water-related threats to security and U.S. interests. An easy and valuable first step would be a series of workshops within the War College system on critical issues and regional threats. Similar workshops could be held with security analysts at the State Department, the Central Intelligence Agency (CIA), and other appropriate and interested agencies. A second step would be to ensure that responsibility for environmental security analysis is clearly delegated in the new presidential administration.

Reducing the risks of water-related conflicts will require that appropriate diplomatic resources be developed and maintained within the State Department, perhaps under the undersecretary of state for global affairs. To the extent possible, the administration should also encourage independent nongovernmental participation in "second-track" negotiations. (See Homer-Dixon and Claussen memos.)

Global Water Crisis and Human Health

The United States should play an active role in improving development aid for nations focusing on meeting basic needs for water. This can include helping United States and international aid organizations refocus spending priorities toward meeting basic water needs rather than building new infrastructure, increasing financial contributions to international organizations with this focus, and providing formal governmental technical assistance. Action is also required to encourage U.S. pharmaceutical companies to develop and disseminate inexpensive medicines targeted at preventable water-related diseases. This action could include federal tax credits for research on new medicines and treatments and credits for donation of effective expertise, equipment, and medicines in developing countries. National health organizations must also carefully monitor the prevalence and sources of water-related disease outbreaks in the United States itself. (See Smith memo.)

Climate Change

Some impacts on U.S. water resources from climate change appear unavoidable. The recent national assessment took the first comprehensive step toward understanding how climatic changes will affect the nation. This work included an analysis of the vulnerability of the nation's water resources to climate changes.[12] The assessment should be an ongoing and regular effort: An update should be initiated during the next four years.

Actions are required at the international level to reduce U.S. contributions to the rate of climate change. In addition, national actions are required to begin to adapt and mitigate changes that are likely to occur. Where extensive infrastructure has been built and is operated by the federal government, there are opportunities for rethinking how we operate and manage our water systems.

Current federal laws and policies affecting water use, management, and development are inefficient and unresponsive to changing conditions. The new administration has several promising opportunities to reduce risks to the nation's water resources from future climate changes. It is vital to note that most of the recommendations below make sense even in the absence of severe climatic changes—hence, they fall under the category of "no regrets" recommendations— we should have no regrets implementing them quickly:

- establish incentives for using, conserving, and protecting water supplies;

- ease constraints on transferring water among competing uses within a basin;

- encourage flexible management of water;

- re-evaluate the operation of existing federal infrastructure to address climatic changes;

- postpone costly and irreversible decisions to build water-related infrastructure; and

- encourage more research into specific impacts on U.S. water resources.

MEMORANDUM TO THE PRESIDENT

From: **Kirk R. Smith**

Subject: **Environment and Health**

PROBLEM

A principal factor driving concern about environmental quality is its connection to human health. Directly, through noxious pollutants, and indirectly, through natural environmental processes, many human health problems are linked to environmental factors. As a result of the near-universal human preoccupation with its improvement, health has been the foundation behind much of the environmental research, legislation, and control efforts undertaken around the world in recent decades. Thus, it is abundantly clear that health is important in the environment arena. What is less clear is how important environment is in the health arena. How much ill health can be attributed to environmental factors, and, conversely, how much health improvement can be achieved by efforts to control environmental factors as opposed to other approaches? And which are the most important environmental factors in this regard?

BACKGROUND

This memorandum focuses on what people know about the current and potential future environmental determinants of human health. Because these terms are often used in different ways in different contexts, it is valuable to define them.

Health

Here, ill health refers to the loss of healthy life years suffered by people through premature death or illness and injury. Thus, the currency of health is time, something that, unlike almost all other resources, is potentially equally allotted to each human, no matter where he or she is born or lives. This assumption is predicated on the belief that every person—whether the poorest beggar in Dhaka or the richest executive in Denver—has the right to the same number of healthy life years. Furthermore, it assumes that if it were not for uncontrolled risk factors, such as poor nutrition, dirty water, air pollution, tobacco smoking, and unsafe sex, everyone would live out the same maximum life expectancy as occurs in the richest, most enlightened, and cleanest societies. The degree that any group does not fulfill this expectancy indicates the extent of ill health affecting people all over the world. Thus, this article will not address the more subtle measures of ill health, such as anxiety, inequity, or discomfort. Nor will it treat the numbers of deaths themselves as a useful measure. Death is easy to determine, but because everyone dies, it tells little without reference to the age at which it occurs. Nor does death tell anything about the disability experienced by the people still living with illness and injury. This lost-time approach fits with the old saying that the purpose of public health is to have everyone die young, at as old an age as possible.

Compared with an accounting of mortality alone, a focus on lost healthy life years reveals a different landscape of important diseases and risk factors—a landscape with profound policy implications.

Environment

In traditional medical terminology, every component of disease that is not genetic is environmental, the classic distinction between nature and nurture. It thus encompasses social risk factors, such as crime, child abuse, and war, as well as behavioral factors such as diet, smoking, and sexual practices. Such an inclusive definition may be useful for some purposes, but this paper takes a more restricted one that fits the public's view of what constitutes environmental factors. Therefore, the only factors counted are measurable physical, chemical, or biological agents passing through environmental pathways to stress humans. In contrast to one common use of the term by the public, this article does not distinguish between those agents set into motion by human activities and those that are entirely natural. The pastoral myth is strong in U.S. culture that if something is natural it must be safe or even benign. People seem to wish to forget that most of humanity has spent most of history trying to protect itself from natural forces and agents and that the majority of the world's population today is still quite vulnerable to them. Thus, in addition to stopping industrial pollution, environmental health also involves protecting ourselves from natural phenomena at all scales, from hurricanes to arsenic atoms and everything in between.

Physical, chemical, and biological agents can be set into motion by a wide range of phenomena, including global change processes (industrialization, urbanization, economic integration, climate change, and biodiversity pauperization). Thus, although the definition of environmental health-risk factors is restricted to measurable insults on humans, this article adopts the increasingly common practice of examining, in the broadest way possible, the risk factors leading to these insults.

Determinant

Determinant is the most difficult term of the three to define. The best definition is a practical one: The degree to which a risk factor is a determinant of a disease is the degree to which the disease would be reduced if exposure to the risk factor were reduced or eliminated. For example, the degree to which poor water quality is a determinant of diarrhea is simply the difference in diarrhea burden (lost years of healthy life) in a group of people who shifted from dirty to clean water and changed nothing else. However, in reality, such simple experiments are not readily available for most environmental risk factors, and the strength of a determinant must be estimated more indirectly and thus with more uncertainty.

That the determinants of a disease burden normally add to more than 100 percent, sometimes much more, is confusing to many scientists and members of the general public. Thus, it might be correct to say that diarrhea in Mexico is caused 30 percent by dirty water, 50 percent by poor sanitation, and 40 percent by malnutrition. This is because the size of each determinant is calculated as if everything else remains the same. This does not imply that eliminating all three determinants would reduce the diarrhea burden by 120 percent (i.e., by more than Mexico started with). Indeed, it is more likely that the reduction would be decidedly less than 100 percent because there are other determinants not mentioned here. Nevertheless, this definition remains intact, because eliminating each determinant alone would produce the change indicated for it. Together they interact, sometimes in complicated ways. The implication for policy discussions is that the sum of risk determinants is intrinsically open ended (i.e., they cannot be judged by whether they add to more than 100 percent). Indeed, it is a blessing in a way when determinants add to much more than 100 percent because it offers several ways of attacking the problem.

Given these definitions, what can be said about the current state of environmental health in the world and where it is heading?

Today's World

Judged by the number and scale of news stories, action groups, research efforts, regulatory actions, monitoring programs, and control expenditures, the biggest environmental health problems in the world seem to lie in the industrial world. This is because the major emergence of environmental health awareness as a political and economic force occurred in the context of industrial and urban pollution in developed countries. However, judged from the perspective of actual ill health, the real environmental health risks lie elsewhere.

Figure 1 shows the burden of disease (lost healthy life years) in the world as a whole according to major region. Adjusted for population, it shows two trends, one better-known than the other. First, it shows the trend in general ill health from poor to rich countries. For example, in sub-Saharan Africa, about 210 days per year of healthy life are lost for every person—a burden that falls to a large extent on children less than 5 years old as it does in most developing countries. By contrast, in the established market economies (Western Europe, Japan, Australia, New Zealand, Canada, and the United States), only 45 days each year are lost per capita—much better than other parts of the world but still indicating room for improvement. Figure 1 also shows that the fraction of the health burden due to environmental factors tends to decline with economic development. In other words, not only are people in richer countries, including the United States, healthier than they are in other countries, but their health status is less dependent on environmental factors than people in poor countries. The major reasons are the huge burdens of environmentally related diseases borne by developing-country children in the form of diarrhea, respiratory infections, and, to a

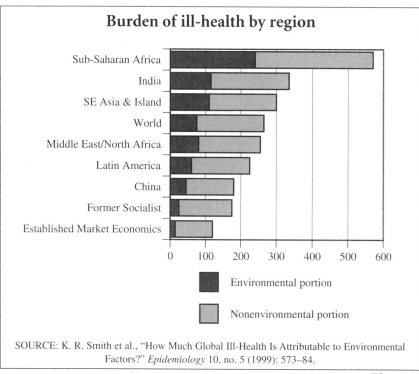

Burden of ill-health by region

SOURCE: K. R. Smith et al., "How Much Global Ill-Health Is Attributable to Environmental Factors?" *Epidemiology* 10, no. 5 (1999): 573–84.

Figure 1

lesser extent, adverse birth outcomes and other factors leading to death in early infancy. These problems exist in developed countries, but at much lower levels. The other major environmental disease in developing countries, malaria, hardly exists at all today in developed countries.

Table 1. Percent of 1999 global burden of ill-health due to specific environmental diseases

Region/disease	Acute respiratory infection	Malaria	Diarrhea
South Asia	2.4	0.2	2.0
Sub-Saharan Africa	1.2	0.8	1.3

Source: World Health Organization, Geneva, Switzerland, 1999

The scale of childhood diarrhea, acute respiratory infections, and malaria as global environmental health issues is sharply illuminated in Table 1. The table shows the fraction of total global burden of disease of all types represented by these largely environmental childhood diseases in just two regions, Africa and South Asia. For example, more than 4 percent of the entire world burden of disease is borne primarily by one relatively small population group (children less than 5 years old) in one country (India) in the form of three environmental diseases. Globally, more than 15 percent of the burden of disease is due to these three conditions alone.

The Environmental Risk Transition

A way to think about the global processes that have led to the situation represented by Table 1 is encapsulated in what has been called the environmental risk transition. This framework is represented in Figure 2, which shows the transitions in environmental risks that tend to occur as economic development proceeds.

In the poorest societies, household risks caused by poor food, air, and water quality tend to dominate. The major risks existing in developing countries today are of this type—diarrhea is attributable to poor water/sanitation/hygiene, acute respiratory diseases to poor housing and indoor air pollution from poor quality household fuels, and malaria to poor housing quality, although all are of course influenced by other factors as well (malnutrition in particular).

The economic development that helps make it possible to bring these problems under control tends to create another set of problems that operate at the community level. These problems include urban outdoor pollution, as noted in Figure 2, and other negative aspects of urbanization, industrialization, and agricultural modernization, such as toxic chemicals, hazardous waste, pesticides, and motor vehicle hazards.

As these problems are brought under control, a new set tends to be created at the regional and global level through long-term and long-range pollutants, such as acid-rain precursors, ozone-depleting chemicals, and greenhouse gases.

Simplistically, this historical process can be seen as a sequential housekeeping effort. First, societies push problems out of the house into the community and then out of the community into the wider global environment. Not illustrated well by Figure 2 is an important characteristic of this sequence: Absolute human

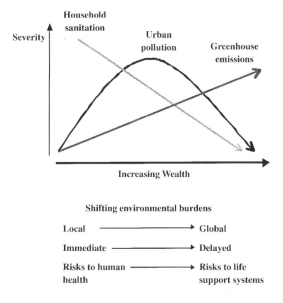

Figure 2

health risk decreases substantially at each stage of development. Thus, those societies still experiencing substantial household environmental risks have much lower overall health status and a higher portion of disease caused by environmental factors than those in the community or global stages, as shown by the regional breakdowns in Figure 1.

This is not to say that even the richest societies do not have residual household and community environmental risks. Nor is it to say that some of the poorest societies are not modestly contributing to global problems. However, the environmental risk transition concept demonstrated in Figure 2 portrays the major trends in links between health and the environment.

Interactions among Regions

The regions of the world represented in the figures above do not exist independently. They coexist in time and, increasingly, in space because of environmental processes that shift risks from one place to another. This is increasingly important as one moves to the right in the second figure. In addition, societal processes leading to increases in trade, tourism, migration, communication, transport, media coverage, drug smuggling, the Internet, and so on are truly shrinking the world.

These processes lead to increasing environmental health interactions of several sorts. Although highly industrialized countries have contributed the most to greenhouse-gas emissions and thus to the risk of climate change, it is the health of people in developing countries that is most vulnerable to changes that might occur because of global warming. Although climate change is likely to cause more economic damage in rich countries, such as the United States, because of the value of the threatened infrastructure, it is likely to cause more health damage in poor countries because of their general vulnerability to environmental stress and lack of supporting infrastructure. Thus, villagers of the developing world are doubly at risk—from household risks and from the late stages of environmental housekeeping by developed countries that have pushed risks off to the global level. The urban poor in developing countries are triply imperiled because they typically experience the worst community-level environmental risks as well.

Although rich countries are not directly threatened by the acute respiratory infections and diarrhea rampant in poor countries, globalization processes do make rich countries increasingly susceptible to other environmentally related infectious diseases. High on this list is tuberculosis (TB), which represents a triple threat:

- It is a function of the same kinds of poor housing, ventilation, fuel, and other household factors that lead to the more localized environmental diseases that currently dominate global disease burdens.

- As the chief outcome of AIDS in poor countries, TB incidence is rising worldwide and now accounts for more than 2 percent of the global burden of disease, half of which is borne by South Asia and sub-Saharan Africa.

- Because there is no effective vaccine, antibiotics currently represent the only viable medical intervention, but antibiotic resistance is growing alarmingly because TB is so difficult to cure with antibiotics.

More exotic and popularized diseases, such as Ebola and Lassa Fever, are also examples of environmentally related diseases emanating from poor countries but potentially threatening rich countries. It is important to be aware of such emerging diseases but also to keep in mind that the more mundane "re-emerging" diseases, such as TB, are vastly more deadly than exotic ones. More people are killed every day from TB than have been killed in 100 years by such exotic diseases.

RECOMMENDATIONS

U.S. Priorities

One of the most profound dilemmas facing decision makers and public health scientists everywhere, and in the United States in particular, is how to address the apparently growing discrepancy between the scientific and public perceptions of environmental risks. Study after study has shown in the last 20 years that environmental hazards truly affecting health status in the country are not those receiving highest attention, whether measured by public opinion polls, news coverage, congressional actions, or government expenditures. Indoor air pollution, in its various forms, receives relatively little attention compared with outdoor sources and yet probably accounts for as much if not more poor health. Hazardous waste dumps, on the other hand, which are difficult to associate with any measurable ill health, garner much attention and resources. The same chemicals in the form of common consumer products, such as household cleaners, pesticides, and fuel (gasoline), account for much more exposure and ill health and yet are comparatively of little concern to the public.

> ...environmental hazards truly affecting health status in the country are not those receiving highest attention....

There are several explanations for this difference in perception, the major ones relating to the fact that the public uses a number of criteria other than health risk to establish its concerns. However, in a world of finite resources, there is a real health cost in focusing attention on risks that have little measurable health impact and, at least by default, thus result in poorer funding of interventions that address significant risks.

An option for consideration is to explicitly separate these risks by keeping those hazards with significant health risks within the health arena and to place others, perhaps equally as important for public policy, but less so for public health (including litter control and wildland preservation), in the category of environmental quality improvement along with many other worthwhile programs of this kind.

In the United States, the environmental programs that definitely ought to remain in the health arena at present are

- controlling household pollution exposures, including radon, environmental tobacco smoke, allergens, lead, consumer products, and wood smoke;

- controlling outdoor air pollution where doing so is more effective than controlling indoor or localized exposure sources of the same pollutants;

- applying stringent criteria in judging any proposed new product or activity that will affect large numbers of people (e.g., new consumer chemical products, household materials, and additives to food or fuel); and

- applying stronger and more uniform restrictions on occupational hazards, which tend to be much larger than those imposed on the general public, and, in contrast, often have demonstrable impacts on health.

International Options for the United States

There are two general categories of international policy options that the United States needs to consider—those that reduce environmental health risks imposed on other countries and those that reduce the environmental health impact on U.S. population.

The most important component of the first category is addressing the U.S. contribution to greenhouse gases. Should a change in climate result, there will be significant health risks imposed on the entire world. There are several actions the United States might take to ameliorate this risk:

> **Should a change in climate result, there will be significant health risks imposed on the entire world.**

- find ways to seriously reduce U.S. greenhouse-gas emissions;

- join the rest of the world in regimes designed to reduce overall emissions;

- push to include health as one of the criteria by which greenhouse-gas reduction measures are evaluated worldwide—studies show that significant improvements in environmental health status can be achieved as part of greenhouse-gas mitigation measures, but only if health considerations are explicitly included in the strategy from the start;

- work to reduce the vulnerability of the poor in developing countries to environmental stresses of all kinds, including stress caused by climate change, through better housing, education, nutrition, and emergency response systems; and

- assist developing countries in reducing the burden of diseases thought to be most enhanced by climate change—recent studies have shown that relatively modest annual investments (e.g., vaccines, clean fuels, and malaria control) that are started today can decrease the incidence of climate-change-related diseases by 2020. Even if climate changes do not occur, these investments will be valuable—a no-regrets policy.

The actions in the first category would not only reduce the big diseases of developing countries but would also reduce the incidence of TB and other infectious diseases that potentially threaten the United States. Thus, they serve to address U.S. direct interests as well. In addition, the United States should consider providing more clout (economic and political) for efforts to develop vaccines for TB, malaria, dengue, and other major environmentally mediated diseases that today mainly affect developing countries but in the future could seriously threaten the United States. Because of the relatively short-term economic outlook of the private vaccine industry, vaccines are unlikely to be developed for such "orphan" diseases in spite of the huge burden they impose on world health.

The United States should also use its clout to move the world development community (World Bank, United Nations Development Programme, U.S. Agency for International Development, and U.S. private foundations) to consider environmental health criteria more explicitly in their loan and grant programs as part of poverty alleviation, energy policy, and other major development efforts.

Finally, the United States can greatly assist in addressing the environmental health hazards that threaten it and the rest of the world by directing a greater proportion of international health research and development efforts toward environmental health problems with serious global burdens as well as those of special scientific interest. Because the U.S. health-related research enterprise is a large fraction of the total global effort, even small shifts in emphasis in the United States can greatly expand the overall size of such efforts in today's world.

Bottom Lines

- Environment is no longer a major determinant of ill health in the United States or other developed countries.

- Public opinion and policy are not well focused on the environmental health risks that do remain in the United States.

- Environment remains an extremely important determinant of health in developing countries and thus the world as a whole.

- Relatively little attention is paid globally to these environmental health hazards in developing countries.

- U.S. domestic and international research and aid policies are partly to blame for this lack of attention and can thus be part of the solution.

- The greatest threat to U.S. health from climate change will probably come through impacts in developing countries on infectious disease that spread globally.

- The need to curb greenhouse-gas emissions provides dramatic opportunities for win-win or no-regrets strategies that improve health as well.

MEMORANDUM TO THE PRESIDENT

From: Walter V. Reid

Subject: **Biodiversity, Ecosystem Change, and International Development**

PROBLEM

During the past decade, the Clinton and Bush administrations regularly included the biodiversity crisis on their public shortlist of global environmental priorities. In practice, they virtually ignored the issue. U.S. policy makers defined the biodiversity crisis as the problem of species extinction, and although they agreed that extinction is morally tragic, they believed that biodiversity had little bearing on U.S. interests and only a small domestic and international constituency. This marginalization of the issue is dangerous and politically misguided. There is another dimension to the problem that is at the very core of U.S. interests. This involves the harmful economic and public health consequences of the wholesale changes humans are making to the structure and function of the world's biodiversity, an issue best characterized as the problem of "ecosystem change."

The new administration needs to reframe the biodiversity issue, taking it from a narrow focus on species extinction to a broader focus on ecosystem change and international development. The latter approach addresses a more critical issue, reinforces international alliances rather than divisions, reinforces international economic and social agendas, and builds political support in the United States. If handled correctly, the issues of biodiversity and ecosystem change could be transformed from a U.S. policy backwater into a visible, popular, and influential opportunity for U.S. leadership.

What is the Biodiversity Problem?

Biodiversity first emerged on the agenda of global environmental concerns in the early 1980s when scientists began to document the threat of global species extinction and habitat loss. By 1993, an international convention on biological diversity had been signed by more than 130 countries. Since then, United Nations agencies have spent more than $1 billion on biodiversity projects around the world—far more than the wildest dreams of conservationists in the 1980s. The warp speed at which this issue gained prominence and became the focus of international action led some to believe that a serious response to this global challenge had begun.

Nobody believes that today. International action has helped some species and habitats, but the pace of species loss and biological resource degradation is accelerating, particularly in developing countries.

The lack of action and the lack of a public constituency stems from the narrow definition of the problem. Biodiversity is the variety of life on Earth. It includes the diversity of species, genetic diversity within species, and the habitats and ecosystems distributed around the world. The biodiversity "problem" is in fact a combination of several interrelated issues concerning changes to the world's biodiversity and how those changes affect people. The issue that has dominated public concern and policy response has been species extinction. Human actions over the past century, in particular the conversion of natural habitats to agriculture and the widespread introduction of nonnative invasive species, have set the stage for an episode of species extinction that, if unchecked, will result in the greatest loss of species in the past 65 million years.[1] Recorded extinctions during the past century already greatly exceed background extinction rates. Scientists predict that tens of thousands of species are likely to go extinct in the coming decades unless major efforts are made to restore habitats and reduce the spread of invasive species. In the United States alone, 1,200 species are currently listed by the federal government as threatened and endangered. The Nature Conservancy estimates that one-third of U.S. flora and fauna is at risk.[2]

> International action has helped some species and habitats, but the pace of species loss and biological resource degradation is accelerating. . . .

Most species that become extinct over the coming decades will have no practical consequences for human livelihoods. This is not to say that extinctions do not sometimes have serious ramifications. For example, before their extinction, New Zealand's moas (elephant birds) were an important source of food. In other cases, such as the extirpation of elephants from parts of Africa, the loss of a species can change the composition, structure, and functioning of entire ecosystems. Moreover, scientists stress that it is difficult to know which species are essential for maintaining various ecosystem processes, and thus the loss of any species is risky. Even so, hundreds of species have gone extinct over the past century, thousands are faced with extinction today, and the economic and social impacts of these extinctions are likely to be minimal. Many of the species that will be lost are rare or restricted to relatively small areas and do not play a unique role in the ecosystem.

For this reason, economic forces rarely help to maintain species diversity. However, there are exceptions. For example, species-rich national parks sometimes generate substantial foreign exchange from ecotourism. But more often, the economic benefits that result from simplifying biological systems and planting crops, cutting forests, or building houses or factories far exceed the direct and indirect economic benefits of protecting species diversity. Protecting species from extinction is thus not a utilitarian choice but a moral one. The extinction of a species is the one truly irreversible impact that humans have on the environment. Edward O. Wilson, Pellegrino Research professor in entomology at Harvard University, has called this the "folly" that future generations are least likely to forgive.[3]

Although the threat of species extinction may be the best known aspect of the biodiversity problem, another has far greater practical consequences for human livelihoods and U.S. interests: ecosystem change. Significant changes to the structure and function of habitats and ecosystems not only result in species loss but also affect the ability of these systems to meet human needs. Humans have extensively changed the world's ecosystems, and the pace of this change is accelerating. Some 40 to 50 percent of land is now transformed or degraded by human actions.[4] Models based on the median UN population projections suggest that an

> **Significant changes to the structure and function of habitats and ecosystems not only result in species loss but also affect the ability of these systems to meet human needs.**

additional one-third of global land cover will be transformed during the next 100 years with the greatest changes occurring in the next three decades.[5] Human actions (the application of fertilizers, cultivation of certain crops, and fossil fuel combustion) now account for the addition of more biologically active nitrogen to ecosystems then all natural pathways combined.[6] These human-caused nitrogen flows will grow rapidly during the next 20 years as fertilizer use rises by an additional 55 percent. Humans have also transformed freshwater ecosystems. People appropriate 54 percent of accessible freshwater runoff, and dams and diversions have slowed rivers to such an extent that the length of time that an average drop of water entering a river takes to reach the sea has tripled.[7] All of these impacts will be compounded by Earth's changing climate.

Ecosystem change is not always harmful. Indeed, most changes to ecosystems have been made intentionally to increase the production of certain goods and services. For example, the growth in the extent of agricultural lands combined with increases in cereal yields have led to net increases in per-capita food availability despite dramatic increases in world population.[8] Similarly, water withdrawals from freshwater ecosystems have been responsible for the growth of agricultural yields and have also met demands of industry and growing urban populations.

Increasingly, however, the costs of these ecosystem changes are mounting. Two processes are at work. First, human actions have often degraded ecosystems so that they are less capable of producing the quantity and quality of products and services demanded.[9] For example, some 40 percent of agricultural land has been strongly or very strongly degraded in the past 50 years by erosion, salinization, compaction, nutrient depletion, biological degradation, or pollution.[10] Similarly, more than 60 percent of the world's major fisheries are in urgent need of actions to restore depleted stocks or to protect stocks from overfishing.[11]

Second, human-made changes to ecosystems to achieve one goal, such as food production or flood control, have resulted in significant and often unforeseen tradeoffs with other important products and services provided by ecosystems. For example, increased use of nitrogen-based fertilizers to increase agricultural production has eutrophied coastal waters, created "dead zones," and destroyed fisheries in rivers and coastal zones in the Mediterranean and Black Seas and the northwestern Gulf of Mexico. These changes in freshwater and coastal systems have also jeopardized human health by contributing to outbreaks of cholera and other diseases. Wetland conversion has increased the frequency and severity of downstream flooding.

The magnitude of human demands on ecosystems is now so great that these tradeoffs among goods and services have become the rule. A nation can increase food supply by converting a forest to agriculture but in so doing decreases the supply of goods, such as clean water, timber, biodiversity, or flood control, that may be of equal or greater importance. A nation can increase timber harvest but only with decreased revenues from downstream hydrofacilities and increased risk of landslides.

Policy Issues

All nations need to modify their ecosystems to meet the needs of growing populations, but the potential environmental, social, and economic damage that will result from inappropriate management actions during the next century have serious implications for U.S. interests in particular. Human demand for the products and services of ecosystems, such as food and clean water, will grow dramatically in coming years. The regions in which demand is growing most rapidly are also the regions in which the capacity of ecosystems to meet this demand has already been degraded. These impacts of ecosystem change will cause the greatest harm to the poor, who depend most directly on forests, fisheries, and agriculture and who are most vulnerable to the environmental problems that result from ecosystem degradation, such as floods and crop failures.

The economic costs of ecosystem degradation directly hinder U.S. efforts to strengthen economies around the world. Africa's economic growth rates will not accelerate while the continent faces increasing problems in meeting basic needs for food and water. Asia's economic growth will be slowed by lower production in its fishing and timber industries and by the health costs associated with declining availability of clean water. The United States needs to help countries confront these issues just as it helps them confront weak financial institutions, corruption, and poorly developed markets.

The United States has even greater reason to be concerned about the social costs of ecosystem degradation. Ecosystem degradation may not be the sole cause of social unrest and political instability, but the overlap between regions of unrest and regions facing serious problems associated with declining agricultural productivity, diminished fisheries production, and water shortages is evident: Peru, Ecuador, Sierra Leone, Ethiopia, Somalia, Haiti. (See Homer-Dixon memo for this forum.)

A scenario of growing economic and social costs of ecosystem degradation is not the only plausible future. An alternative scenario would redirect the pattern of ecosystem change to better meet human needs and strengthen national economies, while simultaneously addressing the species extinction problem. Indeed, this scenario has already played out in parts of the United States. In the 1800s, much of the now-forested East Coast of the United States had been converted to agriculture. But as agricultural productivity grew and the U.S. economy transformed from a resource-based to an industrial economy, rural populations declined and agriculture became increasingly concentrated in the most productive lands of the Midwest. As the human footprint on natural ecosystems is lightened, the capability of those systems to maintain biodiversity increases.

Although a scenario like this could eventually be achieved globally, it is far from inevitable. For example, well-managed forests could allow 20 percent or less of today's forest area to supply world commercial wood demand in the middle of the 21st century.[12] Similarly, if the world farmer reaches the average yield of today's U.S. corn grower during the next century, the expected world population of 10 billion people would need only half of today's cropland area.

The focus of U.S. policy should be to help countries manage the process of ecosystem change to better meet their short-term economic needs and to set the stage for a long-term reduction of the human footprint. Unlike the relatively weak political and economic leverage provided by the issue of species extinction, the issue of ecosystem change is directly tied to important U.S. economic and security concerns.

This approach to the biodiversity issue bears no resemblance to the approach that has been followed thus far. The set of policies and initiatives that have been cobbled together over the past two administrations too often addresses symptoms rather than problems, fails to achieve synergies and often works at cross-purposes, and entirely lacks a coherent strategic focus. The U.S. public cares about forests, coral reefs, elephants, and pandas so the country rails against forest loss, launches a coral reef initiative, brings pandas to the nation's capital, and funds a handful of

> **The set of policies and initiatives that have been cobbled together over the past two administrations too often addresses symptoms rather than problems . . . and entirely lacks a coherent strategic focus.**

protected areas. This "boutique" approach is viewed by most developing countries as post-colonial meddling that undermines their development goals. And it has achieved little.

RECOMMENDATIONS

Around the world, the scale of change to the world's ecosystems is immense and growing rapidly. Many of these changes, such as the expansion of agriculture and the use of fertilizers, have provided tremendous benefits for growing populations. But increasingly, these changes are degrading the productivity of ecosystems, causing growing numbers of species extinctions, diminishing the short-term contributions of ecosystems to meeting human needs, and raising the risk of catastrophic changes to the structure and function of ecosystems that could exact substantial costs on the people of the United States and other nations.

Historically U.S. domestic and international efforts have aimed to slow the degradation of the world's ecosystems. In keeping with the broad transitions that provide the context for action by the new presidential administration, the aim should be to move beyond a defensive posture and take actions that help restore the ability of the living planet to meet the aspirations of U.S. citizens and the needs of the world's poor, in particular. To achieve this end, the administration should take the following steps:

Commit to the creation of a reliable system of ecosystem monitoring and assessment in the United States and internationally.

Until recently, knowledge of the scale of ecosystem change and how best to address the challenge was limited. Advances in remote sensing, environmental monitoring, valuation of nonmarketed ecosystem services, ecological modeling, and ecological forecasting have set the stage for a forward-looking "anticipatory approach" to the problem. International scientific assessment processes, like the Intergovernmental Panel on Climate Change (IPCC) and the proposed Millennium Ecosystem Assessment, can greatly assist decision makers in obtaining state-of-the-art technical information directly relevant to policy choices.[13] This administration should strongly support efforts such as these to communicate the findings of scientific research to policy makers in a manner that directly meets their needs.

At the same time, the research base itself must be strengthened. The U.S. Global Change Research Program (GCRP) has greatly strengthened the capability of the U.S. public and private sector to anticipate, plan for, and mitigate long-term changes resulting from human impacts on the environment and particularly on climate. To meet the needs identified in this paper, GCRP must be bolstered with a strong focus on the life sciences as well.

Renew the commitment to protecting and restoring species and ecosystems within the United States.

Domestically, the United States has made tremendous strides during the past three decades to reduce pressures on its ecosystems and to protect critical ecosystems and endangered species. These efforts are of enormous value because some of the world's most biologically outstanding places are found within U.S. borders. However, the legacy of past mismanagement of the nation's resources and continuing pressures on many ecosystems can be seen in the growing numbers of endangered species and humans' continuing inability to meet such basic and popularly supported domestic goals as "fishable swimable waters." Specific actions include

- Commit to a 10-year goal of achieving the long-stated U.S. policy objective of making the nations rivers and lakes fishable and swimable. As a first step, call on agencies to formulate a plan that goes beyond the existing regulatory approach to nonpoint source pollution and takes full advantage of incentives and market approaches for increasing the efficiency of fertilizer applications and reducing the risk of catastrophic failure of livestock waste facilities. Meeting this goal is important not only for U.S. rivers but for the coastal zone as well. (See Solow memo.) Moreover, by taking steps to address these problems, the United States will become a leader in technology and scientific knowledge that will help the world grapple with the dangerous growth in flows of such nutrients as nitrogen and phosphorus.

- Commit to the goal of reducing the number of threatened species in the United States. The Nature Conservancy regularly publishes statistics on threatened species in the nation. The number has been growing each decade. It is time to reverse this trend by a combination of actions to protect and wisely manage key ecoregions in the nation and by actions to recover species on the federal endangered species list.

- Establish a comprehensive system of marine protection in the coastal waters of the United States. Considerable scientific evidence demonstrates the effectiveness of coastal protected areas in maintaining diversity and helping to maintain and restore harvestable fish populations. Although the United States has one of the world's leading systems of terrestrial protected areas, the country has yet to establish a comparable system for marine and coastal ecosystems. (See Ogden memo.)

Broaden the international approach to the biodiversity crisis to include a strong focus on the need to help countries manage the process of ecosystem change in support of national development.

In the end, the species extinction crisis will be slowed only if we succeed in addressing the broader dimensions of ecosystem change. This does not mean that the United States should not also pursue short-term actions aimed specifically at slowing species extinction. But those short-term actions only make sense if they are part of a long-term strategy addressing nations' prospects and needs for development.

The harmful impacts of poorly managed ecosystem changes are already greater than most of the projected impacts of climate change.

The public cares about the conservation of species and people believe it is morally wrong to cause species extinctions. But everywhere, these concerns take a back seat to people's immediate needs.

However, the issue of ecosystem change is of tremendous importance for U.S. public and private interests and can better motivate action. The harmful impacts of poorly managed ecosystem changes are already greater than most of the projected impacts of climate change. A priority for the U.S. policy agenda should thus be to help other countries manage the process of ecosystem change in support of national development.

- Ratify the United Nations Convention on Biological Diversity. The Convention on Biological Diversity (CBD) has little direct influence on biodiversity because it is a framework convention with few binding commitments. However, the goals of CBD are very much in keeping with a policy focus on ecosystem change and international development. The primary role of the convention has been to shape the standards and norms by which countries address the biodiversity issue. The United States could assume the position of a world leader on this issue if it worked through CBD to promote the approach of managing ecosystem change to help nations prosper. But it can only do this if it has ratified the convention. Moreover, failure to ratify CBD has substantially weakened U.S. influence in important negotiations, such as the negotiation of the Cartagena Protocol on Biosafety.

- Help countries align the benefits of trade liberalization with improved management of ecosystem change. The United States should not dictate choices about the uses other countries make of their ecosystems. For example, it may make perfect sense to clear forests in a heavily forested country to gain access to new agricultural markets liberalized through freer trade. However, it is in the U.S. interest and in the interest of the countries involved that they make wise choices in responding to liberalized markets. The U.S. administration, and particularly the office of the U.S. Trade Representative, should provide technical assistance to countries that will enable them to better understand the costs and benefits of choices they make under freer trade. The United States can also push international institutions such as the World Trade Organization, the International Monetary Fund, and the World Bank to provide similar assistance.

- Mainstream the issue of ecosystem change in foreign policy. The United States is increasingly drawn into situations of social and political unrest created in part by ecosystem degradation. When the United States works with countries to strengthen their social and economic institutions, it should also help them enhance their "biological capital." Two issues that can form the core of U.S. efforts to strengthen nations' abilities to manage ecosystem change are the removal of environmentally damaging subsidies and the "greening" of gross domestic product (GDP). It often makes economic, social, and environmental sense to help countries reduce or eliminate subsidies that achieve economic gains largely by consuming biological capital. Harmful subsidies in the fishing industry are a case in point because they encourage overexploitation of fish resources, causing long-term harm to fishing communities when the harvests crash. Similarly, countries would obtain a clearer picture of their resource dependence and the costs of mismanagement of ecosystem change if they accounted for changes in biological capital in their GDP just as they account for other economic changes.[14]

• Increase support to the protection of biodiversity in the most biologically diverse and threatened ecoregions and hot spots around the world. Species extinction cannot be stopped unless we address the problems associated with ecosystem change. That said, no serious reduction in the human footprint in developing nations is likely until the second half of the 21st century at best. In the span of these 50 or more years, tens of thousands of species could become extinct. The extent and effectiveness of the world's network of protected areas will largely determine the number of species that will survive through the next century. Protected areas are pivotal because the extent of the species extinction crisis is highly localized. Within the coterminous United States, more than half of endangered species of plants, birds, fish, and mollusks are found in less than 2.0 percent of the land area.[15] Globally, 35–45 percent of plants and vertebrate animals are found in hot spots that comprise only 1.4 percent of the Earth's land surface.[16]

• Increase support to regions facing serious problems of ecosystem degradation, particularly where it is having a direct effect on the ability of the poor to meet their needs. At the core of the new approach to the biodiversity crisis described here is the argument that the biodiversity problem is intractable politically and operationally if it is defined only as the problem of species extinction. The United States should increase its efforts to slow species loss in key ecoregions and hot spots, but progress will not be sustained if this is done in isolation without at least as great a commitment to tackling problem areas where ecosystem change is having major impacts on the development prospects of people and nations.

- Commit to the establishment of a fully funded international endowment in support of the maintenance of the world's seedbanks. The world's public-sector seedbanks, maintained by the centers of the Consultative Group on International Agricultural Research (CGIAR) and by national agricultural ministries, house some of the world's most important biodiversity from the standpoint of its importance to human livelihoods. These seedbanks must persist for millennia, yet they struggle to obtain the resources just to last from year to year.

Neither U.S. nor global interests are being well served by the disparate and poorly coordinated U.S. biodiversity policies. By addressing only one aspect of the biodiversity issue, past administrations have made a dangerous and politically shortsighted miscalculation. How countries manage ecosystem change is as close to the center of U.S. interests in many parts of the world as how they manage their economic and human resources. By helping countries manage ecosystem change to support development needs, we would address real concerns of the countries in the context of the mainstream U.S. policy issues of global economic development and national security. And we would steer the course of international development toward a future with a far lighter human footprint on the world's species diversity. This administration could achieve a breakthrough on the biodiversity issue by reframing and mainstreaming the issue of biodiversity, ecosystem change, and international development in U.S. foreign policy.

MEMORANDUM TO THE PRESIDENT

From: **J.C. Ogden**

Subject: **Maintaining Diversity in Our Oceans**

PROBLEM

> *The cod fishery, the herring fishery, the pilchard fishery, the mackerel fishery, and probably all the great sea-fisheries, are inexhaustible; that is to say that nothing we do seriously affects the number of fish. And any attempt to regulate these fisheries seems consequently . . . to be useless.*

The unintended irony of these words, written by Thomas Henry Huxley in a paper presented at The Great International Fishery Exhibition in London in 1884, is a clarion cry for the future of the oceans.[1] At that time, the population of the world was slightly more than one billion, and the oceans were perceived as mysterious and limitless. The H.M.S. Challenger was two years into its epic four-year voyage of discovery, which laid the foundation of modern oceanography and marine science and brought back the first outlines of the ocean's vastness and sketches of its endlessly fascinating animals and plants. However, even then, human beings had drastically reduced populations of the great whales and other marine mammals and turtles—some to extinction.[2] Now, more than a century later, it is said that humans know more about the surface of the moon than about the oceans. But this knowledge is sufficient to understand that the relentless growth of human populations to the present 6 billion is exerting a tremendous influence on the oceans, fundamentally changing their biological diversity and threatening a critical part of the Earth's life support system.

Three recommendations address this alarming decline in marine biological diversity:

- Institute a comprehensive program of ocean resource management and protection based on zoning within the U.S. exclusive economic zone (EEZ);

- establish an integrated monitoring and assessment program encompassing the U.S. EEZ to continuously track the status and trends of key indicators of ocean health; and

- establish an intergovernmental scientific panel within international agencies and conventions that is similar to the Intergovernmental Panel on Climate Change (IPCC) to periodically assess global ocean health and make recommendations on mitigation.

BACKGROUND

What is Biodiversity?

Biological diversity has been the cornerstone of biology since the first century, when Roman naturalist Pliny first described different animals and plants, and it has been a preoccupation of biologists since the 18th century Swedish botanist, Carl Linnaeus, began systematically to name and catalog them.[3] The apparently simple question, Why are there so many different kinds of plants and animals? drives much of the modern science of ecology. In the past three decades, there has been increasing anxiety about the accelerating worldwide loss of biodiversity, including habitat destruction, species extinction, and loss of genetic material and its potential impact upon human dependencies on the environment.

In the 1980s, benchmark meetings of experts heralded a crisis of species extinction largely associated with tropical deforestation.[4] The United Nations Conference on the Environment and Development (UNCED), held in Rio de Janeiro in 1992, developed the Convention on Biological Diversity with more than 150 signatory nations to date pledging conservation action. Because there was no perceived crisis of extinction in the oceans, they were not featured in the convention. However, the collapse of fisheries and the destructive effect of fishing on ocean habitats, the increasing pollution of relentlessly expanding coastal populations, the global decline of coral reefs, and evidence of global warming in the oceans have raised the alarm and pointed to the need for priorities in research, management, and conservation.[5]

The key to understanding marine biodiversity is the salient feature of oceanic life—planktonic larva, which drifts on ocean currents for as little as a few days to as much as a year before settling to begin adult life. Consequently, most marine populations are widely distributed. However, in other areas, such as those in the tropics, the range of tree or bird species may be encompassed within only a few square miles. Modern techniques using genetic markers, combined with satellite observations of currents and water masses and satellite-tracked drifters, have shown great promise in working out patterns of dispersal—surely a key to the design of effective conservation and management strategies. However, scientists now know enough to realize that successful marine resource management and conservation will have to work on local, regional, and, ultimately, global scales.

The oceans cover more than 71 percent of the Earth and, taking depth in account, contain more than 99 percent of the space available for life. Although oceans have fewer species than the terrestrial environment, they contain about twice the phyla (higher order diversity) as land does, with species much more evenly spread among them.[6] In contrast, more than 90 percent of terrestrial diversity is in only two phyla—insects and flowering plants. Just as in the era of the Challenger expedition, the oceans remain remote, difficult to visualize, and poorly understood. For example, deep-sea sediments contain a great biodiversity, yet the total area that has been sampled is the equivalent of only a few tennis courts. Similarly, coral reefs, often called "the rainforests of the sea," are well known in only a few locations.

> ...the oceans remain remote, difficult to visualize, and poorly understood.

How much human disturbance can an ecosystem tolerate? This question is at the center of conservation efforts and attempts to live sustainably with nature. It also lies on the frontier of current ecological research, including indicators of ecosystem functioning, such as plant production and the cycling of essential nutrients in disturbed versus undisturbed sites, comparative studies of sites arrayed along clines of increasing biodiversity, and microcosm experiments.

Other studies look at replacements and adjustments of species numbers and distributions through contemporary and geologic time using well known and well preserved fossil species assemblages. Introductions of nonnative species, such as zebra mussels in the Great Lakes and comb jellies in the Black and Azov Seas principally by ballast-water transport, are accidental "experiments" that have resulted in significant declines of native species and important resources. Some species, called "keystone species" contribute disproportionately to the structure and dynamics of the ecosystem. Identification of these species may provide an indicator of ecosystem health and an early warning to implement intensive conservation efforts in advance of a collapse.[7]

Coral bleaching, a physiological response of corals and their symbiotic algae to high water temperature, was first noted on coral reefs of the greater Caribbean Sea and Florida in 1987. This was the same year that the U.S. Congress began to address global warming. Since then, coral bleaching has been noted periodically all over the world, often associated with El Niño, but always with prolonged elevated seawater temperatures. The 1997–98 El Niño—the largest this century—coincided with the largest, most coherent, and most damaging coral bleaching event in history. All through the world's tropics, corals bleached and unprecedented amounts of coral died. Since 1987, coral bleaching has been a hypothetical early warning signal of global warming in the oceans. The 1997–98 event, combined with recent evidence of warming of the core temperature of the ocean, is great cause for alarm and concern for the future of the most diverse and most beloved shallow-water ecosystem.[8]

Marine ecosystems are major national capital assets. In addition to providing valuable goods, such as fisheries and minerals, they provide critical life support services, such as diluting, dispersing, and metabolizing the effluents of society, thus purifying waters for recreation. The value of a healthy ocean is difficult to overestimate. At a national level, economic evaluation of ecosystem services can guide policy decisions on inevitable development versus environment tradeoffs. For example, Florida's ocean policy estimates an annual economic value of $105 billion to ocean-related industries and tourism. Recent attempts to put a monetary value on global ecosystem services have stimulated much discussion and more comprehensive and ultimately more useful ways to evaluate the importance of nature.[9] Finally, it is important to acknowledge that the value of nature to human society might be even more fundamental. E. O. Wilson, Pellegrino

Research Professor in Entomology at Harvard University, has argued that people have an innate response to biodiversity that links us to our evolutionary origins and stands at the core of humanity and a sense of well-being.[10]

Everything We Do on Land Ends Up in the Ocean

Ahupua'a—from ridgetop to reef—was the ancient Hawaiian scheme for managing human activities from the watershed to the sea, recognizing the inextricable link between them. The coastal seascape—including the watershed (100 miles above sea level) and the coastal ocean and continental shelf (200 miles below sea level)—is the meeting place of the three great provinces of land, sea, and air. It is where 60 percent of the human population lives and it accounts for about 25 percent of global production of plant material, the basis of all food chains, and 90 percent of fish catch. An estimated 80 percent of marine pollution originates from land runoff and atmospheric sources. During the past 100 years of relentless population growth, the seascape's capacity to disperse, dilute, and metabolize the waste products and effluents of human society and its insults to the land has been gradually exceeded. The consequences include damaged coastal economies, pollution, increased frequency and virulence of harmful algal blooms, dead zones off major river mouths, human health concerns, and diseases of marine organisms.[11]

South Florida is a case in point. In 1988, the Everglades National Park sued the state of Florida for discharging nutrient-laden water from the Everglades Agricultural Area into the northern reaches of the park, allowing nonnative plant species to displace the famous river of grass. Downstream, the development of the management plan of the new Florida Keys National Marine Sanctuary targeted declining water quality in the Everglades ecosystem and Florida Bay as a critical impact on contiguous sanctuary waters. The sanctuary plan identified the limitation of freshwater delivery to Florida Bay by decades of freshwater canalization and drainage as the cause. The resolution of these two problems, currently in progress in the Everglades Restoration Project, is the largest effort in U.S. history to restore the functioning of a natural system. In partnership with Florida, it involves a commitment of billions of dollars in property acquisition and drainage engineering to restore more natural freshwater flow through the greater Everglades ecosystem and into the shallow marine waters surrounding the Florida peninsula.[12]

In the west, "shuttling as they do like silver threads between upland and ocean . . . , salmon tightly stitch the interlock between continent, torrent, and tide binding everything humans do to land and water."[13] One has only to look at the reasonably healthy economics and management of the Alaska salmon fishery, where the human population is low, the seascape is relatively undisturbed, and rivers run free of dams, to realize what has been lost in Washington, Oregon, and California. There, disruption of streams and rivers by dams and deforestation, overfishing, and unintentional release of Atlantic salmon and their pathogens from aquaculture are driving genetically distinct Pacific salmon populations to the brink of extinction.

Overfishing

The unfortunate history of fishing is overfishing. The principal reasons are politics and greed. The United States spends approximately $500 million annually on fisheries research and management and has worked out the fisheries-related aspects of the life histories of most commercially important species. Nevertheless, the United States does not effectively manage most of these fisheries.[14] The 1976 Magnuson Fisheries Conservation and Management Act eliminated competition from foreign fishing fleets by establishing eight regional fishery management councils charged with developing management plans for fishery resources and an EEZ of 200 miles. Unfortunately, the act was unclear about overfishing and encouraged the National Marine Fisheries Service and the councils to achieve a vague standard called optimum yield. The shifting definition of optimum yield allowed maximum sustainable yield, another uncertain standard, to be exceeded because of economic and social considerations, driving some fisheries to collapse. The councils mixed the problems of fisheries management with local and regional politics and commerce, shifting emphasis from sustainability to commercial development of hard-pressed fish species and, given frequent disasters, switching effort to underexploited species that become the disasters of the future.

Fish are wildlife. Overfishing causes declines in marine biodiversity and the results recall the history of settlement and development of the land. The development of agriculture required the removal of large land predators, such as bears, wolves, and cats, causing drastic increases in populations of deer and other grazers, which, in turn, disrupted natural and cultivated areas. Overfishing of large predators similarly changes the functioning of marine ecosystems. For example, the shift from reef-building corals to overgrowth by algae on many coral reefs has been attributed to overfishing and associated human distur- bances. In the open ocean, fishing first eliminates the larger top carnivore and then

> . . .trawl fishery has been compared to catching squirrels by cutting down forests. Bottom trawl nets scour and destroy an estimated global area of fish habitat the equivalent of 150 times the area of forests cut annually worldwide. . . .

gradually moves down the food chain, changing the functioning of ocean ecosys- tems in ways that humans do not yet understand.[15]

Fishing gear damages biodiversity. For example, trawl fishery has been com- pared to catching squirrels by cutting down forests. Bottom trawl nets scour and destroy an estimated global area of fish habitat the equivalent of 150 times the area of forests cut annually worldwide, and a great proportion of the catch—the so-called by-catch—is discarded.[16]

The 1996 reauthorized Magnuson Act (renamed the Magnuson-Stevens Sustainable Fisheries Act) addresses the earlier problems of sustainable fisheries and mandates that fisheries management councils use a precautionary approach to evaluate the impact of loss of essential fish habitat (EFH), manage fisheries using ecosystem principles, and mitigate damages. Unfortunately, the act has a fundamental policy flaw in that fisheries management is too narrow in scope to provide the basis for managing the ocean ecosystem implicit in the EFH and ecosystem provisions.

In response largely to concerns of fisheries management, various types of marine protected areas have captured the imagination of policy makers, resource managers, scientists, and the general public as simple, familiar, and demonstrably effective ways of managing fisheries and protecting marine biodiversity. In the years since the National Marine Sanctuaries Act of 1972, 12 marine sanctuaries have been designated. The Florida Keys National Marine Sanctuary (FKNMS), created by Congress in 1991, is one of the largest and the only one with a com- prehensive management plan. The plan uses zoning to separate potentially con- flicting human activities and implements fully protected, fishing prohibition zones, sometimes called "no-take reserves."[17]

Most people are astonished to learn that the total area of fully protected marine habitat in the United States is approximately 50 square miles. The Dry Tortugas Marine Reserve, to be designated as part of the FKNMS in late 2000 after extensive public discussion, will quadruple this area. This tiny and insignificant level of protection stands in stark contrast to land areas in which more than 700 national parks and 93 million acres of national wildlife refuges have been designated, protecting, in total with other areas, approximately 5 percent of the U.S. land area. Clearly U.S. marine sanctuaries are too small and the areas that they protect are tiny and fragmented.

In May 2000, anticipating broad public support, President Clinton ordered the development of a national system of ocean conservation zones centered on fully protected marine reserves with the ultimate goal of protecting 20 percent of U.S. coastal waters. Networks of fully protected marine reserves will support traditional fisheries management by supplying new recruits to the surrounding harvested areas and will enhance fishing in adjacent areas by movement of adults. In addition, the reserves will function as reference or control areas to evaluate the environmental cost of fishing and help to inform management. But the greatest benefit of marine reserves will be the protection of the marine biodiversity.[18]

> **The decline of global fisheries has caused aquaculture to double in the past 15 years . . . . This attempt to make up for the enormous production potential of wild fishes through fish farming is doomed to failure.**

The decline of global fisheries has caused aquaculture to double in the past 15 years, currently accounting for approximately 20 percent of global fisheries production. This attempt to make up for the enormous production potential of wild fishes through fish farming is doomed to failure. More than 220 species of finfish and shellfish are grown in aquaculture, and the collateral damage to the environment has been huge. For example, much of the world's 50 percent decline in mangrove forests can be attributed to the relentless pursuit of the economic potential of shrimp culture. Aquaculture ponds and the culture of nonnative species have caused the introduction of diseases into already stressed native populations. Finally, the most widely consumed aquacultured species are fed a significant portion of their diet on fish meal and oil from wild-caught fishes, further stressing the natural system. Sustainable aquaculture is feasible but not on the industrial scale that has characterized much of the recent growth in aquaculture.[19]

RECOMMENDATIONS

Establish Comprehensive Management and Protection
of Marine Biodiversity in the United States

The pressures on the shallow marine ecosystems in the United States to provide commerce, recreation, and resources and to receive, process, disperse, and dilute the effluents of a complex modern human society are increasing. With the exception of ownership, the United States uses the coastal ocean in much the same way they use the land, and the conflicts between commerce, recreation, development, resource exploitation, and conservation are expensive, contentious, politically sensitive, and very familiar. The recent rapid implementation of marine protected areas has pointed to the need for more comprehensive zoning of the oceans.

The U.S. EEZ is 130 percent of the U.S. land area. It contains most of the country's marine biodiversity and the myriad physical, chemical, and biological linkages that zoning must address. The EEZ is a logical, legally defensible, and ecologically meaningful geographic area in which comprehensive management and protection have the best chance to achieve sustainable balance of resource use and conservation. Zoning brings one of the most familiar tools that has been used on land to separate potentially conflicting human activities and uses—that of the landscape (or land-use) plan, into the ocean. Within the EEZ, humans have the opportunity to step back and assess, with the best available knowledge, the distribution of and threats to coastal ocean biodiversity. The data and information to do this is abundantly available from federal, regional, and state sources. For example, it is not well known that the U.S. EEZ was completely mapped with multibeam sonar in the 1980s. In addition to providing critical information on the distribution of resources, this imagery provides a powerful way for the public to see ocean regions as essentially similar to the land. Armed with this information, the United States can implement a process leading to a seascape (or ocean-use) plan, based upon comprehensive zoning within the EEZ, that will start a whole new course of protection and use of coastal marine resources.

The ocean-use plan, based on zoning, has several immediate benefits. It is familiar and can be put into positive terms. In contrast, concentrating on bottom-up implementation of fishing prohibition zones or no-take marine reserves one at a time targets only one user group and makes the process unduly contentious. However, if the bottom-up efforts are nested within a national commitment to sustainable use of marine biodiversity, all stakeholders—not only fishers—will have a role. The function of marine protected areas will be much clearer and the pain and the benefits will be shared. The ocean-use plan logically links the coastal ocean to the land, a goal that is often stated as basic to coastal ocean management but is rarely achieved.

Finally, a key difference between land and sea is that zoning in the sea is inherently more flexible. The ocean is not owned and zones can be established and moved in response to increased understanding and changing exigencies. The geographically broader approach and the potential flexibility of an ocean-use plan help to deal with a vexing question: How much of a larger area zoned for multiple uses should be fully protected from all human disturbances? The figure of 20 percent has been widely discussed, but there is little scientific justification for it. It seems to be big enough to provide significant protection, yet it is not so big as to be politically impossible to achieve. The implementation of a network of fully protected areas, combined with a scientific monitoring plan, will provide, over time, the key information to answer this question. In other words, adaptive management of the coastal ocean will be inherently easier than management on land.[20]

Establish an Integrated Coastal Ocean Observing System

The great variability, short time scale, and small geographic scale of oceanographic events in the coastal seascape demand state-of-the-art continuous, in situ monitoring equipment, and better access to more refined remote sensing and satellite imagery. For example, there are at present no sensors to monitor the inorganic ions of phosphorus and nitrogen, which are key indicators of pollution of coastal seas. In addition, satellite sensors have not generally been designed for maximum utility in the coastal ocean where most management problems are.

After the 1982–83 El Niño, the United States, in cooperation with France, Japan, and Taiwan, began a 10-year program to build a vast ocean observing system known as the Tropical Atmosphere-Ocean (TAO) Array of 70 buoys spanning the Pacific Ocean. The buoys measure critical surface and subsurface parameters that are telemetered to the National Oceanographic and Atmospheric Administration's (NOAA) Pacific Marine Environmental Laboratory. The TAO Array allowed ocean scientists to accurately predict the 1997–98 El Niño—something that had never before been done.

Following on this success, initial blueprints have been prepared for a national integrated ocean observing system. The data, critical to weather prediction, safer marine operations, and prediction and mitigation of natural disasters, will be among the most valuable for human health and safety in the world.[21] The program will also create opportunities for entrepreneurs. Imagine a nightly weather report including ocean conditions: Temperature gradients, wave fronts, algal blooms, wind patterns, and other key information will be set into motion in full color and become as important to the average person in the United States as cloud patterns and radar images of rain intensity and storm cells are today.

Establish an Intergovernmental Panel on Ocean Health

The reports of IPCC have been extremely influential in directing the energy and atmospheric policies of many nations and have driven demonstrable improvement in human damage to the atmosphere. There is a need for an IPCC-like process directed at marine systems.

In international waters beyond the EEZ, the nations of the world collect a great deal of data and information to inform national programs. Sometimes these data are gathered together in a global summary. For example, the UN Food and Agriculture Organization collects and publishes fishery statistics from every fishing nation. These statistics present a grim recent

There is a need for an IPCC-like process directed at marine systems.

history of fisheries worldwide but are not widely known. Similarly, vast amounts of water quality data critical to understanding the dynamics of the ocean system are collected every year by maritime nations and filed away, largely unused. Taken together, all of these data provide important information on ocean health.

An Intergovernmental Panel on Ocean Health, integrating the information from developing international ocean observing systems, could be as influential as IPCC is on greenhouse gases on national policies involving fishing, waste disposal, mining, energy, and shipping. The United States, having much to gain from comprehensive ocean protection and management, has the power to lead such a development.[22]

Conclusions

Biodiversity is the key to the maintenance of the world as we know it . . . . This is the assembly of life that took a billion years to evolve. It . . . created the world that created us. It holds the world steady. (E. O. Wilson)[23]

Ocean ecosystems are major capital assets and a healthy ocean is a key to the economic and social future of the United States. National polls taken over the past few years clearly show that public awareness of the oceans is growing rapidly and that people are frustrated with our inability to manage and conserve marine biodiversity. The political will is present to support bold new initiatives. A comprehensive long-term program based on zoning the EEZ, developing the scientific and management infrastructure to monitor and manage it, and extending experience in partnership with the maritime nations to the global oceans is an idea commensurate with the scale of these emerging problems. It will not be easy, but the approach demystifies the oceans and lends itself readily to phased timing, partnerships with coastal states and nations, and public education and participation. Stewardship of the last great frontier on Earth will strengthen our global leadership and emerging traditions of environmental sensitivity and do no less than sustain human survival and quality of life.

MEMORANDUM TO THE PRESIDENT

From: Andrew R. Solow

Subject: Red Tides and Dead Zones: Eutrophication in the Marine Environment

PROBLEM

The most widespread and economically costly chronic pollution problem along the world's coasts is eutrophication. Eutrophication occurs when high levels of chemical nutrients stimulate excessive growth of aquatic plants. There is a clear connection between eutrophication and two significant marine environmental problems: the occurrence of harmful algal blooms and the depletion of dissolved oxygen in bottom waters. Harmful algal blooms pose a threat to human health and to commercial and recreational activities at the coast, while oxygen depletion or hypoxia poses a threat to fisheries. Beyond these direct effects on human welfare, both harmful algal blooms and eutrophication can have profound effects on marine food webs and biological diversity. Certain types of harmful algal blooms can destroy ecologically important habitats like seagrass beds and coral reefs, while others can cause illness and death in marine mammals. Oxygen depletion associated with eutrophication can reduce the diversity of biological communities on the seafloor.

BACKGROUND

In the ocean, as on the land, photosynthesis combines energy from the sun, carbon dioxide, and chemical nutrients like nitrogen and phosphorus to produce carbon-rich plant material. This natural process, which is called primary production, forms the base of the marine food chain: without it, the ocean could not support life. However, human activities—notably, the intensification of agriculture; the disposal of human and animal waste; the conversion of riverine, estuarine, and coastal ecosystems; and the combustion of fossil fuels—have increased the discharge of nutrients to coastal waters above its natural level, causing excessive primary production. This is called eutrophication. Although eutrophication is a regional problem, in the sense that its causes and effects tend to be localized, it is also a global problem, in the sense that it occurs along all of the world's inhabited coastlines. The effect of growing nutrient levels on primary production is felt throughout marine ecosystems. As these ecosystems provide commercial, recreational, and other benefits, eutrophication also has effects on human society.

> **...human activities—notably, the intensification of agriculture; the disposal of human and animal waste; the conversion of riverine, estuarine, and coastal ecosystems; and the combustion of fossil fuels—have increased the discharge of nutrients to coastal waters....**

Eutrophication and its associated effects pose a difficult problem in environmental policy. The activities that contribute nutrients to the marine environment are many and varied. The physical and biological processes linking these nutrients to eventual effects are complex and scientific understanding is incomplete. In contrast to the economic value of the activities that produce nutrients, much of the damage due to eutrophication accrues to recreational activities, environmental quality, and biological diversity, so it is difficult to measure in economic terms. Despite the widespread nature of this problem, when measurement is possible, as with the effects on public health and commercial fisheries, these damages appear to be relatively small in aggregate terms, although they can be substantial locally and, unless steps are taken, are likely to grow over time. Taken together, all this suggests that policy makers should begin by looking for measures that reduce nutrient discharge at low or no cost and that have other benefits to society. Two such measures are the use of so-called best management practices in agriculture to reduce the loss of fertilizer and the restoration of wetlands and other buffers to intercept nutrients. In addition, a system for managing growing concentrations of animal wastes needs to be established. Finally, reducing the atmospheric deposition of nitrogen in the marine environment provides an additional rationale for a range of air quality measures.

Harmful algal blooms

There are several thousand species of marine algae. These can be divided into microscopic species, called microalgae, and larger macroalgae, commonly known as seaweeds. Perhaps 100 species of microalgae contain potent toxins. Because high concentrations of some of these species can color the water red or brown, they are sometimes referred to as red or brown tides, although these terms are misleading and are no longer used by scientists. Toxic algae enter the marine food chain when it is consumed by certain kinds of fish, shellfish, and small marine animals called zooplankton. The toxins that accumulate in these consumers are then passed up the food chain to fish, marine mammals, and eventually to humans, where they can cause illness or occasionally death. In the United States, most human illness caused by toxic algae occurs when contaminated shellfish are consumed. These illnesses are collectively known as shellfish poisoning and can cause an array of symptoms from temporary gastric disturbance to permanent neurological damage. In addition to shellfish poisoning, in warmer regions, ciguatera poisoning can occur from ingesting contaminated reef fishes. Toxic algae can cause illness and death in fish, such as in the widely-reported 1991 outbreak of pfiesteria poisoning in the Pamlico River of North Carolina, and pose a particular threat to cultured fish raised in cages and pens. Toxic algae have also been implicated in the deaths of marine mammals, including seals, whales, and dolphins.

Although less dramatic than the effects of toxic microalgae, macroalgae can also cause problems. Large blooms of macroalgae can coat beaches, interfering with recreational activities. Macroalgae can also clog or destroy seagrass beds and coral reefs that provide nursery grounds for commercially important fish and, more generally, support high levels of biological diversity.

Harmful algal blooms occur in every part of the world. In the United States and other developed nations, monitoring efforts and shellfish closures have reduced the incidence of human illness caused by toxic algae. However, both monitoring and closures have economic costs that can be locally substantial. Perhaps the most striking example in the United States is the complete loss of the Alaska wild shellfish resource, which once produced 5 million pounds annually, to persistent paralytic shellfish poisoning. In less developed parts of the world, human illness from the consumption of contaminated fish and shellfish remains a threat to public health. For example, reported cases of ciguatera poisoning currently number about 50,000 annually throughout the world and it is widely believed that the majority of cases go unreported.

It is difficult to assess the role played by human activities in the occurrence of harmful algal blooms. The difficulty stems from the complexity of the physical and biological processes involved and the relatively sparse record of observations. However, while harmful algal blooms can and do occur in relatively pristine conditions, there is a clear relationship between nutrient levels and primary production and it is generally agreed that, other things being equal, factors that favor high levels of primary production also favor harmful algal blooms. Although the observational record is sparse, there is much in it to support this conclusion and little or nothing to contradict it. Beyond the direct effect of increasing nutrient levels on primary production, it has been suggested that the mix of nutrients produced by human activities—predominantly nitrogen and phosphorus, with a little silica—may favor the phytoplankton group with toxic members over less toxic groups.

Hypoxia

The term hypoxia refers to the depletion of dissolved oxygen in ocean bottom waters. In technical terms, hypoxia is said to occur when dissolved oxygen falls below 2 milligrams per liter. Hypoxia occurs when organic material, in the form of dead phytoplankton cells or fecal pellets from predators of phytoplankton, falls to the bottom and is decomposed by oxygen-utilizing bacteria. As long as the bottom waters are well mixed with the oxygen-rich surface waters, the oxygen used by decomposers is renewed. However, under certain conditions, the water column is stratified and there is little mixing. Stratification tends to occur during the summer, when warming at the surface is strongest. The configuration of warm water overlaying cold water is stable and resists mixing. Stratification also tends to occur near the mouths of rivers, where the stable configuration of lighter freshwater overlaying heavier salt water also resists mixing. Finally, stratification is stronger in enclosed or semi-enclosed water bodies that are cut off from large-scale oceanographic processes that promote mixing. When mixing is weak or absent, the oxygen used in decomposition cannot be renewed and hypoxia can occur.

Because animal life depends on the availability of oxygen, the occurrence of hypoxia can have a dramatic effect on marine organisms. The response of marine organisms to hypoxia is varied. Immobile or slow-moving organisms may simply suffocate. While mobile organisms, such as shrimp, lobsters, and fish, can often avoid the direct effects of hypoxia, there can be serious indirect effects. By itself, the loss of once-suitable habitat and the prey that it contains means that the area can only support smaller populations. If all suitable habitat is eventually lost, then the entire population will vanish as well. The occurrence of hypoxic zones can interfere with the offshore migration of animals like shrimp and lobsters. This can delay development and increase predation risk. In extreme cases, hypoxic conditions can trap large numbers of animals in shallow waters, resulting in massive fish kills. Beyond direct damages to economically important species, the occurrence of hypoxia can completely alter the biological community inhabiting the sediments on the ocean floor. Not only is biological diversity lost in this so-called benthic community, but even when the hypoxia itself is broken up by wintertime mixing and commercially important species return, the alteration of the benthic community on which they feed can affect their growth and development.

While the effects of extreme hypoxic conditions on marine species are fairly clear, the effects of less extreme conditions are more difficult to discern. For example, there is an inverse annual correlation between the areal extent of summertime hypoxia and size of shrimp stocks in the northern Gulf of Mexico. However, a similar correlation exists between the areal extent of hypoxia and the size of shrimp stocks outside the hypoxic zone. A possible explanation is that the same regional climatic conditions that favor hypoxia—specifically, high spring rainfall that increases the discharge of nutrients from the Mississippi River system into the Gulf—also have an adverse effect on young shrimp in estuarine nursery areas throughout the Gulf region. Even if this is the case, there is little doubt that continued growth of hypoxia in the Gulf would eventually have an adverse effect on shrimp and other economically important species.

Hypoxia occurs throughout the world. Two of the best known hypoxic areas are in the Black Sea and the Baltic Sea. In the United States, the best known areas of hypoxia are Long Island Sound, the Chesapeake Bay, and the Louisiana Gulf coast (where it is popularly known as the "Dead Zone"). Although there is considerable variability from place to place and observations are limited, there is no doubt that hypoxia has effects on fisheries. In the Black Sea and the Baltic Sea, hypoxia has contributed to the replacement of demersal (i.e., groundfish) fisheries by less profitable pelagic (i.e., mid-water) fisheries. By living up in the water column, pelagic fish are generally unaffected by hypoxia in bottom waters. Also, many pelagic fish prey on phytoplankton and may actually benefit from high levels of primary production. Hypoxia has contributed to the collapse of the Norwegian lobster fishery and the displacement of lobsters in Long Island Sound. Although the hypoxic zone along the Louisiana Gulf coast is large, it has not reached the level of severity seen elsewhere. Nevertheless, there is already some evidence of effects on the important shrimp fishery and a possible replacement of demersal species, like snapper, by pelagic species, like menhaden.

Hypoxia can occur naturally. For example, the bottom waters of the Black Sea have experienced total depletion of oxygen (which is called anoxia) for thousands of years. Naturally occurring hypoxia has occurred in the Chesapeake Bay and along the Louisiana Gulf coast. However, there is no doubt that, by increasing the level of nutrients in surface waters, human activities have increased the frequency, areal extent, and severity of hypoxia in these areas and throughout the coastal environment.

RECOMMENDATIONS

For a variety of reasons, determining an appropriate policy response to eutrophication is difficult. First, many economic activities contribute nutrients to the marine environment. These include agriculture; the disposal of household waste; population growth along rivers, estuaries, and on the coast; the conversion of wetlands; and the burning of fossil fuels. Thus, regulating the flow of nutrients could potentially touch on a large part of the economy. Second, the effects of eutrophication are complex and difficult to measure in economic terms. While certain parts of the problem have received attention by scientists and economists, there is no comprehensive assessment of the potential costs and benefits of alternative strategies to control marine eutrophication. Third, while coastal eutrophication is ubiquitous and increasing, every eutrophic zone is to some extent different in terms of both causes and effects, so that policies will have to be customized to local conditions

In this situation, it seems wise to begin by focusing on low cost options for controlling nutrients, especially those with benefits beyond the reduction of eutrophication; to encourage the development of local and regional approaches; and to support economic and scientific efforts to address key uncertainties and to evaluate the costs and benefits of different strategies. Experience suggests that, within any activity that contributes nutrients to coastal waters, some low-cost reduction is possible. The fact that there are so many such activities suggests, in turn, that there is considerable scope for low-cost reductions. In the case of agriculture, the loss of unutilized fertilizer to the environment itself constitutes an economic loss to producers, so that inexpensive measures to prevent this loss will have benefits beyond the marine environment. Fortunately, a number of relatively inexpensive measures are available to reduce fertilizer loss. These include the use of improved soil and crop testing, remote sensing, and other information to fine-tune fertilizer application over time and across fields and the use of no-till or conservation tillage to reduce erosion and consequent nutrient loss. Curtailing the conversion of wetlands and other buffers that intercept and sequester nutrients and restoring some of those that have already been lost are other promising options, as is upgrading septic facilities and sewage treatment. There is also a clear need for improved treatment of growing concentrations of animal waste. Although these options are more costly, they have benefits beyond reducing coastal eutrophication. For example, wetlands provide refuge for fish, birds, and other animals and thus contribute to the maintenance of biological diversity, while improved handling of sewage is an important priority in managing water quality generally. Finally, the benefits to marine environmental quality should be added to the list of other benefits of reducing atmospheric emissions of nitrogen.

As environmental problems go, coastal eutrophication is not particularly glamorous. While it may be difficult to justify costly measures to eliminate eutrophication, particularly in the short-term, low-cost options do exist to take a step in that direction. Not only would undertaking these options make economic sense today, but they would set us on a course to lighten the tread of society on natural systems.

MEMORANDUM TO THE PRESIDENT

From: Robert W. Kates

Subject: Population and Consumption

PROBLEM

International efforts to address global environmental problems are often characterized by debates as to the proximate causes of environmental degradation that emphasize either growing population numbers of the poor or the conspicuous consumption of the affluent. As with many such classic disputes, both concerns are valid, and efforts to maintain the essential life support systems of the environment will need to address both.

BACKGROUND

A recent report from the National Research Council captures this recurrent debate:

For over two decades, the same frustrating exchange has been repeated countless times in international policy circles. A government official or scientist from a wealthy country would make the following argument:

The world is threatened with environmental disaster because of the depletion of natural resources (or climate change or the loss of biodiversity), and it cannot continue for long to support its rapidly growing population. To preserve the environment for future generations, we need to move quickly to control global population growth, and we must concentrate the effort on the world's poorer countries, where the vast majority of population growth is occurring.

Government officials and scientists from low-income countries would typically respond:

If the world is facing environmental disaster, it is not the fault of the poor, who use few resources. The fault must lie with the world's wealthy countries, where people consume the great bulk of the world's natural resources and energy and cause the great bulk of its environmental degradation. We need to curtail overconsumption in the rich countries which use far more than their fair share, both to preserve the environment and to allow the poorest people on earth to achieve an acceptable standard of living.

Because both concerns are valid, this memorandum begins by laying out what is known about the relative responsibilities of both population and consumption for the environmental crisis and concludes with some policy initiatives to address them. The effort to do so however is hampered by a profound asymmetry that must fuel the frustration of the developing countries' politicians and scientists: namely, how much people know about population and how little they know about consumption.

Population

What population is and how it grows is well understood even if all the forces driving it are not. Population begins with people and their key events of birth, death, and location. Change in the world's population or that of any place is the simple arithmetic of adding births, subtracting deaths, adding immigrants, and subtracting outmigrants. The error in estimates of population for almost all places is probably within 20 percent and, for countries with modern statistical services, under 3 percent—better estimates than for any other living things and for most other environmental concerns.

Current world population is more than six billion people, growing at a rate of 1.3 percent per year. The peak annual growth rate in all history — about 2.1 percent — occurred in the early 1960s, and the peak population increase of around 87 million per year occurred in the late 1980s. About 80 percent or 4.8 billion people live in the less developed areas of the world, with 1.2 billion living in industrialized countries. Population is now projected by the United Nations (U.N.) to be

8.9 billion in 2050, according to its medium fertility assumption, the one usually considered most likely, or as high as 10.6 billion or as low as 7.3 billion.

A general description of how birth rates and death rates are changing over time is a process called the demographic transition. It was first studied in the context of Europe, where in the space of two centuries, societies went from a condition of high births and high deaths to the current situation of low births and low deaths. In such a transition, deaths decline more rapidly than births, and in that gap, population grows rapidly but eventually stabilizes as the birth decline matches or even exceeds the death decline. While the general description of the transition is widely accepted, much is debated about its cause and details.

The world is now in the midst of a global transition that, unlike the European transition, is much more rapid. Both births and deaths dropped faster than experts expected and history foreshadowed. It took 100 years for deaths to drop in Europe compared to the drop in 30 years in the Third World. Today, the global transition to required stability is more than halfway, between the average of five children born to each woman at the post World War II peak of population growth and the 2.1 births required to achieve eventual zero population growth. Three is the current global average births per woman of reproductive age. The death transition is more advanced, life expectancy having grown about three-quarters of the transition between a life expectancy at birth of 40 years to one of 75, and is currently at 64 years. The current rates of decline in births outpace the estimates of the demographers, the U.N. having reduced its latest medium expectation of global population in 2050 to 8.9 billion, a reduction of almost 10 percent from its 1994 projection.

Demographers debate the causes of this rapid birth decline. But even with such differences, it is possible to break down the projected growth of the next century and to identify policies that would reduce projected populations even further. John Bongaarts of the Population Council has decomposed the projected developing country growth into three parts. The first part is unwanted fertility, making available the methods and materials for contraception to the 120 million married women (and the many more unmarried women) who in survey research say they either want fewer children or want to space them better. A basic strategy for doing so links voluntary family planning with other reproductive and child health services.

Yet in many parts of the world, the desired number of children is too high for a stabilized population. A basic strategy for changing this number accelerates three trends that have been shown to lead to lower desired family size: the survival of children, their education, and improvement in the economic, social, and legal status for girls and women. However, even if fertility could immediately be brought down to the replacement level of two surviving children per woman, population growth would continue for many years in most developing countries because so many more young people of reproductive age exist. This youthful momentum of population growth can be reduced by increasing the age of childbearing, primarily by improving secondary education opportunity for girls and by addressing such neglected issues as adolescent sexuality and reproductive behavior.

How much further could population be reduced? In theory, the population of the developing world (using older projections) was expected to reach 10.2 billion by 2100, up from the current developing country population of 4.8 billion. Meeting the unmet need

> **...a 10 percent reduction is both realistic and attainable and could lead to a lessening in projected population numbers by 2050 of upwards of a billion people.**

for contraception could reduce this increase by about two billion. Bringing down desired family size to replacement fertility would reduce the population a billion more, with the remaining two and a half billion growth due to the momentum of a very young population. In practice, however, a recent U.S. National Academy of Sciences report concluded that a 10 percent reduction is both realistic and attainable and could lead to a lessening in projected population numbers by 2050 of upwards of a billion people.

Would a world with 1 billion fewer people be a better world? From the concern with environmental pressures, almost surely. From the needs of developing countries, highly likely. From the needs of the industrialized countries, the conclusion is a bit mixed. The projected doubling of U.S. population by the end of the century to 527 million will put immense but not insurmountable pressures on cities, resources, and environments in this country, while most sectors of the economy will benefit from immigration. To cope with such a doubling will require new ways of dealing with urban growth and sprawl, preserving nature and wildlands, and spreading immigrant communities beyond the few states where they congregate. But the projected declining populations in much of Europe and Japan would leave their aging populations with declining human energy and support unless countered by much higher levels of immigration. Overall, all the world will benefit from a billion less people with smart growth in the places that need it.

Consumption

In contrast to population, where people and their births and deaths are relatively well-defined biological events, there is no consensus as to what consumption includes with physicists, economists, ecologists, and sociologists all differing. For physicists, consumption is what happens when you transform matter or energy. For economists, consumption is what consumers do with their money. For ecologists, consumption is what big fish do to little fish. And for some sociologists, consumption is keeping up with the Joneses.

In 1977, the Councils of the Royal Society of London and the U.S. National Academy of Sciences issued a joint statement on consumption, having previously done so on population. They chose a variant of the physicist's definition:

> *Consumption is the human transformation of materials and energy. Consumption is of concern to the extent that it makes the transformed materials or energy less available for future use, or negatively impacts biophysical systems in such a way as to threaten human health, welfare, or other things people value.*

This memo uses this Society/Academy view with one modification, the addition of information to energy and matter, thus completing the triad of the biophysical and ecological basics that support life. But only limited data and concepts on the transformation of energy, materials, and the role of information exist. There is relatively good global knowledge of energy transformations due in part to the common units of conversion between different technologies. Between 1950 and today, global energy production and use increased more than fourfold.

For material transformations, there are no aggregate data in common units on a global basis, only for some specific classes of materials. A recent analysis finds that materials consumption in the United States averages well over 60 kilos per person per day (excluding water) split between energy and related products (38 percent), minerals for construction (37 percent), with the remainder as industrial minerals (5 percent), metals (2 percent), and products of fields (12 percent) and forest (5 percent).

Over the last century, data on the per capita use of minerals and forestry materials in the United States show a modest doubling between 1900 and the depression of the 1930s (from two to four metric tons), followed by a steep quintupling with economic recovery until the early 1970s (from two to eleven tons), followed by a leveling off since then with fluctuations related to economic downturns.

Trends and projections in agriculture, energy, and economy can serve as surrogates for more detailed data on energy and material transformation. From 1950 to the early 1990s, world population more than doubled (2.2 times), food as measured by grain production almost tripled (2.7 times), energy use more than quadrupled (4.4 times), and the economy quintupled (5.1 times). This 43-year record is similar to a current 55-year projection (1995-2050) that assumes the continuation of current trends or, as some note, "business as usual." In this 55-year projection, growth of half again in population (1.6 times) finds almost a doubling of agriculture (1.8 times), more than twice as much energy use (2.4 times), and a quadrupling of the economy (4.3 times).

Thus, both history and future scenarios predict growth rates of consumption well beyond population, and much of this increased consumption is needed by any standards of human need and equity. Globally, the 20% of the world's people in the highest-income countries account for 86% of total private consumption expenditures—the poorest 20% a minuscule 1.3%. Well over a

...both history and future scenarios predict growth rates of consumption well beyond population....

billion people are deprived of basic consumption needs. Of the 4.4 billion people in developing countries, nearly three-fifths lack basic sanitation. Almost a third have no access to clean water. A quarter do not have adequate housing. A fifth have no access to modern health services. A fifth of children do not attend school to grade 5. About a fifth do not have enough dietary energy and protein. In developing countries only a privileged minority has motorized transport, telecommunications and modern energy.

Thus despite some rhetoric, much consumption is needed and more is desired. Thus it makes sense to focus on the form of consumption that "negatively impacts biophysical systems in such a way as to threaten human health, welfare, or other things people value." By that criterion, globally, there are at least three major groups of consumption products which ought to be reduced or their production changed: products whose production and consumption seriously threaten biodiversity, products whose production or consumption releases large amounts of toxic materials, and fossil fuels that threaten our climate and pollute our air and water.

What can be done to reduce potentially harmful consumption? An attractive similarity exists between a demographic transition that moves over time from high births and high deaths to low births and low deaths with an energy, materials, and information transition. In this transition, societies will use increasing amounts of energy and materials as consumption increases, but over time the energy and materials input per unit of consumption decrease, and information substitutes for more material and energy inputs.

Some encouraging signs surface for such a transition in both energy and materials, and these have been variously labeled as decarbonization and dematerialization. For more than a century, the amount of carbon per unit of energy produced has been decreasing. Over a shorter period, the amount of energy used to produce a unit of production has also steadily declined. There is also evidence for dematerialization, using fewer materials for a unit of production, but only for industrialized countries and for some specific materials. And the inputs of toxics has also been declining.

This transition can be accelerated. It is possible to substitute less damaging and depleting energy and materials for more damaging ones. There is growing experience with encouraging substitution and its difficulties: renewables for non-renewables, toxics with fewer toxics, ozone depleting chemicals for more benign substitutes, natural gas for coal, etc. Beyond substitution, shrinking the energy and materials required per unit of consumption is probably the most effective current means for reducing environmentally damaging consumption. There is growing experience with the three Rs of consumption shrinkage: reduce, recycle, reuse. Perhaps most important in the long run, but possibly least studied, is the potential for and value of substituting information for energy and materials.

Energy and materials per unit of consumption are going down, in part because more and more consumption consists of information.

It may also be possible to reduce consumption by more satisfaction with what we already have, by satiation, no more needing more because there is enough, and by sublimation, having more satisfaction with less to achieve some greater good. This is the least explored area of consumption and the most difficult. There are, of course, many signs of satiation for some goods. For example, people in the industrialized

> **It may also be possible to reduce consumption by more satisfaction with what we already have, by satiation, no more needing more because there is enough. . . .**

world no longer buy additional refrigerators (except in newly formed households) but only replace them. Moreover, the quality of refrigerators has so improved that a 20-year or more life span is commonplace. Yet enterprises are frequently viewed as failures of marketing or entrepreneurship rather than successes in meeting human needs sufficiently and efficiently when their markets have saturated. Is it possible to reverse such views, to create a standard of satiation, a satisfaction in a need well met?

Can people have more satisfaction with what they already have by using it more intensely and having the time to do so? The economist Juliet Schor tells of some overworked Americans who would willingly exchange money for time, time to spend with family and using what they already have, but who are constrained by an uncooperative employment structure. Proposed U.S. legislation would permit the trading of overtime for such compensatory time off, a step in this direction. Sublimation, according to the dictionary, is the diversion of energy from an immediate goal to a higher social, moral, or aesthetic purpose. Can people be more satisfied with less, satisfaction derived from the diversion of immediate consumption for the satisfaction of a smaller ecological footprint? An emergent research field grapples with how to encourage consumer behavior that will lead to change in environmentally damaging consumption, but deeper understanding comes from both humanists and scientists. A small but growing "simplicity" movement tries to fashion new images of "living the good life." Such movements may never much reduce the burdens of consumption, but they facilitate by example and experiment other less-demanding alternatives.

RECOMMENDATIONS

Looking to the future, at least five major opportunities exist to slow population growth, shift consumption to less environmentally damaging forms, and encourage an improved quality of life. While many government programs impinge on each of these objectives, this memo proposes new policy initiatives that provide fresh direction while in some cases bringing together, changing or enlarging upon existing programs.

After-Teens

To slow population growth and reduce future world population by a billion people requires meeting the unmet need for contraception, bringing down desired family size, and postponing marriage and births among the very large numbers of young people. U.S. international aid has long addressed the first of these, in one form or another, by supporting reproductive health services in developing countries, but it only sporadically has addressed the other two determinants. Only rarely do people distributing pills sit down with educators providing crucial education for girls or industrialists who create jobs for them.

Demographers estimate that for each year of postponed births as many as 116 million births might be avoided. This initiative would focus on teenage mothers, seeking to encourage them to postpone child-bearing until they are beyond their teens. A key to such encouragement is schooling, and the "after-teens" initiative would seek to expand the opportunities for girls in the developing world to attend schools and provide incentives for them and their families to take advantage of these opportunities.

> **Demographers estimate that for each year of postponed births as many as 116 million births might be avoided.**

There are a growing number of models for creative programs that expand schooling for girls, provide families with incentives to send girls to school, keep them in school, and create economic opportunities after school. In Bangladesh for example, these include the Bangladesh Rural Advancement Committee's 40,000 village schools for girls, the food for education program that provides poor families with wheat if they keep their children in school, and secondary school stipends if girls remain in secondary school and do not marry before 18. In

Haryana, this state in India deposits the equivalent of $60 for every poor girl born in the State, which can accumulate in savings funds to $600 if she stays unmarried until she is 18; she can then use it either as a dowry, launch some economic activity, or continue to accumulate savings until 22. In Egypt, a new program seeks to provide esteem and earning power to adolescent girls and encourage them to stay unmarried and self-sufficient. Supporting and encouraging the wide expansion of programs such as these could be the core of an after-teens initiative.

Make a Market

The purchasing power of the Federal government is enormous and if channeled can effectively make markets for products that address two major sources of environmentally damaging consumption: fossil fuels and toxic materials. Large scale purchases of products can create markets sufficient for achieving economies of production and marketing scale sufficient to lower costs, increase innovation, and to attract more producers into the market, not only in the United States but in the global economy as well. A requirement for significant proportion of recycled paper in government paper purchases had just such an effect on the market in paper.

Three sets of products may be of particular significance: electricity, cars, and certain recyclable materials. A Federal mandate on the renewable content of electricity generation that it purchases could augment such requirements that some states are currently requiring in face of a massive deregulation of the electrical generating industry with its potential to increase fossil fuel use. A substantial requirement for the purchase of high efficiency automobiles could radically increase the market for such vehicles as hybrid gas-electric cars with a subsequent lowering of cost. To encourage recycling, government can require purchase of low toxic products (e.g. paper produced by chlorine free processes or replacements for polyvinyl chloride (PVC) plastic bottles) or by eliminating obstacles to markets for some recyclable materials that arise from classifying reusable materials as toxic waste for regulatory purposes.

Smart Urban Growth

Growing much faster than the population as a whole, the urban share of population is projected to grow to 60% in a generation and upwards of 75% in two. Of the 4 billion new urban dwellers in 2050, half will be in Asia, and most of the rest in the developing world. For them, the equivalent of 400 cities the size of Buenos Aires, Cairo, Delhi, Manila, Osaka, Tienjing, or Rio de Janeiro will need to be built to house and employ them by 2050. These will not be new cities, of course, but expansions of existing ones.

The challenge that faces the planners, designers, builders, and financiers of those expanded cities is to achieve settlement patterns that make efficient use of land and infrastructure, require less material and energy use, while providing satisfactory levels of living. To do so, we need to bring together the science and technology of habitability, efficiency, and environment, much of it hidden away under disciplinary covers, with the practice of planning, building, and financing the cities of tomorrow. Unfortunately habitability, efficiency, and environment are found separately in different practitioner organizations, academic disciplines, government agencies, and even U.N. organizations. And absent from these are the most important: the speculators and developers transforming the face of many cities. But if we can bring them together, the opportunity to replace and create anew much of the current infrastructure over the next two generations is a key to habitable cities, efficient energy use, and increased biodiversity.

The United States can play an important role in seizing this unique opportunity by initially bringing together the U.S. institutions with important roles in city expansion: our large engineering and design firms, banking institutions, our scientific and practitioner community in urban studies, planning, and architecture, the international agencies such as the World Bank, and the many corporations with appropriate products in a new foreign aid and commercial trade initiative.

Bits for BTUs

The decrease in energy per unit of product in the United States is partly due to greater efficiency but even more so to a shift in product mix from manufactured goods to services of all sorts. Mixed into both these trends is the role of information substituting for energy and materials. Examples are many: fax and e-mail messages clearly substitute for mail that must be flown, trucked or delivered. Do they also reduce travel? A recent study of e-commerce suggests major opportunities for reducing energy consumption but seems flawed in some of its assumptions, for example how much e-commerce might substitute for personal auto trips. Information rich but energy light products such as musical CDs, video films or cable services constitute growing proportions of consumption. But surprisingly there has been relatively little analysis of the full cycle energy and materials costs of such products or the ways in which they may be made even more energy efficient or intentionally substituted for alternative products or services.

A fresh approach for eliminating environmentally degrading consumption is the systematic substitution of digital bits for energy BTUs. Such an initiative would comprise research: identifying better the ways in which web-based services can be developed and expanded to replace travel or other energy intensive activities; how to reduce the energy-intensive aspects of e-commerce, particularly the delivery end; and how knowledge products can be produced and delivered in energy sensitive ways. It would also involve pilot studies, perhaps within government, on such promising features as teleconferencing, distance learning and the like.

Quality Time

Another initiative would address the satisfaction component of consumption by providing opportunities for individuals and families to voluntarily trade time for income and thus have more satisfaction with less material goods. The quality time initiative would bring together and expand a variety of programs that try to address the need for greater flexibility in family life to allow for essential time when needed to cope with childbearing, illness, and child care; flexible time to fit work hours to the increasingly complex schedules of spouses and children; and part time to make possible shared work without loss of essential health and pension benefits. As with changes in welfare benefits, such an initiative could benefit from pilot programs that would better identify needs, problems and interest.

MEMORANDUM TO THE PRESIDENT

From: **Thomas Homer-Dixon**

Subject: **Environmental Scarcities and Civil Violence**

The New York Times, Sunday, April 9, 2000. *"Bolivia Calls An Emergency After Protest Over Water": Bolivia's president declared a state of emergency today, fueling a week of widening unrest that left three people dead in fresh clashes between police and demonstrators. The move came after a week of protests over rising water rates, unemployment and other economic difficulties plaguing the Andean country of eight million people.*

PROBLEM

Recent research shows that scarcities of vital environmental resources—especially of cropland, fresh water, and forests—help cause violence in many parts of the world. These *environmental scarcities* rarely cause wars among countries, but they do generate severe social stresses inside countries, stimulating subnational insurgencies, ethnic clashes, and urban unrest. This internal or *civil* violence particularly affects poor countries, because they tend to be far more dependent on environmental resources and far less able to buffer themselves from the social crises that environmental scarcities cause. This kind of violence may affect poor countries most, but policy makers and citizens in the industrialized world ignore it at their peril. It can harm rich countries' national interests by threatening their trade and economic relations, entangling them in complex humanitarian emergencies, provoking distress migrations, and destabilizing pivotal countries in the developing world.

BACKGROUND

Environmental scarcities have often spurred violence in the past. In coming decades the incidence of such violence will probably rise sharply as scarcities of cropland, fresh water, and forests worsen in many poor countries. Scarcity's role, however, will often be obscure and indirect: it interacts with political, economic, and other factors to generate harsh social effects–from worsening poverty and massive migrations to deeper cleavages among ethnic groups and weakened states–that in turn help produce violence. Analysts often interpret these social effects as the conflict's principal causes, thus overlooking scarcity's influence as an underlying stress. Some examples:

> Scarcity...interacts with political, economic, and other factors to generate harsh social effects–from worsening poverty and massive migrations to deeper cleavages among ethnic groups and weakened states–that in turn help produce violence.

- In South Africa, severe land, water, and fuelwood scarcities in the former black homelands have helped drive millions of poor blacks into squatter settlements around the major cities. The settlements are often constructed on the worst urban land, in depressions prone to flooding, on hillsides vulnerable to slides, or near heavily polluting industries. Scarcities of land, water, and fuelwood in these settlements provoke inter-ethnic rivalries and violent feuds among settlement warlords and their followers. This strife jeopardizes the country's transition to democratic stability and prosperity.

- In the state of Bihar, India, skewed land distribution has combined with rapid population growth and significant soil degradation to produce some of the country's most crippling shortages of cropland. As a result, the last three decades have seen vicious conflicts between marginal farmers and landless laborers, on one side, and middle and upper caste farmers who still own relatively abundant land, on the other. The cycle of violence has polarized Bihar's society and progressively weakened its institutions, from its court system and universities to its financial and agricultural bureaucracies. As the second most populous state in the country, Bihar's chronic political crisis reverberates in the national capital, New Delhi, and has contributed to instability in the country's governing coalition.

- In Pakistan, shortages and maldistribution of good land, water, and forests in the countryside have encouraged millions of the rural poor to migrate into major cities, such as Karachi and Hyderabad. The conjunction of this in-migration with high fertility rates is causing city populations to grow at an astonishing 4 to 5 percent a year, producing fierce competition—and often violence—among ethnic groups over land, basic services, and political and economic power. This turmoil exacts a huge toll on an already struggling national economy.

- In the mid-1990s in Chiapas, Mexico, Zapatista insurgents rose against land scarcity and insecure land tenure caused by ancient inequalities in land distribution, by rapid population growth among groups with the least land, and by changes in laws governing land access. The insurgency rocked Mexico to the core, helped trigger a peso crisis, and reminded the world that Mexico remains—despite the pretenses of the country's economic elites—a poor and profoundly unstable developing country.

The Critical Role of Environmental Resources

It is easy for the billion-odd people living in rich countries to forget that the well being of about half of the world's population of 6 billion remains directly tied to local natural resources. Sixty to seventy percent of the world's poor people live in rural areas, and most depend on agriculture for their main income; a large majority of these people are smallholder farmers, including many who are semi-subsistence (which means they survive mainly by eating what they grow). Over 40 percent of people on the planet—some 2.4 billion—use fuelwood, charcoal, straw, or cow dung as their main source of energy; 50 to 60 percent rely on these biomass fuels for at least some of their primary energy needs. Over 1.2 billion people lack access to clean drinking water; many are forced to walk far to get what water they can find.

The cropland, forests, and water supplies that underpin the livelihoods of these billions are renewable. Unlike non-renewable resources such as oil and iron ore, renewables are replenished over time by natural processes. In most cases, if used prudently, they should sustain an adequate standard of living indefinitely. Unfortunately, in many regions where people rely on renewables, they are being depleted or degraded faster than they are being renewed. From Gaza to the

Philippines to Honduras, the evidence is stark: aquifers are being overdrawn and salinized, coastal fisheries are disappearing, and steep uplands have been stripped of their forests leaving their thin soils to erode into the sea.

This environmental scarcity helps generate chronic, diffuse, subnational violence—exactly the kind of violence that bedevils conventional military institutions. Around the world, we see conventional armies pinned down and often utterly impotent in the face of interethnic violence or attacks by ragtag bands of lightly armed guerrillas and insurgents. As yet, environmental scarcity is not a major factor behind most of these conflicts. But we can expect it to become a more powerful influence in coming decades because of larger populations and higher per capita resource consumption rates.

Currently, the human population is growing by about 1.3 percent a year on a base of just over 6 billion. This figure peaked at about 2.1 percent between 1965 and 1970 and has fallen since then. In recent years, fertility rates have dropped surprisingly fast in most poor countries; women are having, on average, significantly fewer children. But it is wildly premature to declare, as some commentators have, that the problem of the population explosion is behind us. The largest cohorts of girls ever born have yet to reach their reproductive years, which ensures tremendous momentum behind global population growth. So even under the most optimistic projections, the planet's population will expand by almost a third, or by about two billion people, by 2025.

> ...environmental scarcity helps generate chronic, diffuse, subnational violence—exactly the kind of violence that bedevils conventional military institutions.

Real economic product per capita is also currently rising by about 1.0 percent a year. Combined with global population growth, Earth's total economic product is therefore increasing by about 2.3 percent annually. With a doubling time of around thirty years, today's global product of about $30 trillion should exceed $50 trillion in today's dollars by 2025.

A large component of this two-thirds growth will be achieved through yet higher consumption of the planet's natural resources. We will see a further decline in the total area of high-quality cropland, along with the widespread loss of remaining virgin forests. We will also see continued degradation and deple-

tion of rivers, aquifers, and other water resources, and the further impoverish-
ment of wild fisheries.

Regional scarcities of renewable resources are already affecting large populations in poor countries. But during the last decade, global environmental problems, especially climate change and stratospheric ozone depletion, have received
more attention in the popular media in the industrialized world. The social and
economic impacts of these global atmospheric problems, in particular of climate
change, may eventually be very large, but these impacts will probably not be deci-
sively clear until well into this century. And climate change is most likely to have
a major effect on societies, not by acting as an isolated environmental pressure,
but by interacting with other long-present resource pressures, such as degraded
cropland and stressed water supplies. While global atmospheric problems are
important, policy makers, the media, and the public in rich countries should
focus more of their attention on regional environmental scarcities of cropland,
water, and forests in poor countries.

Sources of Environmental Scarcity

Environmental scarcity is caused by the degradation and depletion of renewable resources (say, a specific tract of cropland), the increased demand for these
resources, and/or their unequal distribution. Population growth and increased
per capita resource consumption can cause depletion and degradation, which can
in turn produce a decrease in total resource *supply* or, in other words, a decrease
in the size of the total resource "pie." But population growth and changes in consumption behavior can also cause greater scarcity by boosting the *demand* for a
resource. So if a rapidly growing population depends on a fixed amount of cropland, the amount of cropland per person—the size of each person's slice of the
resource pie—falls inexorably. In many countries, resource availability is being
squeezed by both these supply and demand pressures.

Scarcity is also often caused by a severe imbalance in the distribution of
wealth and power that results in some groups in a society getting disproportionately large slices of the resource pie, while others get slices that are too small to
sustain their livelihoods. Such unequal distribution—or *structural* scarcity—is a
key factor in virtually every case where scarcity contributes to conflict. Often the
imbalance is deeply rooted in institutions and class and ethnic relations inherit-

ed from the colonial period. Often it is sustained and reinforced by international economic relations that trap developing countries into dependence on a few raw material exports. It can also be reinforced by heavy external debts that encourage countries to use their most productive environmental resources—such as their best croplands and forests—to generate hard currency rather than to support the poorest segments of their populations.

In the past, analysts and policy makers have usually addressed these three sources of scarcity independently. But new research shows that supply, demand, and structural scarcities interact and reinforce each other in extraordinarily pernicious ways. Two kinds of interaction are particularly important: *resource capture* and *ecological marginalization*.

Resource capture occurs when powerful groups within a society recognize that a key resource is becoming more scarce (due to both supply and demand pressures) and use their power to shift in their favor the regime governing resource access. This shift imposes severe structural scarcities on weaker groups. In Chiapas, for instance, worsening land scarcities, in part caused by rapid population growth, encouraged powerful land owners and ranchers to exploit weaknesses in the state's land laws in order to seize lands from campesinos and indigenous farmers. Gradually these peasants were forced deeper into the state's lowland rain forest, further away from the state's economic heartland, and further into poverty.

In the Jordan River Basin, Israel's critical dependence on groundwater flowing out of the West Bank—a dependence made acute by a rising Israeli population and salinizing aquifers along the Mediterranean coast—encouraged Israel to restrict groundwater withdrawals on the West Bank during the occupation. These restrictions were far more severe for Palestinians than for Israeli settlers. They contributed to the rapid decline in Palestinian agriculture in the region, to the dependence of Palestinians on day-labor within Israel and, ultimately, to rising frustrations in the Palestinian community.

Ecological marginalization occurs when grave inequality in resource distribution joins with rapid population growth to drive resource-poor people into ecologically marginal areas, such as upland hillsides, areas at risk of desertification, and tropical rainforests. Higher population densities in these vulnerable areas, along with a lack of the capital and knowledge needed to protect local resources, causes local resource depletion, poverty, and eventually further migration, often to cities.

Ecological marginalization affects hundreds of millions of people around the world, across a wide range of geographies and economic and political systems. We see the same process in the Himalayas, Indonesia, Central America, Brazil, India, China, and the Sahel. For example, in the Philippines an extreme imbalance in cropland distribution between landowners and peasants combined with high population growth rates to force large numbers of the landless poor into interior hilly regions of the archipelago. There, the migrants used slash and burn agriculture to clear land for crops. As more millions arrived from the lowlands, new land became hard to find; and as population densities on the steep slopes increased, erosion, landslides, and flash floods became critical. During the 1970s and 1980s, the resulting poverty drove many peasants into the arms of the communist New People's Army insurgency that had a stranglehold on upland regions. Poverty also drove countless others into wretched squatter settlements in cities like Manila.

Links to Civil Violence

Expanding populations, land degradation, and drought spurred the rise of the Sendero Luminoso guerrillas in the southern highlands of Peru. Scarcity-induced resource capture by Moors in Mauritania ignited violence over water and cropland in the Senegal River basin, producing tens of thousands of refugees. In Haiti, forest and soil loss have worsened a persistent economic crisis that generates strife and periodic waves of boat people. And land shortages in Bangladesh, exacerbated by fast population growth, have prompted millions of people to migrate to India—an influx that has, in turn, caused ethnic strife in the state of Assam.

Close study of such cases shows that severe environmental scarcity can restrict local food production, aggravate poverty of marginal groups, spur large migrations, enrich elites that capture resources, deepen divisions among social groups, and undermine a state's moral authority and capacity to govern. Marginal groups that directly depend on renewable resources find themselves trapped in a vise between rising scarcity on one side and institutional and policy failures on the other. These long-term, tectonic stresses can slowly tear apart a poor society's social fabric, causing chronic popular unrest and violence by boosting grievances and changing the balance of power among contending social groups and the state.

So environmental scarcity is mainly an *indirect* cause of violence, and this violence is mainly *internal* to countries. It is not the type of violence that analysts commonly assume will occur when critical resources are scarce—that is, "resource wars" among countries, in which scarcity directly stimulates one country to try to seize the resources of another. Nevertheless, while this internal violence may not be as conspicuous or dramatic as wars among countries, it can have broad implications. The changing nature of the international system—heightened economic interdependence, easier long-distance travel, and increased access to arms—makes previously insignificant regions of interest to policy makers. Crises in small countries, such as Haiti, often create serious foreign policy difficulties for developed countries, and large and significant countries—including Pakistan, China, India, and Indonesia—are not immune to the severe stresses environmental scarcity generates. Major civil violence within states can affect external trade relations, cause refugee flows, and produce humanitarian disasters that call upon the military and financial resources of developed countries and international organizations. Countries destabilized by civil violence often fragment as they become enfeebled and as peripheral regions are seized by renegade authorities and warlords. Their regimes might avoid fragmentation by becoming more authoritarian, intolerant of opposition, and militarized; they might also try to divert attention from domestic grievances by threatening neighboring states.

Environmental scarcity is never a sole or sufficient cause of such crises; it always joins with other economic, political, and social factors to produce its effects. In the Filipino case, for example, the lack of clear property rights in upland areas encouraged migration into these regions and discouraged migrants from conserving the land once they arrived. And President Marcos's corrupt and authoritarian leadership reduced regime legitimacy and closed off options for democratic action by aggrieved groups. Contextual factors like these are often critical, but policy makers must realize that they cannot either adequately understand or respond to many important cases of civil violence around the world—like the Filipino insurgency or the chronic instability in Haiti—if they do not take into account the independent causal role of environmental scarcity.

The Limits of Adaptation

Skeptics often respond that environmental scarcity rarely contributes to conflict, because human societies show great capacity to adapt to resource scarcity, especially through market mechanisms. When a resource becomes scarce, its price increases, which encourages conservation, substitution, and technological innovation. Scarcity also encourages institutional adaptations, such as changes in property rights, that raise incentives to conserve and innovate and that reduce the hardship scarcity produces.

It is true that scarcity often stimulates useful technological and social changes. Yet a society's ability to adapt to rising scarcity depends on the relationship between its requirement for ingenuity to respond to this scarcity and its supply of ingenuity. (*Ingenuity*, as used here, consists of ideas for new technologies and new and reformed institutions.) Societies in which requirement outstrips supply face an *ingenuity gap*; they will be unable to adapt adequately to environmental scarcity and will, consequently, be vulnerable to scarcity's harsh social effects, including economic dislocation, migrations, social cleavages, state weakening, and—ultimately—violence.

In the next decades, population growth, rising average resource demand, and persistent inequalities in resource access ensure that scarcities will affect many environmentally sensitive regions with unprecedented severity, speed, and scale. Ingenuity requirements will therefore rise rapidly. But this situation need not lead to crisis, since, by changing prices and incentives, scarcity often does stimulate a flow of ingenuity sufficient to meet the rising need.

But there are several reasons why this beneficial response may not occur in some poor societies. The prerequisites for effective adaptation to scarcity often do not exist: states are weak, bureaucracies incompetent, judicial systems corrupt, research centers underfunded, and property rights unclear. Markets often do not work well: prices in most developing countries–especially for water, forests, and other common resources–do not adjust to reflect accurately rising scarcity, and therefore incentives for entrepreneurs are inadequate. Low levels of education, technological capacity, and financial capital also depress the supply of ingenuity. Finally, environmental scarcity can actually undermine the ability of developing societies to generate social and technical solutions to scarcity. Under certain circumstances, scarcity mobilizes narrow coalitions and powerful elites to block the institutional reforms that could reduce the scarcity's broader social impact.

Positive economic, social, and technological responses to environmental scarcity are therefore not guaranteed. Some societies will adapt well, others will not. In coming decades, worsening environmental scarcities in many regions will further exaggerate the world's already gaping differentials between rich and poor societies and between the powerful and weak people within those societies. The world's wealthy regions should not

> **In coming decades, worsening environmental scarcities in many regions will further exaggerate the world's already gaping differentials between rich and poor societies and between the powerful and weak people within those societies.**

assume that they will be able to wall themselves off from turmoil in societies that do not adapt well to scarcity. We are living cheek by jowl on this planet now. We are all next door neighbors.

RECOMMENDATIONS

We are passing through a moment in history when political and economic events are fluid and social structures are more malleable than they have been for decades. This situation provides opportunities for reform of our economic, political, and social systems, but it also presents dangers. Many of the choices we make during the next years—even small ones—will have large consequences far into the future. And the future is sometimes not as distant as it seems: well over one third of the people currently alive will still be alive in 2050. The children around us today will live with the consequences of the decisions we make today.

Each case of environmentally induced conflict is complex and unique: each has a specific ecosystem, history, culture, economy, set of actors, and set of power relations among these actors. Policy tools available in one case will not be available in another, for wholly idiosyncratic reasons. Successful policy intervention therefore requires customization based on a careful analysis of the character of the specific case and of the policy tools available in that case.

Yet it is possible to make four general points about policy interventions in this area. First, there is no single solution or "magic bullet" that will always break the links between environmental scarcity and violence. The causal systems in question encompass huge numbers of interacting variables; interventions must therefore operate at many points to capitalize on these systems' natural synergies. Policy makers need to implement a broad and integrated set of responses at the international, regional, national, and community levels.

Second, early intervention is generally better than late intervention. If policy makers wait till widespread violence has broken out, it will probably be too intractable, too complex, and too charged with emotion to resolve. In addition, environmental scarcity tends to produce diffuse and subnational violence of a kind that our conventional military institutions do not, in general, handle well. Policy makers should therefore emphasize proactive interventions that break the early links in the causal chains described here.

Third, policy responses do not have to be capital-intensive: They can be simultaneously effective and relatively inexpensive. Examples include greater support for non-governmental organizations that are rehabilitating local environmental resources and for research on crops that can grow with eroded soil and polluted water.

Fourth and finally, effective policy interventions will not necessarily be unique or special. The analysis above simply presents another set of reasons for a range of interventions—from selective debt relief to enhancement of indigenous technical capacity—that many experts have long believed necessary to produce humane and rapid economic development in poor countries around the world.

In line with these general points, the following six specific actions are proposed:

- As an aid to policymaking, the U.S. administration should seek to develop the internal capacity, within the State Department or intelligence agencies, to track severe environmental and demographic stresses in the developing world and to predict their negative social outcomes, including violence. Within relevant arms of the Executive branch, especially the State Department, financial and other incentives should be introduced to encourage officials to develop expertise and policy on matters relating to environmental security.

- To cope with the additional 2 billion people that will be added to the developing world's population over the next two decades, at a time when these countries' natural resources are under unprecedented stress, the United States should substantially and immediately increase funding to the Consultative Groups on International Agricultural Research (CGIAR) system of agricultural research institutes. The aim should be to reverse the decline in the growth of grain yields in high-intensity agriculture in East and Southeast Asia and to develop crops that can grow in nutrient-depleted soils and water-scarce regions.

- The United States should undertake a major research and policy effort to reform the current system of national income accounts to incorporate the costs of depletion and degradation of our environment. In the short term, leaders of many poor countries see a trade-off between economic growth and environmental protection, and this encourages overuse and degradation of environmental resources. U.S. foreign and aid policies must emphasize that the real trade-off is between short-term unsustainable prosperity and long-term growth potential. This is an answer to the common argument from poor countries that rich countries are using environmental issues to deny them the opportunity to grow: It's in the developing world's self-interest to prevent environmental decline.

- The United States should use its influence with the governments of rich countries, commercial banks, and international financial institutions (IFIs) to reduce the debt burden on poor countries. Developing nations under pressure from banks and lending agencies to pay their foreign debts often use their best lands to grow cash crops for export, which can force large numbers of poor people into marginal and fragile environmental regions. In addition, the stabilization and structural adjustment policies of IFIs, while often essential, must be designed and implemented with environmental consequences in mind. The United States should urge IFIs to recognize that their currency and adjustment policies can have immense effects on the environment; and these institutions need accounting methods that better measure the environmental costs of economic activities in poor countries.

- American development aid should be targeted to build poor countries' technical capacity in environmental management. It is cost-effective for the United States to provide funds for the training of environmental experts in the developing world, including hydrologists, soil and agricultural scientists, foresters, demographers, energy-systems engineers, and fisheries specialists. The emphasis must be on adequately equipping and staffing research and teaching centres in poor countries so that the "brain drain" to rich countries can be stemmed. Networks of such centres established across national boundaries should stimulate wider co-operation among a region's countries.

- The United States should work with other rich countries to coordinate efforts to fund the development and diffusion of environmentally benign technologies for use in poor countries. These technologies include water-conserving irrigation systems and better water purification systems; alternative cooking methods that conserve fuelwood; and aquaculture that does not require destruction of coastal wetlands. Many of these technologies are best developed indigenously in poor countries, using the technical capacity that must be expanded there, but research enterprises in rich countries can help too (and they should be given the financial incentives to do so).

MEMORANDUM TO THE PRESIDENT

From: Eileen Claussen

Subject: Global Environmental Governance

PROBLEM

One of the most important challenges the new president of the United States will face is the challenge of addressing high-stakes environmental issues, such as global climate change, biodiversity loss, and marine conservation—issues that pose serious problems for the United States and the rest of the world in the decades ahead. But the United States and other countries will not be able to deal effectively with these issues without a better system of global environmental governance.

BACKGROUND

The Global Environmental Agenda

The global environmental agenda is an enormous one. The U.S. president will be called upon to respond to problems and potential crises involving the atmosphere (global climate change), oceans (overfishing and pollution), loss of biodiversity (ecosystem and species preservation), transboundary air and water pollution, water and land use issues, forests, and chemicals in international trade, among others. The sheer magnitude of the agenda and the complexity of the issues involved have made it practically impossible for concerned institutions and governments to respond effectively to these problems. Despite high-profile events, such as the 1992 Earth Summit in Rio de Janeiro, and despite the ground-breaking international agreements and the stepped-up national efforts that have taken place in recent years, the world can report little progress on these issues. And the global environment is still at risk.

Why Prevailing Systems Fail the Environment

The size and complexity of the global environmental agenda is only one reason—albeit an important one—why global institutions and national governments have, for the most part, failed to adequately address these high-stakes environmental issues. In assessing the current situation, it is important to recognize six additional factors that have played a part in stalling or putting the brakes on progress. They are:

The role and status of national governments. National governments around the world have entered the 21st century in a position of weakness as the importance of nonstate actors has grown. This is true not only in the United States, where the government has been divided along partisan lines for the better part of the last two decades, but also in other countries where parliamentary majorities often are small. The result is gridlock and a sustained lack of leadership in dealing with global environmental issues. A related problem is an unwillingness to deal with problems when the solutions might involve substantial costs in the short-term or might affect certain industrial sectors disproportionately. The political costs of risking these consequences are simply too high. Compounding these challenges is the fact that even governments in highly developed economies have trouble dealing with an issue as complex and as large as the global environment in addition to issues that are often considered more central or of higher priority (e.g., national security or economic development and growth).

> National governments around the world have entered the 21st century in a position of weakness as the importance of nonstate actors has grown.

Wealth and poverty. In very different ways, wealth and poverty are key drivers behind environmental degradation and a nation's inability to take action on climate change, biodiversity, and other issues. Wealth is a factor because it results in often careless consumption of natural resources and overexploitation of the natural environment. Poverty, on the other hand, is a driver because the poor often have no resources other than the natural environment on which to subsist, a situation that results in pollution and the destruction of such global resources as forests.

Although wealth and poverty are among the major causes of the environmental challenges humans face, they also present obstacles to developing solutions. For example, what obligations are suitable for both rich and poor nations in efforts to reduce human impacts on the natural environment?—i.e., how can we bridge the developed-developing world divide? And, what kinds of regimes can be devised that meet the test of effectiveness as well as fairness, because the rich as well as the poor have to become part of the solution?

Failure to value the future. Governments and individuals around the world are preoccupied with the here and now. The poor are concerned with fulfilling their basic needs for food and shelter. And, for those who are able to fulfill those needs, other day-to-day pressures—including careers, family, and programmed leisure activities—begin to dominate, with the result that there is little time or inclination to consider the interests of future generations. Adding to the problem is that politicians operate on short election cycles, making it hard to shape and adopt forward-looking policies, particularly if those policies incur short-term costs.

The state of science. Recent years have seen the emergence of a sizable body of scientific consensus supporting the need for action on most global environmental issues. Nevertheless, significant uncertainties remain. In the case of global climate change, although there is no longer any dispute that the Earth is warming, there are still skeptical scientists who argue that the impacts cannot be quantified and, in some cases, that they may even be beneficial. On the biodiversity issue, few scientists dispute that the Earth is becoming less and less diverse, but experts and nonexperts alike have failed to recognize the value of those species that are either at risk or already lost.

This lack of scientific understanding—combined with a tendency to focus on uncertainties rather than certainties—has made it difficult for policy makers to take strong or effective action on these issues. The result is that science (which is the necessary underpinning for action) is too often employed in the cause of those who wish to take no action at all.

Fragmentation versus integration. A view of the world at the beginning of the 21st century reveals two countervailing trends in how nations relate to one another. On one hand, there is strong economic integration among nations, with capital moving quickly across international borders and knowledge and innovation spreading at an equally rapid pace around the globe. On the other hand, the increasing number of sovereign nations and an increase in the number of failed states raises the specter of political fragmentation as the order of the day.

> ... lack of scientific understanding—combined with a tendency to focus on uncertainties rather than certainties—has made it difficult for policy makers to take strong or effective action ....

Can such a world establish global regimes in which all countries participate and commit to taking serious action to reduce environmental degradation, often at considerable cost? The ever-shifting nature of national relationships and interactions that has greeted the new millennium suggests that a centralized system of environmental management is unlikely to happen, even if this were a desirable outcome. But it remains unclear exactly what might work in the absence of such a system.

Sovereignty. Sovereignty concerns are at the heart of many of the global environmental governance disputes that have arisen in recent years. The key sovereignty issue centers on the extent to which global institutions and treaties should be the vehicles for action on the environment—i.e., how much sovereignty does a nation give up? In the case of climate change, should the global governance system provide a framework only, with nations deciding what to do based on their own sovereign decisions? Or should the global system prescribe and/or dictate specific national actions that must be taken to achieve an agreed-upon goal for reducing greenhouse gas concentrations in the atmosphere?

To illustrate this point, consider the example of the Amazon rainforest. Is it up to Brazil to decide how to deal with the riches of the Amazon? The Brazilians say it is. But others say the world should play some role in preserving the rainforest because its uniquely rich biodiversity and its role in taking carbon out of the atmosphere affect the entire world. Needless to say, these are difficult issues to resolve.

RECOMMENDATIONS

In large part because of the problems identified above, the system of global environmental governance that exists today is weak. Because of the importance of the issues involved, strengthening this system of governance will be one of the foremost challenges confronting the new presidential administration in the coming years.

However, before considering the options, it is important to define exactly what global governance is and how it works. The answer is that although global governance embraces the institutions of government, it is more encompassing than government. It is a system of rule that often lacks formal authority—a way of getting things done as a matter of practice or, in some cases, as a requirement of law. As structured today, global governance consists of myriad institutions, laws, and nontraditional forms of regulation that achieve varying degrees of success in encouraging and compelling action on the critical global environmental issues of the time.

Institutions

Many institutions deal in one way or another with the global environment. In the United Nations system alone, there are 21 separate agencies that play some role in these issues. In addition to the United Nations, the World Bank and other institutions charged with economic development play an important role in the implementation of policies and projects that affect the global environment. Institutions that deal with trade—e.g., the World Trade Organization (WTO) and the North American Free Trade Agreement (NAFTA)—also affect the global environment, as do institutions that are international but not global in their structure (e.g., the G-8 and the Organisation for Economic Cooperation and Development).

A close look at any or all of these institutions indicates that they are far from able to achieve significant progress in reversing global environmental degradation. Why?

Some fail because they are controlled by a disparate membership with competing interests who are unable to reach consensus on complex and difficult issues. A key example is the UN Food and Agriculture Organization (FAO), under whose auspices only limited progress has been made in dealing with global fishing or agriculture: Although FAO has pursued the collection of statistics on fish stocks, it has not moved to develop systems that would conserve fish stocks.

Other institutions do not succeed because they are responsible only for specific functions or activities and are unable to address whole issues on their own. The World Bank, for example, can provide guidelines for dealing with air pollution or biodiversity preservation only for development projects that use World Bank funds.

Still other institutions have failed to take even the first step in addressing these issues by weaving the environment into their policies and programs as a permanent concern. For example, WTO focuses on trade issues but has yet to confront the nexus of trade, sustainable economic growth, and the environment.

Last but not least are those institutions, such as the G-8, that are hortatory in nature and that lack the ability to control what their members do.

Considering their record, is it possible for the existing array of institutions to improve their performance to such a degree that it would justify a significant U.S. investment in their future? Many would argue that the answer is no. Working within the existing institutions is extremely time-consuming and too often unproductive. There is little coordination

> ... national governments are weak and unable to take risks by which they could be perceived as giving up additional sovereignty or subjecting their nations to new economic costs.

among the numerous actors working on these issues, and, both individually and as a whole, they have been remarkably unsuccessful in overcoming such obstacles to progress as the wealth-poverty conundrum and reluctance to value the future.

Can a new global institution be created? Again, the answer is no. The reality is that there is no political will to create a new body, even if it might make up for the failures of the current, fragmentary approach. The primary reason is that national governments are weak and unable to take risks by which they could be perceived as giving up additional sovereignty or subjecting their nations to new economic costs. The recent attacks on WTO offer a glimpse of the controversy that a new institution might engender.

Therefore, a substantial investment in trying to build a new global institution—or in strengthening the existing ones—is unlikely to yield positive results, either for the United States or for the world as a whole.

Does this mean that the United States should ignore existing institutions? No. The answer instead is to be selective in investing in and working with them. Where the country might be able to make the biggest difference is in steering a new course for the World Bank that would enable it to do a better job of balancing development and environmental interests.

Recent years have seen the World Bank adopt a "do no harm" policy that has reduced investments in infrastructure projects because of often-minimal environmental impacts. The irony is that these types of projects are precisely what developing countries need to build a sustainable and environment-friendly future. A more appropriate agenda might involve national policy reforms that would provide incentives for environmentally sustainable development.

In addition, a stepped-up interest in the United Nations Environment Programme (UNEP) could improve global governance. Although it purports to coordinate all UN activities that deal with the global environment, UNEP's Nairobi location and its policy of accepting "tied grants" (grants given by individual nations for individual projects that reflect one country's interest rather than a global interest) that are not necessarily tied to global goals and priorities have caused it to be unsuccessful in effectively supporting international efforts.

Treaties

Some 150 global environmental treaties have been negotiated since the start of the 20th century. In addition, there are at least 500 bilateral agreements now in effect dealing with cross-border environmental issues. These regimes generally address single issues (e.g., the Framework Convention on Climate Change or the Convention on International Trade in Endangered Species of Wild Fauna and

Flora). And, more often than not, the existing agreements are lacking in ambition or are framed in such a way that they result in little concrete action.

Nevertheless, a few of these agreements have been successful. The most important is the Montreal Protocol on Substances that Deplete the Ozone Layer (originally signed in 1987 and amended in 1990 and 1992), which has achieved remarkable success in phasing out production of the substances that destroy the ozone layer. However, this agreement is an exception to the rule, and the fact that its success is indeed "remarkable" points to how jaded people have become; people simply do not expect these types of agreements to achieve much—if anything—of substance.

Adding to the problem, as green constituencies and green rhetoric have become more dominant in global discussions of these issues, treaty negotiations have become vehicles for political grandstanding. All too often, the result is that decision makers negotiate new regimes that do not have the support or participation of many countries, including the United States. The Kyoto Protocol is such an example.

Even in cases where countries have ratified treaties that have entered into force, parties to the treaties do not always comply with their provisions. An example is Russia's noncompliance with the Montreal Protocol. But there are few penalties for noncompliance other than public scorn, in part because countries are unwilling to give up their sovereignty.

Why is the implementation of global environmental agreements so difficult? One answer is that for most of these regimes to function effectively, participation must be truly global. Yet because of the weakness of individual nations and their differing economies, it is exceedingly difficult to reach meaningful agreement among all the necessary actors. What often results is an ad hoc process driven more by political calls to action than a combined will to act against a common threat. Some nations may play a strong role in the negotiating process, but they then fail to ratify the agreement or implement its requirements. And, if a negotiated agreement requires consensus for adoption, it usually reflects a "lowest common denominator" approach, imposing only those requirements deemed acceptable by the parties most resistant to strong action.

The $64,000 question is how to achieve the necessary balance between what is required to ensure participation and what is required to create an effective regime.

Another obstacle to implementing global environmental agreements is poorer nations' lack of capacity to comply with international treaty requirements. Some treaties have addressed this problem by offering financial assistance to countries that are unable to comply (e.g., the Multilateral Fund of the Montreal Protocol). Other agreements have established more relaxed timetables for compliance for these countries. However, in many cases, the financing has not been forthcoming, and differentiating among countries based on their ability to act has become politically controversial. The Kyoto Protocol, for example, deals with emissions reductions from developed countries only, which has opened the treaty to criticism in the United States. The challenge of developing regimes that are both effective and fair has proved an enormous obstacle to progress.

Despite these problems, treaties are the best traditional tools of global environmental governance. Frameworks for action that are negotiated among different nations are key to leveling the playing field and establishing the rules under which governments, businesses, nongovernmental organizations (NGOs), and citizens can work together toward a common goal.

It is important to remember that treaties have limits. Again, success in combating environmental problems is a question of focus. It requires negotiating skillfully to ensure that a treaty is framed in such a way that it does not overreach but is effective. Is the treaty robust and comprehensive? Is it viable? Is it practical? These three questions will help to forge the international treaties necessary to address the challenges of climate change, biodiversity loss, and threats to the world's oceans.

Nontraditional Governance

Recent years have seen the emergence of nontraditional forms of global environmental governance that show remarkable promise in forcing and encouraging action on key issues confronting the world. It is nontraditional governance—as opposed to the traditional forms of governance embodied in institutions and treaties—that holds the key to future progress on the global environment. Four of these nontraditional forms of governance stand out:

Business. Business—particularly multinational business—is perhaps the most powerful of the nontraditional forms of governance. First, it is globally integrated: Many multinational businesses function in one hundred or more countries and have integrated production and distribution systems throughout the world. Second, because these businesses are the engines of economic growth, they hold significant sway at the local, national, and regional levels. And, because they are multinational, they can influence global institutions and the outcome of global treaties (although their capability to do so has not yet been fully realized). The bottom line is that unlike the more traditional players, business can operate on all levels and can therefore become the most influential actor in setting the rules and making them stick.

> **. . . business can operate on all levels and can therefore become the most influential actor in setting the rules and making them stick.**

In fact, an important reason for the Montreal Protocol's success is that the companies that produced and used many of the ozone-depleting chemicals—and were developing substitutes for them—were very much engaged in the process.

Therefore, the new U.S. president should seek every opportunity to involve business in efforts to address the myriad issues on the global environmental agenda. Business leaders will be essential partners in helping the new administration determine exactly what can and should be done to address these issues in the United States and around the world.

NGOs. Global NGOs, like global businesses, often have the power to exert considerable influence on local and national governments. However, although they are positioned to do so, most of these groups have not played significant roles in global environmental governance. For example, the 1997 Mine Ban Treaty was largely the product of NGOs throughout the world coming together around a common concern and persuading world governments to take action.

As the president considers how best to encourage action on the global environment in the coming years, it is necessary to reach out to those NGOs that already are hard at work on these issues, and by doing so, tap into a wealth of on-the-ground expertise and lobbying clout as well as established systems for educating and mobilizing the public on behalf of the global environmental agenda.

The Media. The news media has a number of very important roles to play in global environmental governance. It is well established that media coverage of specific problems can prod individuals and governments into action. The media also plays an important role by reporting on what is and is not happening to address certain issues and by evaluating whether or not current efforts are delivering as promised.

Of course, the media's role is not always constructive. Media coverage of environmental issues in recent years has caused a shift toward green rhetoric among politicians, businesses, and others, even when there is no intention of matching the rhetoric to reality. The primacy of rhetoric, in turn, has weakened existing institutions and treaties by raising expectations to a level where they cannot possibly be met. Moreover, because the media often fails to follow up on today's big story, it allows governments and businesses to evade responsibility for living up to their rhetoric.

The challenge facing the new administration is to enlist the media as a partner in highlighting the many pressing issues on the global environmental agenda and to use the media to spotlight solutions and encourage broad-based action on these issues in the United States and in other countries.

The Internet. The Internet, like the news media, provides a wide array of opportunities for drawing attention to the global environmental agenda and encouraging substantive action on these issues at all levels. If an issue is to be highlighted or if mobilization of people or ideas is needed to help advance the global environmental agenda, the Internet can provide tools for organizing and communicating the relevant information.

The Internet not only affords new power and capabilities to individuals, but also has created a wealth of new opportunities for businesses, NGOs, and individuals to communicate and discuss specific agendas or topics of interest and to coordinate their activities in ways they never could before. This enhanced communication allows governments and others to create a web of nongovernmental actors who can be as informed and effective at mobilizing and communicating opinions as individual nations or international coalitions.

Therefore, the final recommendation is that the new administration pursue additional ways to tap into the power of the Internet as an organizing tool and a communications network on global environmental issues.

Getting Things Done

Governance, very simply, is about getting people and organizations together to get things done. If governance of the global environment is allowed to remain in the exclusive or near-exclusive realm of national governments and international governmental institutions, the global environment will be poorly served.

Global solutions to such issues as climate change, biodiversity preservation, and the protection of oceans will require the full and enthusiastic participation of businesses, NGOs, and citizens throughout the world. The new administration's challenge in the coming months and years will be to help create the means for all of these diverse actors to get involved in a substantive way in efforts to protect and preserve the global environment.

To meet this challenge, the individuals who manage global environmental issues on the president's behalf, particularly at the Department of State, must do three things:

- Select a minimal number of institutions and treaties on which to focus. It is better to achieve real progress in a limited number of important areas than to attempt to focus more broadly and achieve nothing.

- Open their doors to business and NGO communities. The new administration will succeed in addressing these issues only to the extent that the president is able to enlist these groups and forge whatever degree of consensus is possible between them. Without these players, the odds of success are almost nonexistent.

- Have media and Internet strategies for every global environmental priority.

It is virtually impossible to influence the public or interested parties on a given issue if there is not a deliberate effort to educate the media, get media attention, and use the Internet. These are often the most effective communication tools, and without adoptive communication, there can be no consensus.

MEMORANDUM TO THE PRESIDENT

From: Thomas C. Jorling

Subject: **The New Administration and Setting Environmental Priorities**

PROBLEM

The environmental movement in the United States—hatched in the late 1960's—has been highly successful. Some would even say it was the only successful social movement of that era. Now some thirty years later, that very success has produced conditions which reflect the age-old challenge to successful institutions—how to adjust and adapt to continue to achieve progress. Put more graphically: How can bureaucratic systems avoid ossifying, avoid becoming part of the problem rather than part of the solution.

The fundamental challenge and opportunity of the new administration is to initiate and achieve change in environmental law and its implementing agencies and processes to reflect the changed conditions that now exist. This must be done while maintaining and building on the achievement in environmental performance that has been produced by the system of law and implementing agencies established in the late 60's and early 70's.

BACKGROUND

Understanding the history, even superficially, of these laws and agencies over the past 30-plus years, along with their structure and function, is essential to assessing next steps—and the difficulty in achieving them.

For a host of reasons, the perception in the late 60's of what was morphing in language from conservation and natural resource management to environmental protection or environmentalism was a series of problems—water pollution, air pollution, and later land pollution. Ours is a pragmatic political system—we adopt no heroic schemes, but rather we identify the problem, put bounds around it, and fix it. And we did. We passed the Clean Water Act, the Clean Air Act, and the Solid Waste Act, followed by the Toxic Substances Act and the Safe Drinking Water Act. Then, wrapping up the decade of the 70's and effectively the authorizing phase of the response to the environmental movement, Superfund was passed in 1980. These statutes and what they authorized have produced great progress. They have accomplished much of what the public demanded and expected. In summary terms, we have reduced pollutant loadings into the various media by upward of 90%, even through a period of immense economic growth.

> **. . .we have reduced pollutant loadings into the various media by upward of 90%, even through a period of immense economic growth.**

The statutes were not self-implementing, however. They required the establishment of implementing agencies. The U.S. Environmental Protection Agency (EPA)

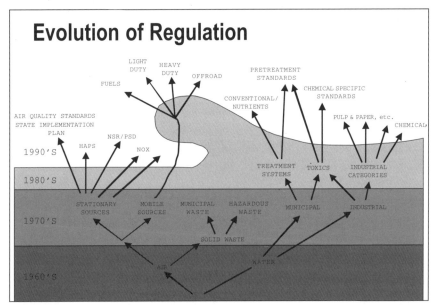

Figure 1

was established in 1970. The new agency was blessed with the leadership of Bill Ruckleshaus, who established a culture of professionalism and quality that was respected across political lines at a time when our political fabric was otherwise under great stress. Its structure matched and grew with the sequence of statutes—a water pollution program, an air pollution program, and so forth.

And how they did grow, from approximately 1,500 staff transferred from other departments in 1970, to now more than twenty thousand! But there was another fundamental premise of these statutes, bred of our Constitutional system, which has resulted in an even more substantial public bureaucracy and one that basically mirrors the EPA. The premise deeply imbedded in our federal environmental statutes is that while the EPA would promulgate the national minimum standards and procedures, the basic authority was to be, and substantively has been, implemented by the States. Consequently, the States have experienced tremendous growth in implementing agencies over the same 30-plus years. These were basically structured the same way as the EPA—water programs, air programs, waste programs—except that in some states these separate functions were lodged in separate agencies. The similar structure is a reflection of the federal and parallel state statutes as well as the program grant funding provided by the EPA to the States. This history of achievement and growth of government is represented somewhat simplistically in Figures 2 and 3.

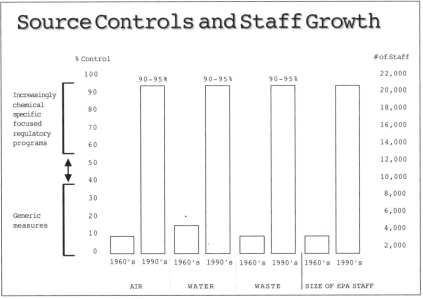

Figure 2

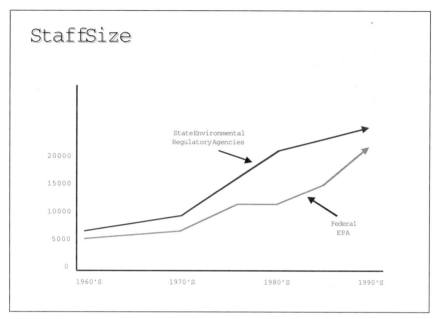

Figure 3

And therein lies the essence of why—today and going forward—change is necessary but also why it will be so difficult to accomplish. Thus the challenge facing the new administration.

We have reached a situation where agencies have imposing personnel and dollar resources (and the consultants those dollars buy, plus the stakeholders who have established mutually dependent relationships with the sub-units and personnel of these agencies). With more inertia than momentum, they are achieving less and less but costing more and more. Most significantly, the pattern of focusing the existing apparatus on problems that have been by and large fixed is leaving unaddressed the compelling issues now facing the human community:

> ...the pattern of focusing the existing apparatus on problems that have been by and large fixed is leaving unaddressed the compelling issues now facing the human community: land and ecosystem disaggregation, climate change, the need to shift from fossil fuels to alternative energy systems, and the greatest environmental threat—poverty....

land and ecosystem disaggregation, climate change, the need to shift from fossil fuels to alternative energy systems, and the greatest environmental threat—poverty—all subsumed under the challenge of the emerging theme of sustainable development.

However, given the distrust and the partisanship that has emerged in recent years around environmental protection, the new administration cannot succeed, nor can Congress, unless it is clear to everyone—the public, the NGOs, the business community and the media—that the progress made to date will be maintained. No effort at creating a program that fits today's and tomorrow's needs will be successful (and this can't be overemphasized) *unless* that condition prevails. It is a fundamental precondition.

But what of the going-forward program? Two levels are necessary. Both include new and different ways of looking at the problems, and both will require not only new statutory authorization but also new agency structures and functions. Both are also informed by a recognition that at either of the two levels we can't do everything. Simply put, there are scarce resources and many competing social and environmental needs, domestic and international, in our increasingly interconnected world. We must make comparative assessments, then make choices, then act.

The first level is the overview level—taking stock and asking the question: What are now the most pressing environmental problems facing the human community—a population of soon to be 8-10 billion, the majority now impoverished, all of whom have, and are entitled to have, aspirations to a decent quality of life. For our purposes a decent life can, in shorthand, be defined in terms of the health, housing, nutrition, education, and amenities enjoyed by a middle class American. This is an awesome undertaking, but it can't paralyze us. We must spend scarce resources doing the things that make the most difference here and around the globe.

There are now many examples where the next round of domestic environmental regulations directed at compelling technology to control this or that chemical or subsystem component will cause massive expenditures, with little or no environmental gain. Neither we in the United States or anyone in the world is rich enough to pursue such a strategy when other important environmental needs are going unaddressed. The basic point is that we as a nation and as a global community have to assess which challenges we should address, just as we did in 1970 when dirty water and dirty air had become unacceptable, and devote public and private resources to address them. The candidates are quite obvious:

- natural resource degradation caused by conditions of raw poverty—the greatest environmental threat, often associated with the absence of the rule of law and human rights;

- the lack of clean drinking water, waste water treatment and basic nutrition for the large, impoverished, mostly developing peoples around the world—especially infants and children;

- climate change and energy systems; and

- balkanization or fragmentation of intact ecosystems with associated losses ranging from biodiversity to amenities.

These really represent components of sustainability, and we need to develop the instruments to address them in their domestic and international context.

The other level of focus is, in effect, nested in the first. It is the level of an operating facility, a manufacturing plant, a power plant, or a municipal water and waste treatment system. Today these facilities are not regulated as systems, but as a disaggregated, disconnected set of sources of water pollution, air pollution, or generators of waste. Often there is a bureau, state or federal, that is motivated and authorized to drive a control on one element of a system—without regard for its impacts on other parts of the system. There may also be no comparative assessment of what that bureau or sub-bureau is charged to do with controls on other parts of that system or even whether there is a risk or environmental or health impact associated with their proposed control. All bureaus apply their authority with energy and vigor—not only as if it is the most important in the world, but the only thing in the world. But no one makes that assessment. The only person who must focus on all of these controls, and who bears responsibility for complying with all of them, is the plant manager.

RECOMMENDATIONS

While preserving the gains we have made, the challenge of the next administration is to seek authority for environmental management and regulation that treats an operating facility as a system. In such a system, comparative, science-based assessments can be made of the environmental benefits and risks from all parts of the enterprise so that those things that can make the greatest difference will be achieved with scarce resources. We can thus cease driving controls of this or that form of pollution, merely because there is authority and a bureaucracy in existence to do it, at the expense of newly emerging and fundamental challenges facing the human community.

> While preserving the gains we have made, the challenge of the next administration is to seek authority for environmental management and regulation that treats an operating facility as a system.

In the area of remaining pollutant loadings from domestic facilities, we need to develop the tools that will enable assessing all releases remaining and judging which, if any, deserve further control. That assessment needs to evaluate risk, cost effectiveness, and effects on jobs and competitiveness.

If all we are doing is improving margins of safety, then it is appropriate and necessary to consider other uses of scarce resources, including maintaining a competitive manufacturing base and the jobs and the families it supports in this global economy. And in this era of globalism, this comparative evaluation should extend to improving the environment and the human condition in other parts of the world. American firms can thus be encouraged to invest in developing countries and to bring their resources, management and manufacturing skills to places now degraded or degrading.

So, in sum, the challenge of the new administration will be to support both the statutory and administrative change necessary to assess facilities as systems and to authorize regulation and permit writers to make comprehensive and comparative assessments of the best way to achieve real environmental improvement, without wasting resources. The EPA has made some tentative steps in this direction, but they are not widespread enough nor based on solid enough legislative authority to make much more than episodic progress.

The task may be beyond the capability of the administration alone, for it will require bipartisan leadership. It will require recognizing that the right answers are not lodged in one group but in a collective wisdom that recognizes the multiple objectives represented in the quest for a decent quality of life. In short, it will require a shift in our political dynamics. But if the evidence of poverty, of resource depletion and degradation, of climate change, of corruption and the absence of the rule of law, of loss of biodiversity and on and on are as compelling as they seem to be, then we had better get on with it.

MEMORANDUM TO THE PRESIDENT

From: William C. Clark

Subject: America's National Interests in Promoting
            a Transition Toward Sustainability

PROBLEM

Among the greatest challenges facing humanity at the dawn of the 21st century is learning how to better meet human needs while restoring and nurturing
the planet's life support systems. Advances in individual sectors of human development, such as food, health, water, and energy, are surely important, as is
progress in addressing individual environmental problems, such as the loss of
biodiversity and climate warming. The proposition advanced here is that these
individual problems are more accurately and helpfully viewed as multiple dimensions of an increasingly interdependent and global relationship between society
and environment—a relationship that has been captured in the phrase "sustainable development." It is not the individual problems alone but rather their interactions that pose the greatest threats and opportunities for the 21st century. If
humanity is to meet these challenges and move forward in a transition toward
sustainability, it will need to craft a vision of the future that encompasses the multiple interactions among the multiple dimensions of development and environment as well as a strategy for action that addresses those interactions.

What ought to be the role of the United States in promoting a sustainability
transition? How this question is answered matters because of the material impact
the United States has on sustainability concerns and because of what many pre-
sume to be the necessity of its leadership in multiple arenas of international
affairs. One set of answers will come from those guided by internationalist and

multilateralist values, another from those focused on the United States's moral obligations to other peoples, a third from those primarily concerned with conserving nature, and so on. All of these views are defensible, and a great deal is to be gained by pluralist strategies that allow each its running room. But a plausible reading of U.S. history suggests that the United States can be expected to provide a high level of unwavering commitment to only a few issues that

> ...the United States can be expected to provide a high level of unwavering commitment to only a few issues that are consensually agreed upon to be central to America's national interests.

are consensually agreed upon to be central to America's national interests. Does the United States in fact have compelling national interests in leading the international effort to craft a vision and strategy for a transition toward sustainability? Answering this question in a way that could help national policy development will require a more structured, rigorous, and hierarchical conceptualization of "national interests" than has been evident in this country's debates about environment and development. This memorandum proposes such a framework and uses it to identify a hierarchy of national interests and related action priorities that could help to guide the United States's engagement in a global transition toward sustainability.

BACKGROUND

Legacy of the Last Two Generations

Many of the challenges facing human development at the beginning of the 21st century are well known. A spectacularly successful 50 years has produced, for the most fortunate, a quality of life unprecedented in human history. For another 3 billion people, it has brought about marked improvements in living standards, including significant increases in life expectancy, infant survival, literacy, and access to safe drinking water. However, this progress notwithstanding, more than 20 percent of today's human population still lives in poverty, 15 percent experiences persistent hunger, and at least 10 percent is homeless. Moreover, the gap between the very rich and very poor is widening, with whole regions clearly losing ground.[1]

Through both its successes and failures, modern human development has transformed the planet on which it has taken place—and on which it depends for its future.[2] Human activities have doubled the planet's rate of nitrogen fixation, tripled the rate of invasion by exotic organisms, increased sediment loads in rivers fivefold, and vastly increased natural rates of metal mobilization and species extinctions. Today's human population takes first bite at more than 40 percent of the world's terrestrial plant production and first sip of more than 50 percent of its freshwater runoff. People have fully- or over-exploited more than 60 percent of the planet's marine fish species, markedly changed the atmosphere's composition, and introduced more than 70,000 synthetic chemicals—including surprise-laden ones like DDT (dichlorodiphenyltrichloroethane) and chlorofluorocarbons (CFCs)—to a planet that had never before experienced their like.[3]

Challenges of the Next Two Generations

Looking ahead, there is a growing consensus that the next 50 years will see a world in which people "are more crowded, more consuming, more connected and, in many parts, more diverse than at any time in human history."[4] The planetary environment in which those people live will be stressed as never before: almost certainly warmer, more polluted, and less species-rich than ever in human history. Many of these trends have had a good deal of discussion of late, under headings ranging from "globalization" to "climate change." Less remarked upon is the fundamental transition under way in the growth of human populations: Rates of increase are now falling almost everywhere in the world, with the result that the number of people on the planet is expected to level off at 10 or 11 billion by the end of the 21st century, reaching around 9 billion—still half again as many as today's count—by 2050.

This transition toward a stable human population, if brought to fruition, could fundamentally transform the challenges of environmentally sustainable human development and also how people think about them. It could allow people to focus, for the first time in modern history, on questions of sustaining increases in the quality, not just the quantity, of human life. Can the transition to a stabilizing human population also be a transition to sustainability in which the people living on Earth over the next half-century meet their needs while nurturing and restoring the planet's life support systems? A recent report from the

National Research Council (NRC) of the U.S. National Academy of Sciences reviewed challenges to a sustainability transition arising from six major development areas initially identified and explored in the 1987 report of the United Nations's World Commission on Environment and Development (the Brundtland Commission).[5] Its findings are summarized below.

Population and settlement. Trends in human population and settlement are leading people toward a world of aging populations, growing more slowly than in the past but with additional growth concentrated as never before in urban areas of the developing world. The space, resources, and waste disposal necessary to provide for the needs of another 4 billion people over the next 50 years seem unlikely to be available without significantly degrading the Earth's life support systems unless quite different patterns of consumption and production can be developed. Since virtually all of this increase will be accommodated in urban areas, the challenges of providing municipal air and water quality, sanitation, and garbage disposal will be particularly acute. For mature, slowly growing, and wealthy urban areas, we almost know how to combine the technology, financing, and administration necessary to provide such waste services. For the young, rapidly growing, and generally underfinanced urban infrastructures that will arise to accommodate 4 billion more city dwellers over the next 50 years, we do not—at least not in ways that do not exact a steep price in human well-being and environmental quality. (See Kates memo.)

Agriculture and food security. Developing secure supplies of food for a world population that, during the next 50 years, will grow to 50 percent again as large as today's is a daunting challenge. World demand for food could easily double during this period, depending on the diets of our children and grandchildren. Unfortunately, many of the sources of the last half-century's phenomenal improvements in agricultural production now appear to be nearing their limits. Moreover, investments are declining in the global agricultural research system that has been responsible for much of the progress made during the past several decades. Substantial private sector investment will almost certainly be necessary to reinvigorate this research system. But as the recent biotechnology debacles show, such investment is a risky business. Learning how to make private investment in agriculture attractive and effective over the long haul—particularly with regard to those aspects of the system most important for enhancing food security and reducing hunger—remains a daunting task for the coming decades. (See Pinstrup-Andersen memo.)

Energy and materials. During the next two generations, global demand for goods and services is likely to increase two- to fourfold. The material and energy use associated with meeting this demand seem less likely than they once did to be constrained by absolute resource shortages. Rather, it is the planet's capacity for waste disposal that now seems most likely to be in short supply. The fundamental challenge today and in the future therefore remains the same as that identified by the Brundtland Commission in the 1980s: to produce more with less. In practice, efforts to meet this challenge have moved along three related but distinct paths: technological substitution to reduce the use of particularly hazardous substances, efficiency improvements in the conversion of energy and materials into end uses, and the reduction of "leakages" in the overall material system through recycling and reuse. In all of these areas, substantial progress is being made. But the absolute quantities of materials released to the environment as a result of human activities continue to grow and already exceed flows associated with natural processes across a wide range of substances. In many cases, these human flows have degraded the performance of crucial life support systems at continental scales and beyond. The potential for future damage is significant, growing, and spreading from the long-industrialized to the newly industrializing portions of the world.[6] (See Holdren memo.)

Living resources. Humans need the other living resources of the planet not only for food and fiber but also for a host of other services ranging from watershed protection and climate maintenance to pollination and the control of disease organisms. Societies have long been aware that overharvesting living resources can undermine subsequent prospects for human development. However, it has become increasingly clear that direct harvest is only one of the pressures placed by humans on living resources, with land use change and habitat destruction often causing even greater damage to the living systems on which our fate so closely depends. Pressures on living resources are increasing across the board, driven by the persistence of a frontier mentality in an increasingly crowded world, excessive harvest demands, heavy-handed recreational activities, and significant perturbations to the chemical and radiation environments of the planet. Significant progress has been made during the last two generations in the protection of a few high-profile vertebrates and a number of especially attractive or unique places. But the ultimate ineffectiveness of protection measures targeted at single links or locations in the complex web of life is becoming ever clearer. And the challenge of conserving whole ecosystems has almost nowhere been met. Indeed, a consensus is only beginning to develop on relevant measures by which the success or failure of such conservation efforts could be evaluated.[7] (See Reid and Ogden memos.)

System effects. Systematic efforts to integrate across all of these development trends and needs for particular parts of the world yield an unsurprising set of environmental threats. Nearly everywhere, problems such as urban air pollution, groundwater contamination, and forest degradation are matters of serious concern. Global issues such as climate change and stratospheric ozone depletion have received lots of attention in some of the more developed and more vulnerable countries but are accorded only secondary attention elsewhere. Reciprocally, disease epidemics, flood, drought, and forest depletion have been the primary focus of attention in many poorer parts of the world. In setting environmental priorities for sustainable development, it is therefore crucial to recognize that there are few universal concerns: Location matters.

> . . .it is becoming increasingly clear that the interactions among problems and activities are significant and that the interdependence of environment and development runs deep.

During the last several decades, most research and policy addressing environment and development issues have focused on one or another of the problems or sectoral activities noted above. Both understanding and management have benefited substantially from these focused approaches. However, it is becoming increasingly clear that the interactions among problems and activities are significant and that the interdependence of environment and development runs deep. The National Research Council concluded:

> most of the individual environmental problems that have occupied most of the world's attention to date are unlikely in themselves to prevent substantial

progress in a transition toward sustainability over the next two generations. Over longer time periods, unmitigated development of even these individual problems could certainly pose serious threats to people and the planet's life support systems. Even more troubling in the medium term that concerns us here, however, are the environmental threats arising from multiple, cumulative, and interactive stresses and driven by a variety of human activities.[8]

Work in Germany has suggested that a dozen or so kinds of interactions characterize many of the most destructive collisions between environment and development. These have been dubbed "degradation syndromes" and have been characterized in three broad groupings of "utilization syndromes" (e.g., the Sahel), "development syndromes" (e.g., green revolution "pesticide treadmills"), and "sink syndromes" (e.g., Black Triangle or Love Canal).[9] However named, they constitute an emerging class of globally embedded but place-based environmental threats that need at least as much attention in managing a transition toward sustainability as do the single-factor problems that have received most of the attention to date.

NRC analysis suggests that the trends described above "could significantly undermine the prospects for sustainability. If they do persist, many human needs will not be met, life support systems will be dangerously degraded, and the numbers of hungry and poor will increase."[10] The study nonetheless concluded

> a successful transition toward sustainability is possible over the next two generations. This transition could be achieved without miraculous technologies or drastic transformations of human societies. What will be required, however, are significant advances in basic knowledge, in the social capacity and technological capabilities to utilize it, and in the political will to turn this knowledge and know-how into action.[11]

America's National Interests in Promoting a Sustainability Transition

America's national interest in promoting such a transition toward sustainability, even in places beyond U.S. borders, is obvious to some. The planet to be sustained is, after all, the only one we have. To others, however, support is of the "yes, but . . . " variety, with the size of the U.S. foreign aid budget suggesting that the "but" is very large indeed. Another response is that U.S. interests lie in whatever interests U.S. citizens. This has the benefit of being more politically viable than the "everywhere" response because it targets attention on a few issues that have broad public support. The problem is that American interest in specific environmental issues has been episodic, flighty, and not particularly well correlated with objective risks posed to the nation, much less the world. Moreover, government programs have dutifully and democratically tracked this fickle public attention, even when this has led to demonstrably inferior policy in both the domestic and international arenas.[12] Such flightiness would be problematic enough in any issue area. For dealing with the long-time scale problems described earlier, it is nothing short of fatal.

These examples suggest that useful conceptualizations of "national interests" must be more structured, rigorous, and hierarchical than those in general use. One framework that meets these criteria was developed by the independent, bipartisan Commission on America's National Interests in the mid-1990s and revised at the turn of the century.[13] This framework distinguishes interests that are vital or strictly necessary to safeguarding and enhancing the well-being of Americans from other interests that are extremely important, merely important, and secondary. It further distinguishes interests from threats to

> **. . .useful conceptualizations of "national interests" must be more structured, rigorous, and hierarchical than those in general use.**

those interests and from policies to advance them. However, it recognizes that people in the United States have repeatedly demonstrated deeply held preferences for the means by which national goals are pursued. These include high—if sometimes conflicting—values placed upon sovereignty and stability in the international arena, upon diffusion of domestic governmental power, and upon openness of governance and markets to outside parties. These fundamental preferences concerning means lead to the identification of *instrumental* national interests as well as *substantive* ones.

Applying this hybrid framework to the analysis of the threats and opportunities around the world presented earlier leads to the following ordered list of America's national interests in promoting sustainable development:

Vital interests, or (in the words of the Commission) "conditions that are strictly necessary to safeguard and enhance Americans' survival and well-being in a free and secure nation":

- Substantively, to prevent the catastrophic collapse of major global life support systems (i.e., those responsible for sequestering toxic materials, cycling and regeneration of nutrients, regulating climate and sea level, screening extraterrestrial radiation, and controlling disease and pest organisms).

- Instrumentally, to develop credible U.S. leadership in dealing with other states on sustainability issues and to build global institutions essential for monitoring, understanding, and protecting Earth's life-support systems.

Extremely important interests, or "conditions that, if compromised, would severely prejudice but not strictly imperil the ability of the U.S. government to safeguard and enhance the well-being of Americans in a free and secure nation":

- Substantively, to prevent and, if possible at reasonable costs, end regional environment/development degradation spirals that could cause major conflicts in strategically important geographic regions (perhaps including North America, East Asia, Russia, Europe, and the Mid-East) or result in massive, uncontrolled immigration across U.S. borders.

- Instrumentally, to promote strong strategic partnerships for sustainable development with such regions.

Important interests, or "conditions that, if compromised, would have major negative consequences for the ability of the U.S. government to safeguard and enhance the well-being of Americans in a free and secure nation":

- Substantively,

    (a) to prevent and, if possible; at low costs, end regional environment/development degradation spirals that could cause major conflicts in strategically less significant geographic regions;

    (b) to prevent cross-border transfer of pollutants or organisms that could affect the health, economy, or ecosystems of the United States; and

    (c) to prevent depletion of global common pool resources in which the

United States has a stake (e.g. fish stocks, forests, biotic diversity).

- Instrumentally, to maintain a strong United Nations and other global, regional, and functional mechanisms for international cooperation.

Secondary interests, or "desirable conditions that . . . have little direct impact on the ability of the U.S. government to safeguard and enhance the well-being of Americans in a free and secure nation":

- Substantively, to protect other aspects of environmental quality.

- Instrumentally, to promote capacity for environmental protection generally.

Threats to America's National Interests

The appropriateness of these particular allocations of U.S. sustainability interests along the Commission on America's National Interests's hierarchy could and should be debated. But independent of their allocation arises the question of threat assessment: How endangered are America's national interests in environment and development? How well is the United States placed to deal with those threats?

Other memos submitted to this forum provide an assessment of environmental threats to this nation's basic interests arising through the quest for human development. More broadly, the World Bank and United Nations Environment Programme have recently completed global surveys of threats but have not matched those surveys to a template of interests.[14] A new international Millennium Ecosystem Assessment is in the works and will join a number of ongoing specialized international assessments, such as that of the Intergovernmental Panel on Climate Change.[15] Several countries have recently completed their own analyses, including that of the U.S. National Academy of Sciences.[16]

Threats to America's *vital* interests. Among all of the problems addressed in these assessments, the only threats that seem to have posed immediate challenges to vital national interests as defined above are fallout from nuclear weapons testing and depletion of the stratospheric ozone layer.[17] In both cases, however, reasonably timely international action seems to have averted disaster—at least for the moment. Surprises may still be in the works. But radioactive fallout from human activities peaked in the early 1960s and is now down to below-natural background levels. And the release of ozone-depleting chemicals has been sufficiently reduced so that stratospheric concentrations have peaked and are expected to return to pre-1980 levels by mid-century.[18] It is worthwhile to note that although the United States shares major responsibility for both of these threats, in both cases U.S. leadership was an essential component of the multilateral efforts that brought the threats under control.

A threat to the Earth's life support systems and humans' vital interests may yet be posed by either climate change or through transformation of the global nitrogen cycle.[19] But these potential threats, whatever else they do, appear unlikely in and of themselves to significantly undermine "the well-being of Americans in a free and secure nation" within the next several decades.[20] And with luck and timely action, they need never undermine these vital national interests at all. Time, however, is precisely what future threats to the Earth's life support systems may not grant. It is sobering to remember that the threat of ozone depletion—especially the potential for run-away depletion suggested by the discovery of the Antarctic ozone hole—emerged suddenly, as a surprise. Scientists' incomplete but indicative understanding of the Earth system gives us every reason to believe that comparable surprises await us in the future.[21] The only defense against these is a general reduction in the pressures the world is placing on its life support systems and a general increase in our social ability to detect and respond to the surprises that will inevitably emerge.

Threats to America's *important* interests. Related to the pressures described above are several threats that could affect important U.S. interests in preventing cross-border transfer of pollutants or organisms that could directly affect the health, economy, or ecosystems of the United States.[22] Most of this nation's attention to such issues to date has focused on the continental-scale transport of acidifying substances originating in Canada or Mexico. These, however, are addressed through bilateral and multilateral agreements (along with the generally greater flows of acidifying substances from the United States to neighboring countries). The

threats they pose to national interests seem unlikely to increase substantially in the future. More alarming is the increasing evidence that tropospheric ozone and other pollutants formed from fossil fuel combustion in Asia
are affecting background levels of ozone in the United States.[23] Given likely growth of Asian emissions during the next decades, the ozone emitted
there has a sufficient impact in the United States to offset its domestic
reductions, cause damage to health and crops, and make domestic control
efforts much more costly. Similar concerns arise over a variety of persistent
organic pollutants that, though regulated because of their health risks in
the United States, are or will soon be produced in sufficient quantities elsewhere to pose an increasing threat to the health of U.S. citizens.[24]

The United States also has important interests relating to the movement of
biological organisms across its national borders. The threats to U.S. interests arising through such movements are clearly increasing.[25] The most
dramatic globalization in biotic linkages has involved the occasional movement (usually aided by human transportation processes) of pest or disease
organisms from their native habitats to places where they have never been
and where the resident people, or other biota they value, have evolved no
protection from the invader. Disease epidemics, other forms of pest outbreaks, and repression or elimination of native species are often the
result.[26] Long-range invasions by other "exotic" organisms are also significant, with perhaps 20 percent of some continental floras now represented
by relatively recent immigrants.[27] The impacts of such long-distance invasions are extensive, representing a major cause of land-use transformation
and species extinction.[28] Data on rates of invasion are sparse but suggest a
rapid acceleration of incidence and extent due to increases in commerce,
tourism, and general travel.[29]

Threats to America's *extremely important* interests. The environmental problems of global scale described above, though posing demonstrable threats to
America's national interests, may not be the most serious threats we will face in
the next several decades. As noted earlier, a general consensus is emerging in the
scientific community that the most serious environmental threats to sustainability in the new century are likely to involve dramatic degradation of regional
systems due to the interactions of multiple, cumulative stresses in places ill-
equipped to deal with them.[30] And a significant program of research has
demonstrated multiple pathways—in particular, scarcity of crucial resources—

through which catastrophic degradation of regional environments has in the past, and likely will in the future, lead to violent conflict among societies in the degraded regions.[31] (See Homer-Dixon memo.)

It is this propensity of regional syndromes of environment/society degradation to precipitate or contribute to violent conflict that makes them a threat to America's national interests. In particular, according to the Commission on America's National Interests's criteria described above, if potentially destabilizing degradation occurs in "strategically important geographic regions" (perhaps including North America, East Asia, Russia, Europe, Mid-East), it threatens an extremely important national interest. If it occurs elsewhere, it threatens an important national interest. By and large, the potential for catastrophic environmental degradation and subsequent violent conflict seems highest in regions with limited resources of economic wealth and state capacity. This view is garnering increasingly serious attention in the United States. The Bureau of Intelligence and Research (INR) at the State Department has concluded that "resource scarcity is much more of an immediate security threat than climate change. Resource degradation tends to be local and will increase ethnic tensions (mostly at a subnational level) between people competing for jobs and land."[32]

RECOMMENDATIONS

Even a highly restrictive concept of America's national interest calls for significant national commitments to promoting environmentally sustainable development. America's vital interests demand an orderly approach to forestall threats to global life support systems that will almost certainly be brought on by excessive emissions of carbon, nitrogen, and other substances not yet identified. Past efforts to mitigate similar threats from radioactive fallout, DDT, and ozone-depleting chemicals provide a model of the sorts of enlightened U.S. leadership that will be required to address such threats. Our extremely important interests demand attention to the risks of conflict-inducing syndromes of regional environment/society degradation in places of strategic concern. No systematic inventory of such risks currently exists; an effort to produce one is urgently needed. Protecting our important interests requires a much broader array of actions. These include preventing regional degradation spirals that might lead to violent

196

conflict anywhere in the world, reducing transborder pollution and movement of organisms, and protecting the global commons in which we have an interest. Although the United States has undertaken a number of measures consistent with these goals, the country has conducted no systematic matching of interests, threats, and action priorities. We should do so in the near future.

Priorities for Multilateral Engagement

Unsurprisingly, much of the United States's ability to protect national interests in sustainable development depends on our ability to undertake effective multilateral action.[33] (See Claussen memo.) In presenting his recent millennium report to the UN General Assembly, Secretary-General Kofi A. Annan argued that

> the overarching challenge of our times is to make globalization mean more than bigger markets. To make a success of this great upheaval, we must learn how to govern better, and—above all—how to govern better together . . . to get (states) working together on global issues . . . (of) freedom from want, freedom from fear, and the freedom of future generations to sustain their lives on this planet.[34]

Even in the United States, there is widespread agreement that strategies for sustainable development ought to involve multilateral engagement. The State Department's "Environmental Initiative for the 21st Century" supports a plausible if predictable range of international and regional initiatives.[35] And no less an authority than then-Secretary of State James Baker argued a decade ago that

> America's entire approach to bilateral and multilateral assistance is based on the concept of sustainable development. . . . When policies of sustainable development are followed, our economic and our environmental objectives are both achieved.[36]

The strategic plan of the U.S. Agency for International Development indeed is focused on sustainability themes. Moreover, the United States has been instrumental in bringing environment to the fore in the new strategies of the World Bank and other international lending institutions. Nonetheless, of the many voices calling for sustainable development initiatives in the United States today, those calling for multilateral engagement have been surprisingly muted. Among those who do call for multilateral approaches, many have advanced proposals that, although almost certainly worth pursuing, do not meet the strict national interest criteria outlined earlier. Among the few that do, however, a few dominant priorities for near-term action emerge.

Significant progress in a transition toward the sustainability goals most central to U.S. interests will be the result not of a few large decisions embodied in international treaties but rather of many small decisions taken by national governments, regional authorities, nongovernmental organizations, private sector enterprises, and individual consumers. Given the complexity of the sustainability challenge and the present state of our understanding, these decisions will often turn out wrong. It is important that those involved in making and living with such inevitably flawed decisions be able to detect and survive their errors, learn from them, and pass the fruits of their experience on to others. In the vast majority of cases, the United States cannot and should not seek to shape individual outcomes of open-ended, regionally embedded decisionmaking in places beyond national borders. Rather, the United States should seek to shape the international environment of norms, rules, information, and incentives in ways that will guide such decisions along pathways consistent with the country's most deeply held substantive and instrumental interests.[37]

In particular, the United States has a significant national interest in, and should commit itself to, multilateral activities that promote

- International law. The United States should push for agreement on norms, standards, legal structures, and indicators for sustainability that are consistent with fundamental U.S. values regarding sovereignty, openness of markets and rule-making processes to multiple parties, and protection of minority rights.

- Global research systems for sustainability science. The United States needs to play a lead role in the development of an international research and decision support system for sustainable development, modeled on the system that supported agriculture's green revolution in the late 20th century, but expanding its mandate to target problems of multiple, cumulative threats to life support systems at the regional scale.[38]

- Incentive systems. The United States should support the design and implementation of incentive systems—including, but not restricted to, market signals and the removal of inappropriate subsidies—that will encourage technical innovation and resource consumption activities consistent with a transition toward sustainability. This will almost certainly require the United States, among other things, to examine the implications of our current tax system for sustainability.[39]

• Social learning. The United States should promote institutionalization of a worldwide capacity for information sharing and social learning regarding sustainable development problems, experiences, and solutions, taking advantage of the strengths and legitimacy of the UN system for such tasks.[40]

Protecting American substantive and instrumental interests while pursuing these sustainability goals in a multilateral context will require active U.S. leadership. The nation's capacity to exert such leadership is the source of the "soft power" that many analysts of international affairs see as increasingly important for the United States in achieving its goals in an increasingly complex, interdependent, and globalizing world.[41] But the feasibility of exerting such international leadership requires credibility that can ultimately derive only from U.S. domestic actions and international reputation for adherence to U.S. commitments and for openhandedness in dealing with others.

> This faltering of credible U.S. leadership for multilateral endeavors in general, and in the realm of sustainable development in particular, is. . .the single greatest threat to the national interests of the United States in the increasingly globalized and interdependent world of the 21st century.

Regarding issues of sustainable development and environment, U.S. actions over the last decade have left the country's credibility as an international leader in short supply. This faltering of credible U.S. leadership for multilateral endeavors in general, and in the realm of sustainable development in particular, is—in the final analysis—the single greatest threat to the national interests of the United States in the increasingly globalized and interdependent world of the 21st century. Fortunately, unlike many other threats, it is one almost wholly in our power to address domestically. Efforts to protect U.S. interests in sustainable development must begin now, and must begin with the examples we set at home.

ENDNOTES AND FURTHER READING

The Energy-Climate Challenge, John Holdren

1. In the early 1990s, a former member of the Council of Economic Advisors asserted to the contrary, that the U.S. economy cannot be very vulnerable to climate change because only 3 percent of the country's gross national product (GNP) depends on the environment. This member was apparently referring to the share generated by agriculture, forestry, and fishing. But in a fundamental sense, GNP all depends on the environment. The economist's assertion is akin to claiming that human beings should not worry about heart attacks insofar as the heart constitutes only 2 percent of the body mass.

2. World use of primary energy forms in 1998 amounted to 440 exajoules (EJ) (1 EJ = 1018 J = 0.95 quadrillion Btu = 22 million tons of oil = 33 million tons of UN standard coal). Of this total, 35 percent came from oil, 23 percent from coal, and 20 percent from natural gas—a total of 78 percent from fossil fuels. Nonfossil contributions were principally 13 percent from biomass fuels (fuelwood, charcoal, crop wastes, dung, and biomass-derived alcohol), 6 percent from nuclear energy, and 2 percent from hydropower. Renewable sources other than biomass and hydropower—notably geothermal, wind, and solar energy—contributed altogether less than 0.5 percent. In the United States, the 1998 primary energy supply of 100 EJ was derived 38 percent from oil, 24 percent each from coal and natural gas, 8.2 percent from nuclear energy, 3.8 percent from biomass, 1.2 percent from hydropower, and 0.4 percent from other renewables.

3. The scenario described here closely resembles scenario IS92a from the 1995 second assessment by the Intergovernmental Panel on Climate Change (IPCC), which was a middle-of-the-road scenario in that study and has been widely employed as a reference case in energy/climate discussions since. Scenarios are not predictions; they serve only to illustrate the consequences of the stated assumptions about the evolution of the contributing factors.

4. Atmospheric particulate matter cools the Earth's surface in some circumstances and warms it in others. The uncertainties associated with these complicated phenomena are considerable, and the investigation of the details—including the prevalence of particulate-warming circumstances versus that of particulate-cooling circumstances—is a vigorous focus of current research. A global-average net cooling effect of the magnitude indicated here was the best estimate of the 1995 assessment of IPCC.

5. This approach tends to underestimate the expected future warming insofar as the most likely deviation from its assumptions is a more rapid decline in particulate concentrations than was assumed as a result of more aggressive programs to control emissions of particulate matter and its gaseous precursors (mainly oxides of sulfur and nitrogen). The dilemma here is that better control of conventional pollutants makes the problem of greenhouse gas-induced climate change worse.

6. That is, the debate among respected analysts. There will always remain a few credentialed skeptics, as there are on such questions as whether cigarette smoking causes lung cancer. This is in the nature of science and the distribution of human characteristics among those who practice it. But the very small and continuously diminishing possibility that the dissidents are right cannot be given much weight in prudent public policy.

7. This means the dissidents have two difficult questions to answer: First, what is the alternative culprit that would account for the observed pattern of effects? Second, how can it be that the measured increase in greenhouse gas concentrations is not causing the pattern of effects that climate science predicts for it (because, by the dissidents' postulate, something else is causing this)? See, for example, Intergovernmental Panel on Climate Change, Climate Change 1995—The Science of Climate Change (U.K.: Cambridge University Press, 1996).

8. National Research Council, Reconciling Observations of Global Temperature Change (Washington, D.C.: National Academy Press, 2000).

9. S. Levitus, J. Antonov, T. Boyer, and C. Stevens, "Warming of the World Ocean," Science 287 no. 5,461 (2000): 2,225-29.

10. It is true, as climate change skeptics are fond of pointing out, that there is considerable natural variability in global climate (arising, for example, from variations in solar output, cycles in the Earth's orbital parameters, and "internal" climate-system oscillations involving the interactions of ice, oceans, and atmosphere). But the size of the climate change "signal" that has emerged over the last few decades from the "noise" of natural variability is large, and, as indicated in the text and in note 7 above, it fits too well the pattern expected from greenhouse gas-induced warming to be plausibly attributed to a hitherto unsuspected and undetected natural cause.

11. These figures take the realized temperature increase from pre-industrial times to 1990 to be 0.5 degrees C. The increase projected between 1990 and 2070 under the BAU scenario is 1.3 degrees C and that between 1990 and 2100 is 2 degrees C.

12. The seeming paradox of having more droughts as well as more floods is explained by the fact that, although a warmed world generates more precipitation with a larger part of it concentrated in extreme events, it also produces greater evaporation and hence more rapid drying out of the soil between precipitation events.

13. The agricultural projections in the IPCC assessment and subsequent ones, such as the recently released draft U.S. National Assessment of Climate-Change Impacts on the United States, are based on analysis of the effects of temperature, moisture, and increased CO2 (which is a plant nutri-

ent) only. They do not account for ecological effects, such as from changes of conditions favorable to plant pests and pathogens. When these ecological factors are taken into account, it seems likely that the net assessment of climate-change effects on agriculture will change from "better in some places, worse in others, balancing out on average" to "more harm than good."

14. The focus of the climate-science community and its literature on the consequences of a doubling, which resulted from an agreement to standardize analyses for the purpose of comparison rather than from any conviction that no more than a doubling is likely, seems to have deflected attention from the full implications of business-as-usual, which would carry the world past any realistic possibility of avoiding a tripling if it persisted through 2075 and past any realistic possibility of avoiding a quadrupling if it persisted through 2100.

15. The heat index combines temperature and humidity into a single measure of discomfort in hot weather. The figures given are 24-hour, 30-day monthly averages. The best way to make these numbers meaningful is to associate what you know to be the current Washington, D.C. climate in July with the figure 86 and then imagine what 109 would mean. See Geophysical Fluid Dynamics Laboratory, "Climate Impact of Quadrupling Atmospheric CO2," available at http://www.gfdl.gov/~fk/climate_dynamics/.

16. The Princeton group only calculated the sea-level rise from thermal expansion, considering that the then-current models were not capable of a credible calculation of the contribution from melting from the Greenland and Antarctic ice sheets.

17. This could also be achieved with other combinations of energy-intensity and carbon-intensity reductions, as long as the century-average reduction rates for the two ratios add up to 2.6 percent per year. Thus, instead of a 2.0 percent per year decline in energy intensity and a 0.6 percent per year decline in carbon intensity, one could do the same job with an energy intensity decline averaging 1.6 percent per year and a carbon intensity decline averaging 1.0 percent per year.

18. To pick but one item on this list for brief elaboration, the vulnerability of air travel to increased summer storminess (a likely consequence of warming and the more vigorous hydrologic cycle that goes with it) should be apparent to anyone who attempted much flying in the summer of 2000.

19. Ending deforestation and improving other land-management practices to reduce greenhouse gas emissions from the managed lands are, of course, forms of emissions control rather than means of removing greenhouse gases that are already in the atmosphere. But the effect is the same, and it is customary for obvious reasons to treat all of the land-use approaches to carbon management together.

20. It is conceivable that another 10 percent could be achieved by fertilizing the oceans to increase the amount of carbon stored in plant material there. But the biology involved is much less well understood than for terrestrial ecosystems, and the chance of unanticipated and unwanted side effects is correspondingly higher.

21. The details of the research programs that need to be pursued under these headings are abundantly spelled out in reports generated over the past few years by IPCC, the U.S. Global Change Research Program, and the U.S. National Academies complex, among others.

22. The merits and demerits of many of these approaches were treated in the two studies of energy strategy conducted by the President's Committee of Advisors on Science and Technology in the second term of the Clinton administration—Federal Energy Research and Development for the Challenges of the Twenty First Century (November 1997), available at http://www.whitehouse.gov/WH/EOP/OSTP/Energy/ and Powerful Partnerships: The Federal Role in International Cooperation on Energy Innovation (June 1999), available at http://www.whitehouse.gov/media/pdf/p2E/pdf—both available from the Office of Science and Technology Policy in the Executive Office of the President.

23. At least one well regarded economic model—that of Dale Jorgenson of Harvard University—indicates that a revenue-neutral carbon tax, wherein the revenues were used to reduce income and capital-gains taxes, would lead in the United States not only to a reduction in CO_2 emissions below business-as-usual but to an increase in GDP compared to the reference (no carbon tax) case. This means that the benefits to the economy from reduced income and capital-gains taxes outweighed the damage to the economy from increased energy costs. See D. Jorgenson and P. J. Wilcoxen, "The Economic Effects of a Carbon Tax," in H. Lee ed., Shaping National Responses to Climate Change (Washington, D.C.: Island Press, 1995), 237–60.

24. A carbon tax of $20 per ton would add 5.5 cents per gallon to the price of gasoline (an increase of about 3 percent on a market price of $1.70 per gallon for regular unleaded); 32 cents per million Btu to the price of natural gas (an increase of about 5 percent on a market price of $6 per million Btu for residential gas); and $11 per short ton to the price of electric-utility coal (an increase of 28 percent on a market price of $40 per short ton). The increment on the price of natural gas would add 0.2 cents per kilowatt hour (kWh) to the 3.5 cents per kWh cost of electricity generation using natural gas in a combined-cycle power plant operating at 50 percent thermal-to-electric efficiency, and the increment on the price of utility coal would add 0.6 cents per kWh to the 6 cents per kWh cost of electricity generation with a conventional pulverized-coal power plant operating at 36 percent efficiency. But the one-tenth of the $30 billion per year total revenue from this tax that would be allocated, by hypothesis, to additional incentives for low-carbon energy choices would be five times larger than the $600 million per year in such incentives proposed in the Clinton administration's initial Climate Change Technologies Initiative.

25. President's Committee of Advisors on Science and Technology, Panel on Energy Research and Development, Federal Energy Research and Development for the Challenges of the Twenty-First Century (Washington, D.C.: Executive Office of the President of the United States, November 1999).

26. The principal recommended increases were (in descending order) in efficiency, renewable, and nuclear (fusion and fission) technologies; recommended initiatives in the fossil category, while they included increases for work on fuel cells, advanced coal technologies, and carbon capture/sequestration technologies, were largely offset by recommended phaseouts. The bipartisan panel that produced these recommendations contained experts in the full range of energy sources—from the private sector as well as from the academic and NGO communities. Its conclusions were all unanimous. Federal Energy Research and Development for the Challenges of the Twenty-First Century, note 25 above.

27. President's Committee of Advisors on Science and Technology, Panel on International Cooperation in Energy Research, Development, Demonstration, and Deployment, Powerful Partnerships: The Federal Role in International Cooperation on Energy Innovation (Washington, D.C.: Executive Office of the President of the United States, June 1999).

28. Most of the multi-hundred-billion dollar per year energy-supply-technology market is outside the United States—and increasingly in developing countries—and this will become even more true as the century wears on.

29. The United States was contributing about one-quarter of worldwide fossil-CO2 emissions at the end of the 20th century, while other industrialized countries contributed about one-half and developing countries the remaining quarter. In a BAU energy future, however, developing countries will become equal to the industrialized ones as emitters of fossil-fuel-derived CO2 by around 2030 and will increasingly dominate global CO2 emissions thereafter.

30. Climate Change Secretariat, UN Framework Convention on Climate Change (Geneva: UN Environment Programme Information Unit for Conventions, 1997).

31. This does not mean that per-capita emissions in all industrialized countries would necessarily have fallen this far by 2035 or that per-capita emissions in all developing countries would necessarily have risen this far; but, under a cap-and-trade scheme, the industrialized countries that had not gotten this low would need to buy emissions permits from the developing countries that had not gotten this high.

Controlling Emissions of Greenhouse Gases, David G. Victor

1. Most adaptation will occur within nations, but some international coordination is needed—for example, nations must work together to plan adaptation within international river basins. In addition, programs are needed to ease adaptation in developing countries, which bear little responsibility for climate change yet are generally more vulnerable to changing weather and less able to pay the costs of adaptation.

2. The most important arbitrary parameter in calculating GWPs is the "time horizon." Different values for the time horizon could raise the GWP for methane to 60 or reduce it to less than

7, with enormous consequences for where the economy focuses mitigation of greenhouse gases. There are no criteria for choosing a time horizon, so most scientists and diplomats choose 100 years for the same reason that Goldilocks made all the middle choices—of the three time horizons that are typically reported, 100 years is longer than 20 years and shorter than 500 years. A better system would compute the value of GWPs according to the goals of the climate treaty and the scenario for future emissions. If the world were approaching a particular goal then the value of short-lived and strong greenhouse gases (e.g., methane) would rise because controls on those gases would have a strong and immediate effect on the climate; if goals are more distant then long-lived gases (notably CO_2) would become relatively more important because the short-term effects of short-lived gases do not matter. The point is simply that the GWP should not be treated as purely a geophysical concept. Rather, it should be adjusted to the political goals and the economic context for achieving those goals.

3. On average, U.S. emissions of carbon dioxide have risen 1% to 1.5% per year since the end of the 1991 recession. In 1998 emissions rose only about 0.1%, which led some analysts to conclude that the "new economy" was rapidly decoupling wealth from energy consumption and therefore it would be relatively easy for the United States to comply with the Kyoto targets. In reality, the slow growth in emissions for 1998 was the consequence of an unusually warm winter that reduced demand for heating; preliminary data for 1999 show a rise in emissions of about 1%, which is consistent with the historical rate. Indeed, the economy is slowly decoupling from fossil energy—economic growth of about 3% per year causes a rise in greenhouse gas emissions of only about one-third that amount. However, the decoupling process is slow and will not deliver much change by 2008; nor has it fully decoupled industrial wealth from emissions. Some new wealth goes to airplane trips, gas guzzling cars and other activities that cause emissions—the "new" economy has not eliminated old pleasures and needs.

4. Critics of this suggestion will argue that industrialized nations have already tried (without success) the nonbinding approach starting in 1988 with the nonbinding "Toronto Target" that urged countries to cut CO_2 emissions 20% by 2005. But the Toronto Target was not a serious effort. Rather, the Toronto target was a symbolic goal invented with no attention to whether it was feasible— no advanced industrialized country has come close to achieving the Toronto limits. Nor did the Toronto conference include any effort to follow-up targets with plans for action and periodic reviews of those plans—yet experience in other areas of international environmental cooperation (e.g., the successful effort to clean up the North Sea) show that ambitious nonbinding plans work best when they are followed by serious efforts to develop national action plans and to review implementation of those plans.

5. Tackling these technical problems will also reveal that it is especially difficult for developing countries to make legally binding commitments to cap their emissions of greenhouse gases at particular levels—the approach taken in the Kyoto Protocol—because the development process is somewhat unpredictable and leads to unpredictable levels of greenhouse gas emissions. Instead, it would be better to codify commitments in terms that correspond more closely with the levers that

policy makers actually control—for example, targets could be set for improving energy efficiency, which can be measured as the ratio of energy consumption to economic output. By that measure, China is already making rapid improvement, but efficiency in Brazil and India is more stagnant.

6. We could make these property rights more secure by linking them with other benefits in the international system. For example, we could attempt to link compliance with the emission trading system with the benefits of the WTO. However, doing so would raise many problems—it could severely harm the WTO's mission of liberalizing trade, and it would encounter blistering opposition from developing countries who are already wary of efforts to link the WTO with environmental and labor standards.

7. In brief, the central problem is that countries would implement emission taxes on top of existing distortions in the tax code, such as existing energy taxes and subsidies. Thus it would be impossible to measure the practical effect of an emission tax and therefore impossible to determine whether a country was complying with its international commitments.

Food and Agriculture, Per Pinstrup-Andersen

1. Accessed via http://www.worldbank.org/poverty/data/trends/income.htm on 15 October 1999.

2. A. Deaton, The Analysis of Household Surveys: A Microeconomic Approach to Development Policy (Baltimore and London: Johns Hopkins University Press for The World Bank, 1997).

3. Food and Agriculture Organization of the United Nations (FAO), The State of Food Insecurity in the World, 1999 (Rome: FAO, 1999).

4. Accessed via http://www.ers.usda.gov/briefing/foodsecurity on 6 June 2000.

5. United Nations Administrative Committee on Coordination/Subcommittee on Nutrition (ACC/SCN) and International Food Policy Research Institute (IFPRI), Fourth Report on the World Nutrition Situation (Geneva: ACC/SCN and Washington, D.C.: IFPRI, 2000); and World Health Organization, Malnutrition Worldwide, accessed via http://www.who.int/nut on 6 June 2000.

6. P. Pinstrup-Andersen, R. Pandya-Lorch, and M. W. Rosegrant, World Food Prospects: Critical Issues for the Early Twenty-First Century, 2020 Vision Food Policy Report (Washington, D.C.: IFPRI, 1999).

7. United Nations Children's Fund, The State of the World's Children 1998 (New York: Oxford University Press, 1998).

8. ACC/SCN and IFPRI, note 5 above, pages 23–32; and ACC/SCN, Third Report on the World Nutrition Situation (Geneva: ACC/SCN, 1997).

9. Pinstrup-Andersen, Pandya-Lorch, and Rosegrant, note 6 above, pages 8–18.

10. Ibid., pages 23–24; E. Diaz-Bonilla and S. Robinson, eds., Getting Ready for the Millennium Round Trade Negotiations, 2020 Vision Focus 1 (Washington, D.C.: IFPRI, 1999); and P.

Pinstrup-Andersen, R. Pandya-Lorch, and M. W. Rosegrant, The World Food Situation: Recent Developments, Emerging Issues, and Long-Term Prospects, 2020 Vision Food Policy Report (Washington, D.C.: IFPRI, 1997).

11. FAO, The State of Food and Agriculture in Figures, 1999 (Rome: FAO, 1999).

12. P. Pinstrup-Andersen and M. J. Cohen, Aid to Developing Country Agriculture: Investing in Poverty Reduction and New Export Opportunities, 2020 Vision Brief no. 56 (Washington, D.C.: IFPRI, 1998).

13. FAO, Investment in Agriculture: Evolution and Prospects, World Food Summit technical background document no. 10 (Rome: FAO, 1996).

14. Accessed via http://www.oecd.org/dac on 6 June 2000.

15. Accessed via http://www.wfp.org on 6 June 2000.

16. Accessed via http://www.unhcr.ch and http://www.refugees.org on 19 July 2000.

17. E. Messer, M. J. Cohen, and J. D'Costa, "Food from Peace: Breaking the Links Between Conflict and Hunger," Food, Agriculture, and the Environment Discussion Paper no. 24 (Washington, D.C.: IFPRI, 1998).

18. Pinstrup-Andersen, Pandya-Lorch, and Rosegrant, note 6 above, pages 24–26; "Global Study Reveals New Warning Signals: Degraded Agricultural Lands Threaten World's Food Production Capacity," IFPRI News Release (21 May 2000), accessed via http://www.cgiar.org/ifpri/press-rel/052500.htm on 6 June 2000.

19. E. C. Oerke, H. W. Dehne, F. Schonbeck, and A. Weber, Crop Production and Crop Protection: Estimated Losses in Major Food and Cash Crops (Amsterdam: Elsevier, 1994).

20. M. Yudelman, A. Ratta, and D. Nygaard, "Issues in Pest Management and Food Production: Looking to the Future" Food, Agriculture, and the Environment Discussion Paper no. 26 (Washington, D.C.: IFPRI, 1998); 1998–99 World Resources Guide to the Global Environment: Environmental Change and Human Health (New York: Oxford University Press, 1998); and P. Pinstrup-Andersen and R. Pandya-Lorch, "Food for All in 2020: Can the World Be Fed without Damaging the Environment?" Environmental Conservation 23, no. 3 (1996): 226–34.

21. Pinstrup-Andersen, Pandya-Lorch, and Rosegrant, note 10 above, pages 23–5.

22. S. J. Scherr, Soil Degradation: A Threat to Developing-Country Food Security by 2020? 2020 Vision Brief no. 58 (Washington, D.C.: IFPRI, 1999).

23. A. F. McCalla and W. S. Ayres, Rural Development: From Vision to Action (Washington, D.C.: The World Bank, 1997).

24. C. L. Delgado et al., Agricultural Growth Linkages in Sub-Saharan Africa, Research Report no. 107 (Washington, D.C.: IFPRI, 1998).

25. FAO, note 13 above, page 33; and FAO, "Public Assistance and Agricultural Development in Africa," accessed via http://www.fao.org.docrep/meeting/x3977e.htm on 21 February 2000.

26. P. G. Pardey and J. M. Alston, Revamping Agricultural R & D, 2020 Vision Brief no. 24 (Washington, D.C.: IFPRI, 1996).

27. P. G. Pardey, J. M. Alston, J. E. Christian, and S. Fan, Hidden Harvest: U.S. Benefits from International Research Aid, Food Policy Report (Washington, D.C.: IFPRI, 1996). The 16 Future Harvest international agricultural research centers are supported by the Consultative Group on International Agricultural Research, an informal association of 58 governments, international organizations, and private foundations that seeks to contribute to food security and poverty eradication in developing countries through research, partnership, capacity-building, and policy support.

28. For more on this topic, see G. Persley, ed., Biotechnology for Developing Countries: Problems and Opportunities, 2020 Vision Focus 2 (Washington, D.C.: IFPRI, 1999); P. Pinstrup-Andersen and M. J. Cohen, "Modern Biotechnology for Food and Agriculture: Risks and Opportunities for the Poor," in G. J. Persley and M. M. Lantin, eds., Agricultural Biotechnology and the Poor (Washington, D.C.: The World Bank, 2000); and P. Pinstrup-Andersen and M. J. Cohen, "Food Security in the 21st Century and the Role of Biotechnology," foresight 1, no. 5 (1999): 399–412.

29. C. James, Global Status of Commercialized Transgenic Crops: 1999, ISAAA Briefs no. 12: Preview (Ithaca, N.Y.: International Service for the Acquisition of Agri-Biotech Applications, 1999).

30. Accessed via http://www.bls.gov, http://www.census.gov, and http://www.usda.gov/nass on 18 November 1999.

31. "Sachs on Development: Helping the World's Poorest," The Economist, 14 August 1999, 17–20.

32. I. Serageldin, "Biotechnology and Food Security in the 21st Century," Science, 16 July 1999, 387–89.

33. L. C. Smith and L. Haddad, "Overcoming Child Malnutrition in Developing Countries," Food, Agriculture, and the Environment discussion paper no. 30 (Washington, D.C.: IFPRI, 2000).

34. U.S. Department of Agriculture, A Time to Act: A Report of the USDA National Commission on Small Farms (Washington, D.C.: USDA, 1998).

Global Water: Threats and Challenges Facing the United States, Peter H. Gleick

1. P. H. Gleick, The World's Water 1998–1999: The Biennial Report on Freshwater Resources (Washington, D.C.: Island Press, 1998).

2. W. R. Solley, R. Pierce, and H. A. Perlman, Estimated Use of Water in the United States in 1995 (Denver, Colo.: U.S. Geological Survey Circular 1,200, 1998).

3. P. H. Gleick, "Water and Conflict," International Security 18, no. 1 (1993): 79–112.

4. For quotes and references relevant to environmental security issues, see Environmental Change and Security Project Report, the regular report from the Woodrow Wilson Center, Washington, D.C. By summer 1999, five issues had been published.

5. For detailed information on water-related diseases, see the World Health Organization web site at http://www.who.org. Specific data on access to basic water services can be found in Gleick, note 1 above; and http://www.worldwater.org.

6. Detailed information on climate change science and impacts can be found in the reports of the Intergovernmental Panel on Climate Change (IPCC) published by Cambridge University Press, in 1996. For detailed information on the impacts of climate change on U.S. water resources, see the newly released report from the Water Sector of the National Assessment of Impacts of Climate Variability and Change for the United States: P. H. Gleick, Water: The Potential Consequences of Climate Vulnerability and Change for the Water Resources of the United States (Washington, D.C.: The National Assessment—U.S. Global Change Research Program, 2000).

7. United Nations Framework Convention on Climate Change (UNFCCC), International Legal Materials 31(1992): 849. See also http://www.unfccc.de.

8. P. E. Waggoner, ed., Climate Change and U.S. Water Resources (New York: John Wiley and Sons, Inc., 1990).

9. Intergovernmental Panel on Climate Change (IPCC), Climate Change 1995: Impacts, Adaptations and Mitigating Climate Change: Scientific-Technical Analysis, contribution of working group II to the Second Assessment Report of IPCC, (New York: Cambridge University Press, 1996).

10. American Water Works Association (AWWA), "Climate Change and Water Resources," Committee Report of the AWWA Public Advisory Forum in Journal of the American Water Works Association 89, no. 11 (1997): 107–10.

11. The report of the president's Water Resources Policy Commission, A Water Policy for the American People (Washington, D.C.: U.S. Government Printing Office, 1950).

12. Gleick, note 6 above.

Environment and Health, Kirk R. Smith—Further Reading

P. Lichtenstein et al., "Environmental and Heritable Factors in the Causation of Cancer—Analyses of Cohorts of Twins from Sweden, Denmark, and Finland," New England Journal of Medicine 343, no. 2 (2000): 78–85.

J. M. McGinnis and W. H. Foege, "Actual Causes of Death in the United States," Journal of American Medical Association 270, no. 18 (1993): 2,207–12.

J. M. McGinnis and W. H. Foege, "Mortality and Morbidity Attributable to Use of Addictive Substances in the United States," Proceedings of the Association of American Physicians 111, no. 2 (1999): 109–18.

G. McGranahan et al., Citizens at Risk: From Urban Sanitation to Sustainable Cities (London: Earthscan, 2000).

A. J. McMichael, Surviving Uncertain Futures: Environments, Societies and Patterns of Disease (U.K.: Cambridge University Press, forthcoming 2000).

C. Murray and A. Lopez, eds., The Global Burden of Disease: A Comprehensive Assessment of Mortality and Disability from Diseases, Injuries, and Risk Factors in 1990 and Projected to 2020, Global Burden of Disease and Injury Series (Cambridge, Mass.: Harvard School of Public Health on behalf of the World Health Organization and the World Bank, 1996).

C. Murray and A. Lopez, Global Health Statistics: A Compendium of Incidence, Prevalence, and Mortality Estimates for over 200 Conditions (Cambridge, Mass.: Harvard School of Public Health on behalf of the World Health Organization and the World Bank, 1996).

National Center for Health Statistics (NCHS), Health People 2000: National Health Promotion and Disease Prevention Objectives (Hyattsville, Mass.: NCHS, Public Health Service, 2000).

National Research Council, Grand Challenges in Environmental Science (Washington, D.C.: National Academy Press, 2000).

D. Pimentel et al., "Ecology of Increasing Disease," BioScience 48, no. 10 (1998): 817–26.

K. R. Smith, "The Risk Transition, "International Environmental Affairs 2, no. 3 (1990): 227–51.

K. R. Smith, "National Burden of Disease in India from Indoor Air Pollution," Proceedings of the National Academy of Sciences 97 (forthcoming 2000).

K. R. Smith et al., "How Much Global Ill-Health Is Attributable to Environmental Factors?" Epidemiology 10, no. 5 (1999): 573–84.

K. R. Smith and M. Desai, "The Contribution of Global Environmental Factors to Ill-Health," in P. Martens and A. J. McMichael, Environment, Climate Change, and Health: Concepts and Methods (U.K.: Cambridge University Press, forthcoming 2000).

K. R. Smith et al., " Indoor Air Pollution in Developing Countries and Acute Lower Respiratory Infections in Children," Thorax 55 (2000): 518–32.

L. Weicker et al., America's Environmental Health Gap (Baltimore, Md.: Pew Environmental Health Commission, School of Public Health, Johns Hopkins University, 2000).

World Health Organization (WHO), Health and Environment in Sustainable Development, (Geneva: WHO, 2000), 242.

WHO, World Health Report (Geneva: WHO, 1999).

Biodiversity, Ecosystem Change, and International Development, Walter V. Reid

1. W. V. Reid, "How Many Species Will There Be?" in T. Whitmore and J. Sayer, eds., Tropical Deforestation and Species Extinction (London: Chapman and Hall, 1992).

2. B. A. Stein, L. S. Kutner, and J. S. Adams, eds., Precious Heritage: The Status of Biodiversity in the United States (New York: Oxford University Press, 2000).

3. N. Myers, ed., Gaia: An Atlas of Planet Management (New York: Anchor/Doubleday, 1984), 159.

4. P. M. Vitousek, H. A. Mooney, J. Lubchenco, and J. M. Melillo, "Human Domination of Earth's Ecosystems," Science, 25 July 1997, 494–99.

5. B. H. Walker, W. L. Steffen, and J. Langridge, "Interactive and Integrated Effects of Global Change on Terrestrial Ecosystems," in B. Walker et al., eds., The Terrestrial Biosphere and Global Change (U.K.: Cambridge University Press, 1999), 329–75.

6. P. M. Vitousek et al., "Human Alteration of the Global Nitrogen Cycle: Causes and Consequences," Issues in Ecology, no. 1 (1997): 1–15.

7. S. L. Postel, G. C. Daily, and P. R. Ehrlich, "Human Appropriation of Renewable Fresh Water," Science, 9 February 1996, 785–88; and C. Rosen, ed., World Resources 2000–2001: People and Ecosystems: The Fraying Web of Life (Washington, D.C.: United Nations Development Programme, United Nations Environment Programme, World Bank, and World Resources Institute, 2000).

8. P. Pinstrup-Andersen, R. Pandya-Lorch, and M. W. Rosegrant, The World Food Situation: Recent Developments, Emerging Issues and Long-term Prospects (Washington, D.C.: International Food Policy Research Institute, 1997).

9. G. C. Daily, ed., Nature's Services: Societal Dependence on Natural Ecosystems (Covelo, Calif.: Island Press, 1997).

10. Rosen, note 7 above.

11. R. J. R. Grainger and S. M. Garcia, Fisheries Technical Paper 359 (Rome: Food and Agriculture Organization of the United Nations, 1996).

12. R. A. Sedjo and D. Botkin, "Using Forest Plantations To Spare Natural Forests," Environment, December 1997, 14–20, 30.

13. W. V. Reid, "Ecosystem Data To Guide Hard Choices," Issues in Science and Technology 16, no. 3 (2000): 37–44; and E. Ayensu et al., "International Ecosystem Assessment," Science, 22 October 1999, 685–86.

14. R. Repetto and W. B. Magrath, Wasting Assets: Natural Resources in the National Income Accounts. (Washington, D.C.: World Resources Institute, 1989).

15. W. V. Reid, "Biodiversity Hotspots," Trends in Ecology and Evolution 13, no. 7 (1998): 275–80.

16. N. Myers, R. A. Mittermeier, C. G. Mittermeier, G. A. B. da Fonseca, and J. Kent, "Biodiversity Hotspots for Conservation Priorities," Nature 403, no. 6,772 (2000): 853–58

Maintaining Diversiy in Our Oceans, J. C. Ogden

1. T. H. Huxley, Fisheries Exhibition Literature 4, Inaugural Address, 1884, 1–22. This quotation should be understood in context. A Practical Fishermen's Congress, organized at the same time, recommended that "the question of the destruction of immature fish is one of international importance. . .[it is] imperative. . .that an International Conference be held to consider the desirability of recommending legislation upon the subject."

2. At the time of its scientific discovery in 1741 on the ill-fated Russian Alaskan exploring expedition, the gigantic Steller's sea cow (more than 20 feet long and weighing 5 tons) was already reduced in range by hunting to two small subarctic islands. By 1768, it was extinct.

3. Although often thought of only as numbers of species, the term biodiversity refers to three components: species (i.e., the different kinds of animals and plants), their genetic material, and the habitats that sustain them.

4. E. O. Wilson, ed., Biodiversity (Washington, D.C.: National Academy Press, 1986); and M. L. Reaka-Kudla, D. E. Wilson, and E. O. Wilson, eds., Biodiversity II (Washington, D.C.: Joseph Henry Press, 1996).

5. National Research Council, Understanding Marine Biodiversity (Washington, D.C.: National Academy Press, 1995); and E. A. Norse, Global Marine Biodiversity: A Strategy for Building Conservation into Decision Making (Washington, D.C.: Island Press, 1993).

6. The total number of marine species is controversial. Some scientists suggest that it is as low as 200,000. See, J. C. Briggs, "Species Diversity: Land and Sea Compared," Systematic Biology 43 (1994): 130–35. On the other hand, others cite a figure of 10 million. See, J. F. Grassle, "Deep-Sea Benthic Biodiversity," BioScience 41 (1991): 464–69. There is no controversy about the higher order diversity of the ocean. See, G. C. Ray and J. F. Grassle, "Marine Biological Diversity," BioScience 41 (1991): 453–57.

7. F. S. Chapin III et al., "Consequences of Changing Biodiversity," Nature 405 (2000): 234–42. Keystone species are top predators that, when disturbed or removed, cause dramatic changes in prey species populations. See R. T. Paine, "Food Web Complexity and Species Diversity," American Naturalist 100 (1966): 65–75.

8. Coral bleaching occurs when unusually elevated or prolonged high seawater temperatures disrupt the relationship between corals and their intracellular symbiotic algae. The algae are expelled from the coral tissue causing it to turn pale or white in color. Bleached corals can recover, but prolonged temperature stress can kill them. B. E. Brown, "Coral Bleaching: Causes and Consequences," Coral Reefs 16 (Suppl.) (1997): S129–38; O. Hoegh-Guldberg, "Coral Bleaching, Climate Change, and the Future of the World's Coral Reefs," Marine and Freshwater Research 50 (1999): 839–66; and C. Wilkinson et al., "Ecological and Socioeconomic Impacts of 1998 Coral Mortality in the Indian Ocean: An ENSO Impact and a Warning for Future Change?" Ambio 28 (1999): 188–96. For a detailed discussion of biodiversity and functioning of the coral reef ecosystem

see T. J. Done, J. C. Ogden, W. J. Wiebe, and B. R. Rosen, "Biodiversity and Ecosystem Function of Coral Reefs," in H. A. Mooney, J. H. Cushman, E. Medina, O. E. Sala, and E. D. Schulze, eds., Functional Roles of Biodiversity: A Global Perspective (New York: John Wiley and Sons, 1996), 393–430. Documentation of warming of the global ocean was recently reported. See S. Levitus, J. I. Antonov, T. P. Boyer, and C. Stephens, "Warming of the World Ocean," Science 287 (2000): 2,225–29.

9. R. Costanza et al., "The Value of the World's Ecosystem Services and Natural Capital," Nature 387 (1997): 253–60; G. C. Daily et al., "The Value of Nature and the Nature of Value," Science 289 (2000): 395–96; and G. C. Daily, Nature's Services (Washington, D.C.: Island Press, 1997).

10. E. O. Wilson, Biophilia: The Human Bond with Other Species (Cambridge, Mass.: Harvard University Press, 1984).

11. Kam Schools Hawaiian Studies Institute, Life in Early Hawai'i, The Ahupua'a 3rd ed. (Kam Schools Hawaiian Studies Institute, 1994); J. C. Pernetta, and J. D. Milliman, eds., "Land-Ocean Interactions in the Coastal Zone: Implementation Plan," Global Change Report No. 33, International Geosphere-Biosphere Programme of ICSU, Stockholm, 1995; P. M. Vitousek et al., "Human Alteration of the Global Nitrogen Cycle: Sources and Consequences," Ecological Applications (1997): 737–50.

12. K. Kloor, "Everglades Restoration Plan Hits Rough Waters," Science 288 (2000): 1,166–67.

13. C. Safina, Song for a Blue Ocean: Encounters Along the World's Coasts and Beneath the Seas (New York: Henry Holt and Co., 1998).

14. D. Ludwig, R. Hilborn, and C. Walters, "Uncertainty, Resource Exploitation, and Conservation: Lessons from History," Science 260 (1998): 17, 36.

15. J. A. Estes and J. F. Palmisano, "Sea Otters: Their Role in Structuring Nearshore Communities, Science 185 (1974): 1,058–60; J. A. Estes et al., "Killer Whale Predation on Sea Otters Linking Oceanic and Nearshore Ecosystems," Science 282 (1998): 473–76; and D. Pauly, V. Christensen, J. Dalsgaard, R. Froese, and F. Torres Jr., "Fishing Down Marine Food Webs," Science 279 (1998): 860–63.

16. E. A. Norse, and L. Watling, "Impacts of Mobile Fishing Gear: The Biodiversity Perspective," American Fishing Society Symposium 22 (1999): 31–40.

17. S. N. Murray et al., "No Take Reserve Networks: Sustaining Fishery Populations and Marine Ecosystems," Fisheries 24 (1999): 11–25.

18. In the fall of 2000, major reports from the National Academy of Sciences and the National Center for Ecological Analysis and Synthesis will show that fully protected marine reserves can work to conserve fisheries and biodiversity.

19. R. L. Naylor et al., "Effect of Aquaculture on World Fish Supplies," Nature 405 (2000): 1,017–24.

20. The Oceans Act of 2000 contains action items relating to most of the points of this memorandum. For example, the act specifies the creation of a National Ocean Commission to make recommendations on a broad set of ocean issues, including changes in existing law to improve management, conservation and use of ocean resources; an assessment of ocean-related facilities and technologies; a review of federal ocean activities to eliminate duplication; a review of known and anticipated supply and demand for ocean resources; a review of the relationship between federal, state, and local governments in planning ocean activities; and a review of opportunities for the development of ocean products and technologies.

21. National Research Council, The Global Ocean Observing System: Users, Benefits, and Priorities, (Washington, D.C.: National Academy Press, 1997); and U.S. Coastal-Global Ocean Observing System, Challenges and Promise of Designing and Implementing an Ocean Observing System for U.S. Coastal Waters, Report No. 3,217 (University of Maryland, Center for Environmental Studies Contribution, 1999).

22. This proposal for an IPOH recognizes the Millennium Ecosystem Assessment (MEA), which is a 4-year international scientific assessment of the world's ecosystems. The MEA, reporting to the Convention on Biological Diversity, the Desertification Convention, and the Ramsar Convention, among others, will cover marine ecosystems in part, but does not involve the relevant audiences for the marine environment, such as the Intergovernmental Oceanographic Commission, the UN Environment Programme's Regional Seas Program, and the various fisheries conventions. The proposed IPOH will strengthen considerably the MEA in these critical areas.

23. E. 0. Wilson, The Diversity of Life (Cambridge, Mass.: Harvard University Press, 1992).

Red Tides and Dead Zones: Eutrophication in the Marine Environment, Andrew Solow—Further Reading

Harmful algal blooms

Anderson, D.M. 1994. Red tides. Scientific American 271: 52-58.

Anderson, D.M. 1995. Toxic red tides and harmful algal blooms: A practical challenge in coastal oceanography. Reviews of Geophysics, Supplement.

Anderson, D.M. 1997. Turning back the harmful red tide. Nature 388: 513-514.

Hallengraeff, G.M. 1993. A review of harmful algal blooms and their apparent global increase. Phycologia 32: 79-99.

Shumway, S.E. 1988. A review of the effects of algal blooms on shellfish and aquaculture. Journal of the World Aquaculture Society 21: 65-104.

Smayda, T.J. 1989. Primary production and the global epidemic of phytoplankton blooms in the sea: A linkage? In: Novel Phytoplankton Blooms: Causes and Impacts of Recurrent Brown Tide and Other Unusual Blooms (E. Cosper, et al., eds.). Springer-Verlag, New York.

Turner, J.T. and Tester, P.A. 1997. Toxic marine phytoplankton, zooplankton grazers, and pelagic food webs. Limnology and Oceanography 42: 1203-1214.

Hypoxia

Caddy, J. 1993. Toward a comparative evaluation on fishery ecosystems of enclosed and semi-enclosed seas. Review of Fisheries Science 1: 57-95.

Diaz, R.J. and Rosenberg, R. 1995. Marine benthic hypoxia: A review of its ecological effects and the behavioural response of benthic macrofauna. Oceanography and Marine Biology Annual Review 33: 245-303.

Harding, L.W. and Perry, E.S. 1997. Long-term increase of phytoplankton biomass in Chesapeake Bay, 1950-1994. Marine Ecology Progress Series 157: 39-52.

Larsson, U., Elmgren, R., and Wolff, F. 1985. Eutrophication and the Baltic Sea: Causes and consequences. Ambio 14: 9-14.

Turner, R.E. and Rabalais, N.N. 1991. Changes in Mississippi River water quality this century: Implications for coastal food webs. Bioscience 41: 140-147.

Zaitsev, Y.P. 1991. Cultural eutrophication of the Black Sea and other European seas. La Mer 29: 1-7.

Population and Consumption, Robert W. Kates

1. P. Stern, T. Dietz, V. Ruttan, R. H. Socolow, and J. L. Sweeney, eds., Environmentally Significant Consumption: Research Direction (Washington, D.C.: National Academy Press, 1997)

2. United Nations, Population Division, World Population Prospects: The 1998 Revision (New York: United Nations, 1999).

3. K. Davis, "Population and Resources: Fact and Interpretation," in Resources, Environment and Population: Present knowledge, Future Options, K. Davis and M. S. Bernstam, eds.; supplement to Vol. 16, 1990 Population and Development Review (New York: Oxford University Press, 1990), 1–21.

4. Population Reference Bureau, 1997 World Population Data Sheet of the Population Reference Bureau (Washington, D.C.: Population Reference Bureau, 1997).

5. J. Bongaarts, "Population Policy Options in the Developing World," Science, 263: (1994), 771–776; J. Bongaarts and J. Bruce, "What Can Be Done to Address Population Growth?" (unpublished background paper for The Rockefeller Foundation, 1997).

6. National Research Council, Board on Sustainable Development, Our Common Journey: A Transition Toward Sustainability (Washington, D.C.: National Academy Press, 1999), pp.303-305.

7. http://www.census.gov/population/projections/nation/summary/np-t1.pdf

8. Royal Society of London and the U.S. National Academy of Sciences, "Towards Sustainable Consumption," reprinted in Population and Development Review, 1977, 23 (3): 683–686.

9. For the available data and concepts, I have drawn heavily from J. H. Ausubel and H. D. Langford, eds., Technological Trajectories and the Human Environment. (Washington, D.C.: National Academy Press, 1997).

10.L. R. Brown, H. Kane, and D. Roodman, Vital Signs 1994: The Trends That Are Shaping Our Future (New York: W. W. Norton and Co., 1994).

11. Wernick. and J. Ausubel, "National Materials Flow and the Environment," Annual Review of Energy and Environment, 20 (1995): 463–492.

12. I. Wernick, "Consuming Materials: The American Way," Technological Forecasting and Social Change, 53 (1996): 111–122.

13. Historic data from L. R. Brown, H. Kane, and. M. Roodman, Vital Signs 1994: The Trends That Are Shaping Our Future (New York: W. W. Norton, 1994).

14. One of several projections from P. Raskin, G. Gallopin, P. Gutman, A. Hammond, and R. Swart, Bending the Curve: Toward Global Sustainability, a report of the Global Scenario Group, Polestar Series, Report No. 8 (Boston: Stockholm Environmental Institute, 1995).

15. UNDP (UN Development Programme) Human Development Report, 1998 [New York; Oxford University Press, 1998]

16. Royal Society of London and the U.S. National Academy of Sciences, "Towards Sustainable Consumption," reprinted in Population and Development Review, 1977, 23 (3): 683–686.

17. N. Nakicenovic, "Freeing Energy from Carbon," in Technological Trajectories and the Human Environment, eds., J. H. Ausubel and H. D. Langford. (Washington, D.C.: National Academy Press, 1997); I. Wernick, R. Herman, S. Govind, and J. Ausubel, "Materialization and Dematerialization: Measures and Trends," in J. Ausubel and H. Langford, eds., Technological Trajectories and the Human Environment (Washington, D.C.: National Academy Press, 1997), 135–156.

18. For a helpful perspective on what might be achieved using Europe as a model see; N. Meyers, "Sustainable Consumption: the meta-problem" in B. Heap and J. Kent eds. Towards Sustainable Consumption: A European Perspective (London: the Royal Society, 2000).

19. J. Schor, The Overworked American (New York: Basic Books, 1991).

20. A. Durning, How Much Is Enough? (New York: W.W. Norton and Co., 1992); Center for a New American Dream, Enough!: A Quarterly Report on Consumption, Quality of Life and the Environment, 1:1 Summer 1997 (Burlington, VT: The Center for a New American Dream, 1997); M. Wackernagel and W. Ress, Our Ecological Footprint.: Reducing Human Impact on the Earth (Philadelphia, Pa.: New Society Publishers, 1996).

21. W.Jager, M. van Asselt, J. Rotmans, C. Vlek, and P. Costerman Boodt, Consumer Behavior: A Modeling Perspective in the Context of Integrated Assessment of Global Change, RIVM Report No. 461502017 (Bilthoven, Netherlands: National Institute for Public Health and the

Environment, 1997); P. Vellinga, S. de Bryn, R. Heintz, and P. Mulder, eds., Industrial Transformation: An Inventory of Research. IHDP-IT No. 8 (Amsterdam: Institute for Environmental Studies, 1997).

22. A recent compilation of essays, R. Rosenblatt, ed., Consuming Desires: Consumption, Culture, and the Pursuit of Happiness (Washington, D.C.: Island Press, 1999)., explores many of these issues. These elegant essays by 14 well-known writers and academics ask the fundamental question of why more never seems to be enough, and why satiation and sublimation are so difficult in a culture of consumption. Indeed, how is the culture of consumption different for mainstream America, women, inner-city children, South Asian immigrants, or newly industrializing countries?

23. H. Nearing and S. Nearing, The Good Life: Helen and Scott Nearing's Sixty Years of Self-Sufficient Living (New York: Schocken, 1990); D. Elgin, Voluntary Simplicity: Toward a Way of Life That Is Outwardly Simple Inwardly Rich (New York: William Morrow, 1993

24. J. Bongaarts, personal communication.

25. Population Council, South and East Asia Regional Office, Our Daughters, Our Wealth: Investing in Young Girls: Apni Beti Apna Dhan, Government of Haryana [New York: Population Council, 1999]; S. Amin and G. Sedgh, Incentive Schemes for School Attendance in Rural Bangladesh, Policy Research Division Working Paper No. 106 [New York, Population Council, 1998]; M. Assaad and J. Bruce, "Empowering the Next Generation: Girls of the Maqattam Garbage Settlement," Seeds No. 19, 1997

26. National Research Council, Board on Sustainable Development, Our Common Journey: A Transition Toward Sustainability (Washington, D.C.: National Academy Press, 1999), pp.62-64.

America's National Interests in Promoting a Transition Toward Sustainability, William C. Clark

Prepared for the Aspen Environmental Forum, 8–11 July 2000. The text of this memo draws extensively on material appearing in the National Research Council's (NRC), Our Common Journey: A Transition Toward Sustainability (Washington, D.C.: National Academy Press, 1999), available at http://books.nap.edu/books/0309067839/html/index.html, a report emerging from a study Clark cochaired with Robert W. Kates for the NRC's Board on Sustainable Development. It also makes substantial use of the report of the Commission on America's National Interests, published as R. Ellsworth, A. Goodpaster, and R. Hauser, Cochairs, America's National Interests: A Report from The Commission on America's National Interests; G. T. Allison, D. K. Simes, and J. Thomson, executive directors. (Cambridge, Mass.: Belfer Center for Science and International Affairs, Harvard University, 2000), also available at http://ksgnotes1.harvard.edu/BCSIA/Library.nsf/pubs/Nat-Interest2. Early versions of portions of this paper were presented at The Ecology Law Quarterly's symposium "Environment 2000—New Issues for a New Century," 25–26 February 2000; and at a meeting of the

Overseas Development Council's project "America's National Interests in Multilateral Engagement: A Bipartisan Dialogue," 16 May 2000. The current draft has benefited greatly from comments of the participants in those meetings and the Aspen Forum itself, plus additional feedback from Joe H. Clark, Richard Falkenrath of Harvard, and John A. Riggs of the Aspen Institute.

1. NRC, Our Common Journey: A Transition Toward Sustainability (Washington, D.C.: National Academy Press, 1999), chapter 2, available at http://books.nap.edu/books/0309067839/html/index.html.

2. See, for example, B. L. Turner et al., eds., The Earth as Transformed by Human Action: Global and Regional Changes in the Biosphere over the Past 300 Years (New York: Cambridge University Press, 1990).

3. Ibid.; and P. Vitousek et al., "Human Domination of the Earth's Ecosystems," Science, 25 July 1997, 494–99.

4. NRC, note 1 above, page 1.

5. Ibid.; and World Commission on Environment and Development, Our Common Future (New York: Oxford University Press, 1987).

6. A. McDonald, "Combating Acid Deposition and Climate Change: Priorities for Asia," Environment, April 1999, 4–11, 34–41; and N. Nakićénovíc, A. Grubler, and A. McDonald, eds., Global Energy Perspectives (U.K.: Cambridge University Press, 1998).

7. NRC Committee to Evaluate Indicators for Monitoring Aquatic and Terrestrial Environments, Ecological Indicators for the Nation (Washington, D.C.: National Academy Press, 2000), also available at http://www.nap.edu/catalog/9720.html; Millennium Ecosystem Assessment, http://www.ma-secretariat.org/; The John H. Heinz III Center for Science, Economics and the Environment, Designing a Report on the State of the Nation's Ecosystems (Washington, D.C.: The Heinz Center, 1999), also available at http://www.us-ecosystems.org; see also R. O'Malley and K. Wing, "Forging a New Tool for Ecosystem Reporting," Environment, April 2000, 20–31.

8. NRC, note 1 above, page 8.

9. German Advisory Council on Global Change (WGBU), World in Transition: The Research Challenge (Berlin: Springer Verlag, 1997), also available at http://www.wbgu.de/wbgu_jg1996_engl.html.

10. NRC, note 1 above, page 4.

11. Ibid., page 7.

12. For example, in the mid-1980s the U.S. Environmental Protection Agency (EPA) found that whereas an objective assessment of environmental risks to U.S. people, property, and ecosystems would have led them to focus on such issues as indoor air pollution, coastal and ocean degradation, pesticide risks, and stratospheric ozone depletion, public and congressional concerns had pushed them to focus instead on the relatively low risks posed by hazardous waste sites, underground storage tanks, and municipal land fills. See U.S. EPA, Unfinished Business: A Comparative Assessment of Environmental Problems (Washington, D.C.:

EPA, 1987); see also a summary by the study directors R. Morgenstern and S. Sessions, "Weighing Environmental Risks: EPA's Unfinished Business," Environment, July/August 1988, 15–17, 34–39. Our international priorities have been no more disciplined or consistent. An early interest in establishing a Law of the Sea, initiated under President Richard Nixon, was repudiated by President Ronald Reagan. The Carter administration's pioneering Global 2000 report made a strong case for America's national interests in addressing global environmental problems and then vanished along with the president who had requested it. Two decades later, Secretary of State Warren Christopher's much-heralded announcement that the United States would subsequently produce an "annual report on Global Environmental Challenges . . . setting U.S. priorities for the coming year" did not even require a change of administration to fall by the wayside—only one such report was ever produced. See Warren Christopher, U.S. Secretary of State, "American Diplomacy and the Global Environmental Challenges of the 21st Century," speech delivered at Stanford University on 9 April 1996. Available at http://dosfan.lib.uic.edu/ERC/briefing/dossec/1996/9604/960409dossec.html.

13. R. Ellsworth, A. Goodpaster, and R. Hauser, cochairs, America's National Interests: A Report from The Commission on America's National Interests, 2000. To offset something of a bias in the Commission's report toward a military security frame of reference, its approach can usefully be supplemented with Roger Porter and Raymond Vernon's appraisal of how basic values and abiding characteristics of the United States ought to figure in the U.S. approach to foreign economic policymaking. See R. Porter and R. Vernon, Foreign Economic Policymaking in the United States (Cambridge, Mass.: Center for Business and Government, John F. Kennedy School of Government, Harvard University, 1989).

14. United Nations Environment Programme (UNEP), Global Environmental Outlook–2000 (London: Earthscan, 1999); and R. Watson et al., Protecting Our Planet, Securing Our Future (Nairobi: UNEP, 1998).

15. Millennium Ecosystem Assessment, note 7 above.

16. WGBU, note 9 above; and NRC, note 7 above.

17. Most of the reports alluded to in notes 14–16 above discuss the usual suspects as threats to sustainability in the 21st century: overuse of renewable resources, climate change, physical transformation of landscapes and coastal zones with resultant loss of habitat for biodiversity, the degradation or depletion of freshwater supplies, the ubiquitous spread of persistent biocides and other chemicals throughout the environment, disruption of the major biogeochemical cycles (especially carbon, nitrogen, and sulfur), spread of exotic organisms, nuclear contamination, and ozone depletion.

18. NRC Committee on Global Change Research, Global Environmental Change: Research Pathways for the Next Decade (Washington, D.C.: National Academy Press, 1999).

19. See, for example, the reports of the Intergovernmental Panel on Climate Change, or P. Vitousek et al., "Human Alteration of the Global Nitrogen Cycle: Causes and Consequences," Issues in Ecology no. 1 (1997), available at http://esa.sdsc.edu/issues.htm.

20. NRC, note 1 above, pages 223–24.

21. NRC, note 18 above; and R. W. Kates and W. C. Clark, "Expecting the Unexpected?" Environment, March 1996, 6–11, 28–34; and UNEP, note 14 above, page 336.

22. On the globalizing dimensions of environmental disruptions, see W. C. Clark, "Environmental Globalization," forthcoming in J. Nye and J. Donahue, eds., Visions of Governance for the Twenty-First Century (Washington, D.C.: Brookings Institution Press, 2000).

23. D. J. Jacob, J. A. Logan, and P. P. Murti, "Effect of Rising Asian Emissions on Surface Ozone in the United States," Geophysical Research Letters 26, no. 14 (1999): 2,175–78, available at http://www.agu.org/GRL/articles/1999GL900450/GL110P01.html.

24. UNEP, Report of the Second Session of the Criteria Expert Group for Persistent Organic Pollutants UNEP/POPS/INC/CEG/2/3 (Vienna, Austria, 18 June 1999).

25. As one perceptive analysis has observed, "Human transport of species around the Earth is homogenizing the Earth's biota," Vitousek, et al., note 3 above.

26. Several excellent historical studies have traced the impacts on world affairs of transcontinental disease migrations. See W. McNeill, Plagues and Peoples (Garden City, New York: Doubleday, 1976); A. Crosby, Ecological Imperialism: The Biological Expansion of Europe, 900–1900 (U.K.: Cambridge University Press, 1986); and J. Diamond, Guns, Germs and Steel: The Fates of Human Societies (New York: Norton, 1997).

27. M. Rejmanek and J. Randall, Madrono 41 (1994): 161.

28. Vitousek et al., note 3 above.

29. R. N. Mack et al., "Biotic Invasions: Causes, Epidemiology, Global Consequences and Control," Issues in Ecology no. 5, available at http://esa.sdsc.edu/issues5.htm; J. A. Drake and H. A. Mooney, eds., Biological Invasions: A Global Perspective (New York: Wiley, 1986); and V. H. Heywood, ed., Global Biodiversity Assessment (New York: Cambridge University Press, 1995).

30. Thus, for example, climate variability plus excessive water withdrawals plus chemical pollution plus a minimal capacity for social response have come together to destroy the prospects for sustainable development in places like the Aral Sea. The German Advisory Committee on Global Change has identified more than a dozen such regional degradation "syndromes" occurring in multiple places around the world. See WGBU, note 9 above. Other studies have documented "critical zones" of enhanced vulnerability; see J. X. Kasperson, R. E. Kasperson, and B. L. Turner II, Regions at Risk: Comparisons of Threatened Environments (Tokyo: United Nations University Press, 1995).

31. See the "Project on Environmental Scarcities, State Capacity and Civil Violence" at http://www.utlink.utoronto.ca/www/pcs/state.htm. Many of the results of the project are summarized in T. Homer-Dixon, Environment, Scarcity, and Violence (New Jersey: Princeton University Press, 1999).

32. Center for Environmental Security http://www.pnl.gov/ces/dialogue/ww_5_f5.htm. In a recent speech on how the environment figures in foreign affairs, Secretary of State Madeleine K. Albright

stated with reference to the former Soviet Union, "(W)e know that easing that region's environmental challenges must be part of any real democratic transition there. We also know that regional conflicts pose a major threat to international stability, and that competition for natural resources can contribute to political extremism and civil strife. Somalia was an example of this, and the Congo now is another. And as we have seen in Africa, Haiti, and the Balkans, environmental problems slow recovery from conflict, and make the transition to stability that much harder." Madeleine K. Albright, U.S. Secretary of State, "An Alliance for Global Water Security in the 21st Century," remarks in recognition of Earth Day, 10 April 2000, http://secretary.state.gov/www/statements/2000/000410.html.

33. Gro Harlem Brundtland stressed in her foreword to the 1987 report of the World Commission on Environment and Development that "perhaps our most urgent task today is to persuade nations of the need to return to multilateralism . . . . The challenge of finding sustainable development paths ought to provide the impetus—indeed the imperative—for a renewed search for multilateral solutions and a restructured international economic system of cooperation." See G. H. Brundtland, foreword in the World Commission on Environment and Development, note 5 above, page x.

34. Kofi A. Annan, statement to the General Assembly on presentation of his millennium report, We the Peoples: The Role of the United Nations in the 21st Century, UN Doc. SG/SM/7343; GA/9705 (New York: 3 April 2000). The report is available at http://un.org/millennium/sg/report/summ.htm. See also, Kofi A. Annan, "Sustaining the Earth in the New Millennium," Environment, October 2000, 22–30.

35. U.S. Department of State, "Environmental Initiative for the 21st Century," available at http://www.state.gov/www/global/oes/init.html.

36. J. Baker, "Diplomacy for the Environment," address before the National Governors Association, Washington, D.C., 26 February 1990. U.S. Department of State Dispatch, 3 September 1990, 17–20.

37. J. S. Nye, Jr. Bound to Lead: The Changing Nature of American Power (New York: Basic Books, 1990).

38. NRC, note 1 above, pages 296–302; and Carnegie Commission on Science, Technology and Government, International Environmental Research and Assessment: Proposals for Better Organization and Decision Making (New York: Carnegie Commission, 1992).

39. T. Sandler, Global Challenges: An Approach to Environmental, Political and Economic Problems (U.K.: Cambridge University Press, 1997).

40. Social Learning Group, Learning To Manage Global Environmental Risk (Cambridge, Mass.: MIT Press, forthcoming 2001).

41. Nye, note 37 above.